# THE RECONSTRUCTION
# OF IRAQ: 1950-1957

## By Fahim I. Qubain

*foreword by*

# THE FOREIGN POLICY RESEARCH INSTITUTE SERIES

*The Foreign Policy Research Institute*
*University of Pennsylvania*

**Number 6**

THE FOREIGN POLICY RESEARCH INSTITUTE

UNIVERSITY OF PENNSYLVANIA

# THE RECONSTRUCTION OF IRAQ: 1950-1957

by Fahim I. Qubain

with a foreword by
ROBERT STRAUSZ-HUPÉ

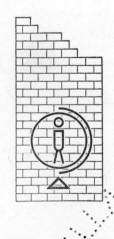

FREDERICK A. PRAEGER · Publisher

NEW YORK · N.Y.

# BOOKS THAT MATTER

First published in the United States of America in 1958
by Frederick A. Praeger, Inc., Publishers
15 West 47th Street, New York 36, N. Y.

© 1958 in the United States of America
by The Foreign Policy Research Institute

Library of Congress catalog card number 58-10098
Printed in the United States of America

This is the sixth in a series of studies to be published by
Frederick A. Praeger, Publishers, under the auspices of the
Foreign Policy Research Institute at the University of Pennsylvania, established under a grant of the Richardson Foundation, Greensboro, North Carolina. This study was subjected
to the extensive and critical discussion of the Associates of
the Foreign Policy Research Institute. However, the views
expressed in THE RECONSTRUCTION OF IRAQ are the author's own.

# ACKNOWLEDGMENTS

The publication of this study was made possible by a grant from the Foreign Policy Research Institute of the University of Pennsylvania. This grant permitted me to revise and bring up to date a manuscript which had its origins in a Ph.D. dissertation written at the University of Wisconsin under the direction of Professor Llewellyn Pfankuchen of the Department of Political Science.

The Staff Conference of the Associates of the Foreign Policy Research Institute reviewed the manuscript and offered many helpful comments on my work. The Institute arranged for the editing of the entire manuscript and its preparation for publication by Mr. William Sands, Editor of the *Middle East Journal*.

Many people helped me during both my research and writing. I especially want to express my heartfelt gratitude to my friend and teacher Professor Pfankuchen, who never failed to give me his support and counsel. He supervised my early research and criticized the original manuscript. Thanks are also due to Professors James McCamy, Richard Hartshorne and Theodore Morgan, all of the University of Wisconsin, for their helpful advice and encouragement. The financial aid of the Social Science Research Council enabled me to do field work in Iraq and neighboring countries.

Special thanks are due to Professor Robert Strausz-Hupé and Mr. Erasmus H. Kloman, Jr., both of the Foreign Policy Research Institute. They offered many valuable criticisms and suggestions concerning content and manner of presentation.

Needless to say, I am alone responsible for all statements—whether of fact or opinion—made in this book.

Fahim I. Qubain

*Washington, D. C.*
*March 31, 1958*

# FOREWORD

In July, 1958 the pro-Western government of Iraq was abruptly and violently overthrown by a military *coup*. The revolution in Iraq raised grave questions for American foreign-policy makers. Since Iraq was the one Arab state which adhered to the Baghdad Pact concluded in 1955, the tremors of the upheaval in Iraq were bound to affect fundamentally the West's strategic position in the Middle East. But even more importantly, the fall of the Hashemite Kingdom raised a question of vital concern to the entire range of America's foreign economic policies.

No country of the Middle East had progressed farther along the path of economic progress than had Iraq under the direction of King Faisal and Nuri as-Sa'id. The program of the Iraqi Development Board represented a well-considered and systematic utilization of 70 per cent of Iraq's oil resources for the development of the national economy. But economic development did not assure political stability. The obvious question raised by events in Iraq is whether efforts to promote economic growth have any significant effect on political alignments and ideological orientation.

Regardless of the political complexion of the future regimes, Iraq's basic problems of development will remain the same. In all probability the Development Board or a device similar to it will continue to be the principal instrument for promoting economic growth. This study by Dr. Fahim Qubain provides an objective and detached view of the basic problems involved in the transformation of a rural and static society into an urban and dynamic one. Dr. Qubain's study, although enlivened by a deep awareness of the social and economic changes which are taking place throughout the Middle East, avoids political controversy. It focuses on the underlying economic problems which must be understood before judgment can be passed on Iraq's politics and role in regional affairs.

Among the Ottoman Empire's outlying Arab possessions, the vilayets of Mosul, Baghdad and Basrah, comprising most of ancient Mesopotamia, were among the most neglected and the poorest. The ministrations of the Sultan's government were largely confined to the collection of taxes. The population was sparse and, especially in the river valleys, ridden by endemic diseases. From these three provinces was formed, upon the breakup of the Ottoman Empire in 1918, the state of Iraq. Its first king, Amir Faisal, was crowned in 1921. Yet, only in 1932, when Great Britain relinquished her League of Nations mandate, did Iraq acquire full sovereignty. Thus, independent Iraq has existed for less than three decades. The achievements of Iraq in the field of economic and social development must be measured by the burden of neglect, inherited from Turkish rule, and the short span of national experience.

Unlike most of the states carved from the territory of the Ottoman Empire, Iraq had to start virtually from scratch in laying the foundations of a modern state. Ever since the beginning of the nineteenth century, Syria, Lebanon and Egypt had been open to Western influences. In these Arab-speaking countries of the Levant, long before they won national independence, Western education and trade had fostered the growth of a middle class composed of Western-trained physicians, engineers, teachers, public servants and businessmen. The newly created state of Iraq, situated at the eastern periphery of the Middle East and isolated by distance and desert from the lively, prosperous Levant, could boast of but a small cadre of Western-trained army officers and a handful of graduates from Ottoman Western academic institutions. That Iraq has been able, amidst the trouble of the turbulent Arab world and great power conflicts converging upon the Middle East, to assemble a corps of civil servants and technical experts capable of administering so complex and so sophisticated an undertaking as the program of the Iraq Development Board bespeaks the tenacity and inborn intelligence of the Iraqi people. Although foreign administrative and technical advisers assisted in the task of modernization—and where in the Middle East have they been absent?—native talent now operates Iraq's departments of government, including the economic services.

Iraq has put its own resources to work in developing an

"infrastructure"—the basic public services—as well as agricultural productivity and light industries. The Iraqi performance compares favorably with that of other Afro-Asian nations who are now launched on various programs of accelerated economic development. True enough, relatively few among the latter enjoy the economic potential of Iraq. Not every "underdeveloped" country can rival Iraq's economic endowment and hence hope to equal Iraq's economic progress. The unequal distribution of natural resources among countries is one, although not the only, reason that invalidates a global, albeit superficial, approach to the problem of international economic development. A country that can call freely upon all the capital it can use for social, agricultural and industrial investment enjoys an obvious advantage over those nations which cannot wring sizeable savings from their subsistence economies. Iraq has benefited from a steadily and rapidly growing international demand for oil. In a sense, oil revenues provided the artificial stimulant of an economy which, but for this fortuitous boon, could not hope to break the vicious circle of oppressive penury and a rapidly increasing population.

But the problems facing Iraq in the present stage of its development are by no means devoid of meaning for other underdeveloped countries. In the first place, Iraq is far from the richest of the oil-producing countries of the Middle East. Many of the presently "underdeveloped' countries in Africa and Asia are discovering resources which, once their rational exploitation has been undertaken, will find ready markets. Secondly, Iraq's central problem is one which, to a greater or lesser degree, confronts all backward economies—the inadequate supply of technically trained personnel capable of meeting the demands of an expanding economy. Despite the remarkable increase of native talent, Iraq has not been able to dispense with the assistance of foreign technicians and advisers. The very rate of Iraq's economic progress and the increase of trained personnel are racing one another. Iraq, just as many other countries, appears to have labored under the illusion that plenty of capital, a pile of imported industrial equipment and a battalion of foreign experts and technicians somehow add up to national economic development. These factors, necessary and desirable as they are, cannot work lasting results within a society that is indifferent or hostile to the exacting disciplines of Western technology. This lesson Iraq had to learn the hard way. There has been waste; there have been failures. Current planning places more emphasis, than in the past, upon the development of human resources as the first and indispensable step towards the exploitation of the country's natural wealth. The successes and failures of the Iraq government in joining native skills to the nation's physical assets provide significant lessons to other nations.

Iraq's unusually favorable position is based on a combination of several factors: a low density of population; an abundant supply of water; large tracts of fallow land that can be brought under cultivation by irrigation; a vast potential supply of hydroelectric energy; and, most importantly, the revenue from proven and producing oil deposits sufficient to meet all of Iraq's capital requirements for the foreseeable future. The low population density suggests, in fact, that Iraq might be able to relieve the serious overcrowding in other Middle Eastern areas. Although the prospects for large-scale immigration to Iraq are barred at present by international political controversies, Iraq could furnish a safety valve of Middle Eastern population pressure. The unity of Arab-Islamic culture and the evident trend towards union among the Arab states will no doubt operate to diminish the obstacles which mass migration encounters in less homogeneous areas.

The plans of the Development Board are comprehensive and ambitious; they must be both, for the forces of social change are all-pervasive—and the Middle East is not one of those few remaining tranquil regions where comparative remoteness insulates domestic affairs from world politics. The Iraqi model of economic progress is being scrutinized by all the peoples of the Middle East, and not all critics are friendly. The men of the Development Board are in a hurry, for not only must they prove the worth of their scheme to their own people, but they also know that the eyes of all Arabs are upon them. It is all the more to their credit that, notwithstanding these pressures, their approach to the task of planned development has been refreshingly undogmatic. Their main objective has been the gradual transformation of a pre-industrial and predominantly agricultural system into a modern and diversified economy. As tenant farmers are settled upon new land, wrested by irrigation from heretofore arid or swampy soil, the hold of feudal tenure is being broken. Furthermore, the pool of agricultural labor reserves is being drained into the work of reclamation and into new industries. Large land holdings, since their operation benefits from their very size, are left intact. Yet the expanding demand for labor and the increase of independent peasant holdings, as well as the mechanization of large-scale agricultural production, tend to raise agricultural wages and modify the traditional relationship between landlord and peasant. The increasing mobility of labor—"horizontal" as well as "vertical"—has triggered an unideological, albeit real and far-reaching, revolution.

The theoretical assumptions underlying the Board's investment policies reflect a healthy skepticism towards the idea of "economic growth"—at bargain rates. The estimate accepted by some Iraqi planners of a marginal capital-output ratio of $6:1$ lies above the United Nations estimate of $8:1$ but is far more cautious than that of, for example, the Indian Planning Commission $(3:1)$. The fact is that a theory of economic growth is as yet a matter of abstruse controversy and, as a guide to economic policy, does not exist. For testing such a theory, the statistical data available are far from adequate even in the most advanced states, not to speak of the emergent nation states of Asia and Africa. In truth, little is known about the real capital needs and absorptive capacity of the underdeveloped countries. The Iraqi Board's policies, although applying theoretical assumptions as a rough measure of the course, are commendably pragmatic. They are informed, so it seems, by the variety of experience rather than by the simplicity of dogma.

Many of the Development Board's projects are entrusted to foreign private contractors. This practice, although it is not always immune to abuses, has paid off well, for the con-

xii

tracting firms have submitted their bids on a competitive basis. Sometimes, this competition has been rugged, and the Board as well as the Iraqi people have been the principal beneficiaries of this wholesome international rivalry.

The economic development of each country is a unique experience, and its lessons are not easily transferable to another one. There is no model of economic growth; there are some preconceived notions about what economic growth, its cause and rate, might be, provided all other things were equal—which they never are. Thus the Iraqi experience should not be compared without stringent qualifications with that of, let us say, Egypt or Syria or Iran. Yet the Iraqi record will be scanned closely by many peoples in the throes of transition from a static to a dynamic economy and, especially, by the peoples of the Middle East.

Not so long ago, Mesopotamia could look to little else but the sunken ruins of the past and their enigmatic message of futility. Today's Mesopotamia, Iraq, is a new country. Its people are swept along in a universal tide: the "revolution of rising expectations." Not all the new in Iraq has been built well; not all the expectations aroused by the popular slogans of progress can be fulfilled. This is not surprising; even in the richest and most advanced countries, the benefits of progress are contested by the pains of dislocation; and performance hardly ever lives up to expectation.

ROBERT STRAUSZ-HUPÉ

*Philadelphia*
*July, 1958*

# CONTENTS

## LIST OF MAPS AND CHARTS

# GLOSSARY OF TERMS

| | |
|---|---|
| FALLAH | A peasant, a farmer. The word can also refer to the whole class of peasants or farmers. |
| FALLAHEEN | Plural of fallah. |
| IRAQI FILS | 1,000 fils equal one dinar (*see below*). |
| IRAQI DINAR (ID.) | A currency unit equal to one pound sterling or $2.80. |
| IRAQI DUNUM | A land unit measurement equal to 0.62 acres. |
| LIWA | A province. An administrative division. |
| MESHARA | An Iraqi dunum (*see above*). |
| MUTASSARIF | A governor of a liwa, or province. |
| NAHIYA | A sub-district, a county. An administrative division. |
| QADA | A district. An administrative division. |
| SHAIKH | The head of a tribe. Can also mean a Muslim religious leader, or a teacher of the Quran. |
| VILAYET OR WILAYET | A political and/or administrative division. |

*The Reconstruction of Iraq:*

*1950-1957*

# INTRODUCTION

Today a silent social and economic revolution is taking place in Iraq. Its inspirational roots go back to a glorious past when, during the Abbassid Caliphate (754 A. D.-1258 A. D.), the country is said to have supported a population of some twenty million people. During this era, Baghdad became the cultural center of the civilized world. The arts, philosophy, science, and medicine, as well as commerce and navigation, flourished and prospered. An intricate irrigation system was constructed, and Iraq was the granary of a great empire. The canal system being developed today follows, to an amazing degree, the ruins of its ancient counterpart.

In 1258, following a period of political decline, Iraq was invaded by Mongol hordes who reduced its splendor into dust. The canal system was virtually destroyed; the desert gradually encroached on the farmland; security was absent; the population decreased rapidly and nomadism spread. This era is regarded as the darkest period in Iraq's history. Only in recent years has the country begun to recover from the ravages wrought by the Mongol invasions.

In 1534 the Ottoman Turks under Sulaiman the Magnificent invaded Iraq. With the exception of a brief period (1621-38), the country remained an insignificant Ottoman province until World War I. Generally speaking, Ottoman rule was characterized by weakness and corruption. Governors were virtually independent from the central authorities; tribal chieftains ravaged the countryside, warred against each other, and were a constant menace to the cities.

In the nineteenth century some measures of reform were effected. The country was reorganized into three administrative provinces. The bureaucracy and the financial arrangements were improved. During the governorship of Midhat Pasha (1869-72), an enlightened reformer, land tenure reform was initiated, a more effective police system introduced, and an attempt at town-planning and at enforcement of modern laws was made. In addition, a few secular schools were established, and the tribes were brought under much closer discipline. The genesis of the modern irrigation system dates back to the last years of Turkish rule, just before the outbreak of World War I, when Sir W. Willcocks made his famous report on the control and utilization of the waters of the Tigris-Euphrates river system.

When the war broke out, the Arabs, under the leadership of Sherif Husayn of Mecca, joined the Allies with the understanding that their independence would be recognized. For various reasons not within the scope of this book, their expectations did not materialize. At the San Remo Conference on April 25, 1920, Iraq was awarded to Britain as a mandated territory.

The announcement of the mandate was immediately followed by a general uprising which lasted from July to October (1920). Some 133,000 troops, including huge reinforcements from India, were employed to suppress the rebellion. The losses in human life, money and property were staggering. When the end came, the toll had risen to some 10,000 casualties. The number of Iraqis killed has never been accurately ascertained, but is estimated at about 4,000 in addition to those injured. Over 400 British lost their lives in addition to over 1,880 wounded or missing. The cost to the British treasury was over forty million pounds. The damage to property was immense.

The rebellion demonstrated to the British the need for some concessions to national sentiment. In October (1920), Sir Percy Cox, an able statesman, arrived in Baghdad as British High Commissioner. He immediately organized a provisional Arab government with limited powers, composed of ten leading Iraqi personalities. On August 23, 1921, Amir Faisal, son of Sherif Husayn, was proclaimed king. An Anglo-Iraqi treaty was signed on October 10, 1922, and the drafting of a constitution completed in the fall of 1923. Both were approved by the Constituent Assembly which was convoked for the first time in March, 1924.

The treaty, and not the constitution, was in fact the basic instrument. It established the foundation and framework of the new state, as well as defining its relations with Britain and the League of Nations. Iraq was nominally recognized as a sovereign state, yet the conditions imposed left it in a mandate status. This anomalous position became popularly known in Iraq as *al-Wad' al-shadh* (the abnormal position). On June 30, 1930, a new Anglo-Iraqi treaty was signed which recognized the full independence of Iraq but, at the same time, protected British interests. The treaty remained in force until 1955, when all special ties with Britain were terminated. On October 3, 1932, upon the recommendation of the British government, Iraq was admitted as a full-fledged member of the League of Nations.

Iraq is a constitutional monarchy with a king, a Parliament composed of two chambers, a cabinet theoretically responsible to Parliament, and an independent judiciary. The government, however, is highly centralized and is characterized by the subordination of Parliament—and sometimes even the judiciary—to executive power. The cabinet, modeled after the British system, functions in actual practice after the French. This is due to the absence of an organized party system and the lack of party solidarity.

The exploitation of the oil wealth of Iraq has a long political history. Rivalry between British and German interests began in the opening years of the twentieth century. In 1914 the two parties joined forces when the Foreign Office Agreement was signed. The Agreement stipulated that the Anglo-Persian Oil Company receive a 50 per cent interest in the newly created Turkish Petroleum Company (T. P. C.), and that Deutsche Bank and Anglo-Saxon Company (a subsidiary of Royal Dutch Shell) receive 25 per cent each. Following the agreement, T.P.C., supported by the British and German governments, pressed the Turkish government for a concession. On June 28, 1914, the Grand Vizier agreed to lease the company the oil rights in the provinces of Mosul and Baghdad. Further negotiations were suspended by the outbreak of the war.

After the war, following several years of negotiations among British, French, and American interests on both the business and diplomatic levels, T.P.C. (renamed in 1931 Iraq Petroleum Company) was reconstituted by the famous Red Line Agreement of 1928 providing for the present division of ownership. In the meantime, T.P.C. received its first concession from the Iraqi Government on March 14, 1925. Oil was struck in commercial quantities at Baba Gurgur near Kirkuk on June 27, 1927.

Oil is Iraq's Third River. The Tigris and Euphrates, properly harnessed, supply life-giving water to the vast but hitherto idle lands of the country. Oil, in addition to its industrial potentialities, supplies the funds to finance the development of its natural and human resources. Oil revenue began to assume some significance in the late twenties. After 1950 a new fifty-fifty profit-sharing agreement was signed, and a Development Board was established to utilize the vastly increased revenue. What the Iraqis have done and are doing with these great resources will be the subject matter of this book.

# PART I  *The Background*

# CHAPTER 1

## THE POPULATION STRUCTURE OF IRAQ

In 1934, the population of Iraq was estimated to be around 3.8 million persons. In 1947, when the first census in the history of the country was taken, it was found to be 4,816,185. In 1955, it was put at about 5,113,000.[1]

Iraq is not a nation in the Western sense of the term. It is rather a conglomeration of ethnic, religious, linguistic, and ecological groups. Primary loyalties in many cases still belong to immediate social units rather than to the nation-state.

Strong forces are at work, however, gradually welding the various groups into a whole and effectuating a transference of primary loyalty to the state. In the first place, the culture, traditions and socio-economic institutions of the country have an Arab-Muslim base. This, in itself, is a strong unifying force which has proved its effectiveness in times of external danger. Others which appeared recently are: nationalism, the spread of education, secularization and a rational view of the universe; patriotic indoctrination of the young in the educational system; vast expansion in the social and economic activity of the state; urbanization; and, finally, increased population mobility.

*The Muslim Arabs*

Over four million or about 93 per cent of the population of Iraq are Muslims divided into two main sects: Shi'a and Sunni.

Since the 1947 census ignored sectarian divisions among the Muslim population, no accurate statistical data exist as to the number of the Shi'a. They do constitute the largest single community in the country, and it is generally believed that they form between 50 and 60 per cent of the total population, concentrated mostly in the central and southern part of the country. With the exception of a small number of Kurds, Lurs, Shabaks, and some Iranians, the Shi'a are Arabs.

Despite their numerical majority, the Shi'a have traditionally played the role of a minority group in the country. This is because, despised as heretics, they have suffered almost continuous persecution at the hands of Sunni rulers from the Abbassid Caliphate (est. 750 A. D.) to the end of the Ottoman Empire after World War I.

The exact number of the Sunni Arabs is not known. It is, however, believed that with the Kurds, the majority of whom are also Sunni, they are numerically almost equal to the Shi'a.

The Sunni Arabs are not as geographically concentrated as the Shi'a. They engage in a wide variety of occupations including a majority in agriculture. In economic status, they range over the whole spectrum from the wealthiest to the poorest. However, they are heavily represented in government, and most of the members of the economic, political, and intellectual élite are drawn from among them. They play an influential role in the country.

*The Kurds and Other Muslims*

Second in numbers after the Arab Muslims are the Kurds. They are Sunni by religion and speak several Kurdish dialects, although they are gradually adopting the Arabic language. The latest considered estimate, that of Hourani in 1947, placed their number at about 800,000 persons, or about 16 per cent of the total population of Iraq.

In the 1920's, there was a fairly strong movement for the formation of a Kurdish state, including also the Kurds of Iran and Turkey. The state did not materialize, and, after the failure of their movement, the Kurds began to play an important role in the life of Iraq. This is in part because they share the Sunni faith with the Arab political majority and in part because their leading families identified themselves with Arab-Iraqi nationalism. Several Kurds have occupied cabinet and other high posts in the government and particularly in the army.

The Kurds are concentrated in the mountain border regions of the North and Northeast. The Sulaimaniya province is almost exclusively Kurdish, and the provinces of Mosul, Arbil, Kirkuk, and Diyala contain large majorities. In many respects they still maintain a tribal form of social organization and are characterized by extreme clannishness.

In addition to the Kurds, there are some 75,000 Turkomans who are Sunni by religion; about 60,000 Lurs who are Shi'a; and about 12,000 Shabak who practice another variant of the Shi'a faith. All these groups, however, are being gradually Arabicized.

*The Yezidis*

The Yezidi minority, according to the 1947 census, numbered 32,434 persons. It is one of the two most interesting minorities in Iraq, the other being the Mandaean community. Inbreeding will probably result in extinction of the Yezidis before long.

The religious beliefs of the Yezidis are held in strict secrecy. They have been erroneously called devil worshipers. Basically, their religion is dualistic and recognizes two forces in the universe: good and evil. These two are in perpetual struggle, but *Shaitan* (Satan) is most powerful on earth and therefore must be appeased. To escape his attention, the Yezidis avoid the use of words beginning with the sound *sh*.

During the Ottoman regime they were regarded as a heretical Muslim sect. As such they were not allowed, like the Christians and the Jews, the status of *millet* (sect) and were consequently deprived of all the attendant legal benefits. They were subjected instead to constant persecution and periodic raids from their Turkish rulers and Kurdish neighbors.

This struggle for survival has made them the most tightly-knit and most regimented community in Iraq. Their social organization is both semi-political and religious. This brings them occasionally into conflict with the central authorities. In addition, some of their religious beliefs inhibit the education of children, which makes the task of government difficult.

The Yezidis speak a Kurdish dialect but many of them speak Arabic also. Almost all of them live in the province of Mosul. Because of their religious beliefs and their social isolation, they stand apart from the main stream of Iraqi life. They fall into the lowest economic brackets in the country.

### The Mandaeans

The Mandaeans are another picturesque religious minority. In 1947 they constituted an urban community of 6,597 persons scattered in various towns south of Baghdad. Their main town is Suq al-Shuyukh in the southern province of Muntafiq.

Assimilation may soon lead to the extinction of the Mandaeans, whose number is rapidly diminishing even now. Mandaean women are highly in demand by other groups as wives, since they are renowned for their beauty. The Mandaeans do not object to marrying off their women to outsiders.

Their religion appears to be of gnostic origin. They are sometimes called the "Followers of St. John" or the "Christians of St. John," and they themselves claim descent from the ancient Sabaeans. Two outward manifestations of their religion are pacifism and baptism. The latter is observed not only once, as in the Christian faith, but after the commission of any sin. They are reputed for their honesty, gentleness, and industry.

### The Jews

In 1947, according to the census, the Jewish community numbered some 118,000 persons. Estimates, however, ran as high as 150,000. In 1950-51 the bulk of the Jewish community left the country for Israel, India, Europe, and the United States. It is estimated that some 10,000 are still left in Iraq.

Before their exodus, the Jews were an urban community holding a very important position in the economic life of the country. They were prominent in business and banking and had almost exclusive monopoly of the money-changing trade.

## *The Christians*

In 1947 there were some 150,000 Christians of all denominations. Half live in Mosul—the traditional Christian center in Iraq. The other half are scattered throughout the country, but particularly in urban centers such as Baghdad, Basrah, Kirkuk, and Ramadi.

As in all Arab countries, the Christians in Iraq were the first to avail themselves of the advantages, such as education, offered by the West and to adopt Western techniques and attitudes. At the same time, however, they generally identified themselves with the Arab nationalists and took over the outlook and aspirations of the Sunni political majority. On the whole, they live in harmony with their fellow nationals and cannot be distinguished from the rest of the population.

An exception are the Nestorians, who claim descent from the ancient Assyrians. Until recent years they have been in constant conflict with both the government and the majority. Although no reliable data are available, it is believed that they number around 25,000 in Iraq.

There are two main sources of conflict. The Nestorians claim to be a nation and in the twenties attempted to establish a state in the north of Iraq along the Turkish border. Their patriarch, who now resides in the United States, still claims political as well as religious authority over them. This fact, along with the tendency of many constantly to petition foreign governments and international bodies for redress of real or imaginary wrongs, has created considerable resentment against them among other Iraqis.

A second factor contributing to their unpopularity is that, being in opposition to the national aspirations of the population, they identified themselves completely with the British mandatory power, and placed themselves under the latter's protection. For example, the "Iraqi Levies" (disbanded in 1941), which acted as a protective force for British military installations in Iraq, were composed almost exclusively of Assyrians (Nestorians).

In recent years, the Assyrians seem more inclined to identify themselves with Iraqi life. This may be explained by the waning of British power there, and the recognition by many of them that their best hope lies not in foreign protection, nor in petitions to foreign organizations, but in integrating and identifying themselves with the rest of the population.

*Foreign Nationals*

The 1947 census recorded 73,828 persons as residents of Iraq but nationals of other states. All of them were residents of urban centers and the large majority (63,886) lived in the three cities of Baghdad, Basrah, and Karbala.

The largest foreign community is the Iranian, which, in 1947, constituted 52,430 persons, or more than 75 per cent of all aliens. The majority of the Iranians live in Shi'a religious centers such as Karbala, Najaf, and Baghdad. In addition to the Iranians, there are about 1,000 Afghans living in Shi'a holy cities. The Shi'a of Iraq exert a strong pull on their co-religionists in Iran. On the other hand, many of the Shi'a religious leaders in Iraq are Iranians.

The second largest foreign group are the Pakistanis who, in 1947, numbered 4,790 persons. Half of them live near Shi'a shrines and the other half in the Basrah area.

Other foreign residents in 1947 included some 3,400 Saudi Arabs; about 3,000 Lebanese and Syrians; 3,000 from all other Arab countries; about 3,000 British subjects, the majority of whom were non-Europeans; and about 1,000 Turks. In 1948 about 5,000 Palestinian refugees entered the country, and since then there has been some further influx.

*Geographic Distribution of the Population*

The total population in 1947 was 4,816,185 persons, divided into 2,257,345 males or 46.6 per cent, and 2,558,840 females or 53.4 per cent. There is reason to believe that there was considerable under-reporting of both males and females— the former to escape military conscription and the latter because of Islamic tradition.

The country is divided into fourteen administrative provinces with an average density for the whole country (excluding desert areas) of twenty-one persons per square kilometer. The provinces of Baghdad and Dulaim have the highest and lowest densities with sixty-seven and five persons per square kilometer respectively.

The urban population comprises about 34 per cent of the population. In fact, this figure is not a precise one, for urban population is defined by the census as all persons living within municipalities.

TABLE 1

POPULATION OF IRAQ: 1947

| Liwa | Total | Male | Female | Nomads | Density Per Square Km. | Per Cent Urban Population. |
|---|---|---|---|---|---|---|
| Baghdad | 817,205 | 408,404 | 408,801 | | 64 | 67 |
| Mosul | 595,190 | 288,199 | 306,991 | 70,000 | 20 | 35 |
| Diwaniya | 378,118 | 159,875 | 218,243 | | 25 | 21 |
| Muntafiq | 371,867 | 148,034 | 223,833 | 30,000 | 25 | 15 |
| Basrah | 368,799 | 183,723 | 185,076 | | 30 | 40 |
| Amara | 307,021 | 138,207 | 168,814 | | 17 | 20 |
| Kirkuk | 286,005 | 129,365 | 156,640 | | 14 | 33 |
| Karbala | 274,264 | 132,116 | 142,148 | 125,000 | 45 | 42 |
| Diyala | 272,413 | 133,749 | 138,664 | | 17 | 19 |
| Hilla | 261,206 | 124,897 | 136,309 | | 48 | 28 |
| Arbil | 239,776 | 108,488 | 131,288 | | 13 | 21 |
| Sulaimaniya | 226,400 | 101,767 | 124,633 | | 24 | 24 |
| Kut | 224,938 | 103,987 | 120,951 | | 14 | 22 |
| Dulaim | 192,983 | 96,534 | 96,449 | 25,000 | 5 | 20 |
| | 4,816,185[a] | 2,257,345 | 2,558,840 | 250,000 | 21 | 34 |

[a] In 1957 a new census was completed. The preliminary results, which have just been published, are incorporated as Appendixes I and II at the end of the book. (Table continued on following page)

| Cities | Total | Male | Female |
|---|---|---|---|
| Greater | | | |
| Baghdad | 523,870 | 270,685 | 253,185 |
| Greater Basrah | 101,535 | 53,762 | 47,773 |
| Mosul | 133,625 | 67,392 | 66,233 |
| Kirkuk | 68,308 | 36,852 | 31,456 |
| | | | |
| Najaf | 56,261 | 25,683 | 30,578 |
| Amara | 48,110 | 23,719 | 24,391 |
| Kazimain | 48,676 | 24,390 | 24,286 |
| Karbala | 44,150 | 20,964 | 23,186 |

Source: *1947 Census*, I, 3. Percentage figures tabulated.

Close to 550,000 live in the city of Baghdad and its suburbs, 300,000 in the three cities of Basrah, Mosul, and Kirkuk, and about 350,000 in towns with a population of 15,000 and over. This brings the total urban population to about 1.25 million, or about 25 per cent of the total population.

About half a million people live in a hundred or so towns of less than 15,000 population. These are usually the administrative and market centers of minor political subdivisions. Most of them are no more than large villages. They constitute a semi-rural category intermediate between the village and the town.

The population can then be divided as follows: 250,000 or 5 per cent are nomadic (it is believed that the number is larger); 1,250,000 or 25 per cent are urban; 500,000 or 10 per cent are semi-rural; and 3 million or 60 per cent are rural. The city of Baghdad accounts for 11 per cent of the total population and for 44 per cent of the urban population.

## Age-Sex Distribution

Iraq is a very young nation. 34.5 per cent of the total population—excluding nomads—was, in 1947, between the ages of one and nine; and 16 per cent fifty years and over. In other words, the economically productive population ranging between the ages of ten and forty-nine constituted, in 1947, 51.5 per cent of the total population (*see Table 2*). This is a picture fairly representative of underdeveloped countries, where both fertility and mortality rates are very high.

TABLE 2

POPULATION OF IRAQ BY AGE AND SEX: 1947
(Nomads Excluded)

| Age | Male | Female | Total | Percentage Male | Percentage Female | Total |
|---|---|---|---|---|---|---|
| Under 5 | 409,039 | 430,101 | 839,140 | 9.0 | 9.4 | 18.4 |
| 5-9 | 337,433 | 399,231 | 736,664 | 7.4 | 8.7 | 16.1 |
| 10-19 | 317,967 | 415,448 | 733,415 | 7.0 | 9.1 | 16.1 |
| 20-29 | 201,224 | 285,468 | 486,692 | 4.4 | 6.3 | 10.7 |
| 30-39 | 250,650 | 301,695 | 552,345 | 5.5 | 6.6 | 12.1 |
| 40-49 | 252,224 | 232,262 | 484,486 | 5.5 | 5.1 | 10.6 |
| 50-59 | 148,176 | 144,576 | 292,752 | 3.2 | 3.2 | 6.4 |
| 60 & Over | 209,561 | 228,980 | 438,541 | 4.6 | 5.0 | 9.6 |
|  | 2,126,274 | 2,437,761 | 4,564,035 | 46.6 | 53.4 | 100.0 |

Source: *1955 Statistical Abstract*, p. 16. Data based on 1947 census. Percentage figures tabulated by the writer from the data.

## Marital Status

In 1947, 56 per cent of those aged ten and over (2,958,231) among the settled population were married. An additional ten per cent were widowed, divorced, or separated. Of those married, 92.3 per cent had one wife, 7 per cent had two wives, and a little over one-half per cent, three wives or more (*see Table 3*). The figures indicate that marriage and the family are an established institution in Iraq. They also show that polygamy has to all practical purposes ceased to be an acceptable social institution among the Muslims. The factors operating to limit polygamy are the gradual conversion from subsistence to money economy with concomitant economic pressures on the poorer classes; education and westernization, especially among the upper strata of society; and, finally, the appearance of new prestige values.

## Death and Birth Rates

According to government sources in 1950, the crude birth rate in Iraq is twenty-seven per thousand; the crude death rate, twelve per thousand, and the infant mortality rate ninety-seven per thousand babies born.[2]

Estimates of medical authorities and other writers, however, indicate that the above figures are way off the mark.

TABLE 3

MARITAL STATUS: 1947

(Nomads Excluded)

|  | Male | Female | Total |
|---|---|---|---|
| Single | 542,502 | 494,511 | 1,037,013 |
| Divorced, separated, or widowed[a] | 37,137 | 253,673 | 290,810 |
| *Married:* |  |  |  |
| One wife or married | 738,515 | 860,846 | 1,599,361 |
| Two wives | 56,283 |  | 56,283 |
| Three wives | 5,304 |  | 5,304 |
| Four wives | 1,131 |  | 1,131 |
| Total Married | 801,233 | 860,846 | 1,662,079 |

Source: *1955 Statistical Abstract*, p. 18. Data based on 1947 census.

[a]This category is composed mostly of "widowed." There were 34,271 widowed men and 243,197 widowed women.

Adams, writing in 1956, estimated the crude birth rate at about fifty per thousand, the crude death rate at thirty per thousand, and the infant mortality rate for the whole country at 300-350 per thousand with regional variations going as high as 500 per 1,000 babies born in malarial areas.[3]

*Prima facie* evidence indicates that mortality is on the decline, and that the rate of decline will accelerate quickly over the next few years. The effects of the new public health program are not as yet recorded, but drastic measures are being taken to eradicate malaria and other endemic diseases. Sanitation, pure water, and medical facilities are being increasingly introduced to towns as well as to rural areas. Education is being provided to a much larger segment of the population, and real income is rising.

On the other hand, evidence also indicates that the birth rate is extremely high, and the traditional beliefs of the population favor high fertility. It has been stated that government activity will soon reduce mortality considerably. No such measures can be imposed to limit fertility. Social mores and traditions have a way of hanging on for years and cannot be changed by legislation. The conclusion is obvious: the rate of net natural increase will steadily climb higher for some years to come. Fortunately for Iraq, no Malthusian doom need be predicted. The country at present is under-populated. It has large resources which, if properly developed, as is now being done, can support a much larger population at a higher standard of living. However, the high rate of growth does place a considerable burden on the state in providing adequate social services such as educational and health facilities.

*Internal Migration*

In recent years there has been very heavy migration from rural areas to urban centers. The main recipients have been Baghdad and Basrah, where literally thousands of immigrants have created *sarifa* camps and barely exist in makeshift reed and mud huts under the most unhygienic conditions.

As can be expected, most of these rural immigrants are young adults or adolescents, mostly male. An index of the rate of the movement to the city is that the 1947 census showed a high proportion of the very young (under ten) and the very old (over fifty) living in rural areas, as well as a high proportion of females.

The flight to the city has not subsided since 1947, but has, on the contrary, increased. Recently, the director of the agricultural machinery administration stated that "recent official agricultural statistics show that less than 15 per cent of the manpower on the farm remain to work in the field, while 85 per cent migrated to the main cities."[4]

The "pull factor" in this migration follows the same pattern as that of other areas where the process of urbanization and industrialization takes place: the expectation of better wages and advancement, the lure of city pleasures, comparative freedom from traditional ties and from the tyranny of the family are the usual incentives. The "push factor" is the depressed condition of the *fallah* in rural areas. This latter is probably the predominant factor.

The heavy migration to urban centers has in recent years created rather serious problems in the cities. In the first place, the immigrants have aggravated the housing shortage;

secondly, the makeshift hut camps which they build create slums which become breeding places for disease and epidemics; finally, being willing to accept low wages, they compete with city labor and tend to depress wage rates.

*Literacy*

Of the five million people in Iraq only 369,864 persons, or 8 per cent, could read and write in 1947. Of these, 312,319 persons, or 79 per cent, were men and 85,545 persons, or 21 per cent, were women. The literate males were 14 per cent of the total male population, while the literate women constituted 3 per cent of all females.

The provinces of Baghdad and Muntafiq had the highest and the lowest percentages, respectively, of literates in the country with 18 and 3 per cent. Baghdad Province had 34.5 per cent of all literate men and 48 per cent of all literate women. Literacy in 1947 was still a city luxury. The provinces of Baghdad, Basrah, Mosul, and Kirkuk, with large urban centers, accounted for about 50 per cent of the total literate male population and 76 per cent of literate women.[5]

*Distribution of the Labor Force*

Statistics on occupational distribution in Iraq hardly exist. Data gathered by the 1947 census can serve only as a general guide since they contain wide margins of error. According to the census, there were in 1947, 1.3 million people economically active in the following occupations:

|                                     | Percentages of Employed |
|-------------------------------------|:-----------------------:|
| Agriculture                         | 56                      |
| Service; government and private     | 12                      |
| Commerce                            | 10                      |
| Manufacture                         | 7                       |
| Workers (not specified)             | 9                       |
| Miscellaneous                       | 1                       |
| Apprentices (under ten)             | 1                       |
|                                     | ——                      |
|                                     | 100                     |

The above percentage figures for agriculture (fifty-six) and industry (seven) do not coincide with other data. It would seem, from what is generally known, that a much higher percentage of the labor force is engaged in agriculture. This contention is supported by the Agricultural Census of 1952-53 which gave the number of those actually employed on farms as 1,400,152 persons.[6] Similarly, the percentage allotted to industry seems high for 1947, although it may not be far off the mark today after ten years of further industrialization. The Industrial Census of 1954 gave the number of those employed in industry (of all categories) as 90,291 persons.[7]

In any case, there is no dispute as to the order of importance. The majority of the labor force is engaged in agriculture, followed in descending order by government and private services, commerce, and industry.

*National and Per Capita Income*

In 1949 the Statistical Office of the United Nations estimated the national and per capita incomes of Iraq at 424 million dollars and eighty-five dollars a year respectively.[8] Two years later, the International Bank Mission to Iraq attempted to make a rough estimate, but the reports were so conflicting and important data either so unreliable or unavailable that the attempt was abandoned. It did, however, reach the conclusion that the estimate of the Statistical Office was roughly correct.[9] In fact, the above estimate is at best an informed guess.

Since 1951 two developments have taken place: a sharp increase in oil revenues, coupled with a consistent policy of plowing back the major part of these revenues into the development of the idle resources of the country.

Oil revenue rose from 5.35 million dinars in 1950 to 73.74 million ($206.5 million) in 1955, an increase of over fourteen times. If we assume that the oil revenue today averages about 200 million dollars a year (it is actually more) and if we also assume that, as a result of capital investment in flood control, land, agriculture, industry, roads, health, etc., the national income from all sources other than oil rose to 500 million dollars a year, then, roughly speaking, the total national income of Iraq in 1957 was about 700 million dollars. If we divide by five million, the number of the population, then the annual per capita income would now be around 140 dollars.

It should be noted that the per capita income figures are national averages which, in fact, do not reflect enough such income frequencies to make them representative. They are only broad estimates that can only show general orders of magnitude. In a certain sense they are almost meaningless, for it is only too well known that, with the exception of a small middle income group, there is a large majority whose income falls much below the national average and a small wealthy minority whose income is much above.

*Disposition of Family Income*

There is hardly any information on this subject. It is reasonable to assume that a fairly large part of the income of wealthy families goes to luxury items. On the other end of the scale, among laborers and *fallaheen*, most, if not all, of the income goes to the maintenance of a minimum level of existence.

In January and February, 1954, a sample survey of households with monthly incomes of twenty dinars or less was conducted in Baghdad to determine the expenditure habits of various economic groups. The households were selected so as to provide a representative cross-section.

Two hundred ninety-one households covering 2,025 persons were selected in the built-up area. The mean family size among this group was found to be 6.96 persons. Fifty-nine more households covering 335 persons in a *sarifa* camp were also selected. The mean family size of this group was 5.68 persons. The results of the survey were as follows:

| Item | Built-Up Area | | Sarifa Camp | |
|---|---|---|---|---|
| | Dinar | Per Cent | Dinar | Per Cent |
| Food | | | | |
| Cereals | 4.674 | 23.65 | 4.042 | 33.17 |
| Meat | 2.092 | 10.59 | 1.252 | 10.28 |
| Fats | 1.307 | 6.61 | .463 | 3.80 |
| Vegetables | .887 | 4.49 | .536 | 4.40 |
| Fruits | .291 | 1.47 | .000 | 0.00 |
| Sugar | .664 | 3.36 | .836 | 6.86 |
| Tea | .523 | 2.65 | .549 | 4.51 |
| Eggs | .252 | 1.28 | .051 | 0.42 |
| Other | .557 | 2.82 | .257 | 2.11 |
| Total Foods | 11.247 | 56.92 | 7.986 | 65.55 |
| Clothing | 1.408 | 7.13 | .935 | 7.67 |
| Fuel & Light | | | | |
| Electricity | .198 | 1.00 | .000 | 0.00 |
| Other Fuels | 1.236 | 6.26 | 1.240 | 10.18 |
| Total Fuel & Light | 1.434 | 7.26 | 1.240 | 10.18 |
| Cleaning Material | .686 | 3.48 | .358 | 2.94 |
| Furniture & Utensils | .309 | 1.56 | .137 | 1.12 |
| Rent | 1.786 | 9.03 | .000 | 0.00 |
| Misc. (cigarettes, movies, cafes, buses, etc.) | 2.889 | 14.62 | 1.528 | 12.54 |
| Grand Total | 19.759 | 100.00 | 12.184 | 100.00 |

Source: *Statistical Abstract for 1955*, pp. 132-33.

The survey shows that in the case of both the dwellers in the built-up area and the *sarifa* camp, over 80 per cent of the family income goes to the absolute necessities of life: food, clothing, rent, and fuel. It is also to be noted that the *sarifa* dwellers do not use electricity and do not pay rent. This is because the *sarifas* are huts made up of reeds and mud which the occupants, mostly immigrant laborers from rural areas, built themselves.

Under the food category, cereals (mainly wheat and rice), meat, and fats receive the major share of expenditures. Vegetables are consumed in small quantities, and fruits only in the built-up area. Expenditures on sugar and tea are particularly high among the *sarifa* dwellers. Very sweet hot tea is the national drink of Iraq.

Cigarettes are evidently regarded as a necessity. They account for 5.43 per cent of expenditures in the built-up area and for 6.72 per cent in the *sarifa* camp. Coffee houses are still the chief entertainment and account for 3.23 and 2.27 per cent respectively. Movies have become popular in the built-up area (1.17 per cent), but *sarifa* dwellers probably cannot afford them (0.38 per cent).

To be noted also is the comparatively high percentage spent on fuel, and the very small percentage spent on house furniture—an index of the low level of existence of these people.

1. Iraq Government, Ministry of Economics, *Statistical Abstract, 1955* (Baghdad: 1956), p. 8. Henceforth referred to as *Statistical Abstract* followed by year. A second census was completed in 1957. See preliminary results in Appendix I at end of book.
2. Iraq Government, Directorate General of Health, *Annual Bulletin of Health and Vital Statistics for 1950* (Baghhad: 1952), pp. 1-4.
3. Doris Adams, "Current Population Trends in Iraq," *The Middle East Journal*, Vol. 10 (Spring, 1956, pp. 159, 161.)
4. *Iraq Times*, May 2, 1956.
5. Data based on 1947 census.
6. Iraq Government, Ministry of Economics, *Report on the Agricultural and Livestock Census of Iraq, 1952-53* (Baghdad: 1954), Vol. I, p. 18). Henceforth referred to as the Agricultural Census.
7. Iraq, Ministry of Economics, *Report on the Industrial Census of Iraq, 1954* (Baghdad: 1956), p. 9. Henceforth referred to as the Industrial Census.
8. U. N. Dept. of Economic Affairs, Statistical Office, *National and Per Capita Income of Seventy Countries* (New York: 1951), pp. 14, 22.
9. International Bank for Reconstruction & Development, *The Economic Development of Iraq* (Baltimore: The Johns Hopkins Press, 1952), pp. 131-32 Henceforth referred to as IBRD.

CHAPTER

# 2

## THE BACKGROUND OF DEVELOPMENT

*Conditions in 1920-21*

Iraq has a comparatively vast natural wealth in land, water, and minerals, in addition to its human resources. When the state came into being, however, conditions in the country were, in the words of an early Iraqi Health Director, "like those described in the Book of Genesis."

The native provisional government took over from the British in the midst of widespread unrest and tension; the government administrative machinery itself had to be organized; the form of government had to be decided upon; out of the heterogeneous religious, linguistic, racial, and tribal blocs a nation had to be created; the traditional schism between government and people so characteristic of Middle East society, with its resultant fears and suspicions, had to be overcome. There were no statistical data and no surveys[1] upon which to establish criteria.

*Health and Education.* Over 98 per cent of the population were illiterate. In 1920, the country had eighty-four primary schools, all for boys, with 363 teachers and 6,743 students. There were also three trade schools, one secondary school, and one small law college.[2]

Medical facilities were equally lacking. During the same year, there were one or two hospitals worthy of the name, although twenty-eight so-called hospitals were listed, as well as fifty-one dispensaries and a few specialist institutions. There were twenty-five Iraqi doctors and forty British medical officers.[3]

*Agriculture.* Of the country's vast land wealth, less than 5 per cent was under cultivation. Control and utilization of the water resources were to all practical purposes non-existent. The country was subject to disastrous floods in the spring and to severe droughts in the summer. There was always the danger of frequent drastic shifts in the courses of the twin rivers and their tributaries.

Age-old methods of production were used in agriculture and yields were very low. Few landholders were certain of their claims to the land. In addition to floods, a variety of insects, including locusts, and diseases plagued the main industry of the country. Livestock production was primarily an occupation of the nomads.

*Industry, Trade, and Transport.* Aside from handicrafts and some cottage industry, there was no other industry worth mentioning. Factories were virtually unknown. Commerce and trade were the main occupations of the people after agriculture.

The communications system was still in an embryonic stage. In 1920 there were some 3,500 miles of dirt roads, the majority of which were impassable in the winter.[4] Before 1914, there had been no mechanized vehicles.[5] Postal and telegraph services were in the process of organization.[6] The total length of the railroad system was 1,139 miles, consisting of "a number of unconnected sections built, for the most part, of secondhand rails...and the rolling stock was a heterogeneous collection of such secondhand or worse vehicles as could be spared from the Indian Railways."[7] The port of Basrah, which was brought by the military into fairly good working condition during the war, was able to handle 428 ships in 1920-21.[8]

An inefficient installation pumped crude river water into

Baghdad, but no other town in the country had either electricity or piped water.[9]

*Experiments in Progress*

It is against the above background that the progress of Iraq must be considered. There was an early awareness of the potentialities of the resources of the country and the need to develop them. The three decades between 1920 and 1950 witnessed faltering attempts by the government to translate the dreams of a better future for Iraq and its people into reality.

For illustrative purposes, some of the laws regarding development which were enacted year after year and summaries of their contents, are cited below. The general principle followed throughout this period, was to have one budget, an "ordinary budget," to take care of current expenses of government, and another, an "extraordinary budget," the accounts of which would be exclusively devoted to "productive capital works." The sources of income for the extraordinary budget were to come from oil royalties, profits of the Iraqi Currency Board, sales of government land and loans. The difference between the two budgets, however, remained more theoretical than real. Some of the laws enacted are as follows:

1.    *Law No. 79 (1931).*    This law provided for the expenditure of 2,210,000 dinars* from oil revenue to be spent on "capital works" from 1931-35 inclusive.

2.    *Law No. 39. (1934).*    This revoked the above law. Instead, it allotted 3,237,000 dinars to be spent from 1934-38 inclusive. The revenue was to be provided from the government reserve account.

3.    *Ordinance No. 26 (1935) and Law No. 26 (1936).*    These created the Three-Year Plan. They provided for the expenditure of 761,180 dinars from 1935-37 inclusive. The money was to be provided from the excess funds of the ordinary budget.

4.    *Ordinance No. 28 (1935) and Law No. 33 (1936).* These revoked Law No. 39 (1934). Instead, they allotted

*For value of the dinar see *Glossary of terms* for Arabic words used in the text.

4,120,000 dinars to be spent during 1936-40. The program was to be financed from oil revenues.

5.   *Law No. 45 (1938).*   This law revoked Law No. 33 (1936). It provided, however, for the expenditure of 8,230,000 dinars between 1938-42 inclusive. The program was to be financed from oil revenue, profits of the Currency Board, revenue from repatriated loans to municipalities, the railways, the Port Authority, and from sales of state land.

6.   *Law No. 37 (1939).*   This replaced the above law. It allotted 11,135,000 dinars to be spent on capital works during 1939-42. The sources of income were to be oil royalties, revenue from the Currency Board, the I.P.C. loan to the Government, sale of state land, and from repatriated loans to municipalities and the railways.

Each of these laws had a schedule attached, specifying how and on what the funds were to be spent. The contemplated projects covered the whole spectrum of social and economic life: the construction of government buildings, schools, hospitals, clinics, special schools for mothers, museums, cultural and athletic clubs, low-cost housing, resort hostels, and a refinery. They also included the building of roads, bridges, dams, reservoirs, canals, grain stores and silos, quarantine stations, wireless, telephone and telegraph lines, as well as the establishment of an agricultural-industrial bank, land settlement schemes, loans and grants to local industries, loans to farmers in times of crop failure and, finally, price support for agricultural products.

In actual fact, however, "capital productive works" within the extraordinary budget consisted mainly of irrigation and flood control projects, such as the Kut Barrage on the Tigris, construction of roads, bridges and other means of communications and public buildings, including schools and hospitals. These works excluded development projects of the Basrah Port Authority, the Fao Dredging Scheme, the Railways Administration, the Tobacco Monopoly, and similar other public undertakings. Each of these has been a semi-autonomous organization, has its own budget separate from the government budget, and carries out its own development programs. They also excluded other development undertakings carried out by the various government ministries and credited to the ordinary budget. Therefore, expenditures under the "extraordinary" budget do not in actual fact reflect the full attempt of the government to develop the resources of the country.

Table 4 below gives a statistical summary of expenditures on "capital works" from 1933 to 1950, and their percentile relationship to total government expenditures. It will be noted that during the thirties expenditures were constantly rising in absolute terms. In relative terms they rose from 18 per cent of the budget in 1935 to an all-time high of 30 per cent in 1936. During the war years and in the immediate post-war era, they dropped considerably. The drop was much more severe than indicated in the table because the the real purchasing power of the dinar had dropped to about half its prewar level. Expenditures on capital works did not

TABLE 4

EXPENDITURES ON CAPITAL WORKS IN MILLIONS
OF IRAQI DINARS AND EXPENDITURES AS PER CENT
OF TOTAL GOVERNMENT EXPENDITURES

| Year | Million Dinars | Per Cent |
|------|------|------|
| 1933 | .43 | 10.3 |
| 1934 | .42 | 9.8 |
| 1935 | 1.03 | 18.2 |
| 1936 | 2.18 | 30.5 |
| 1937 | 2.37 | 27.6 |
| 1938 | 2.46 | 27.2 |
| 1939 | 2.23 | 24.6 |
| 1940 | 2.71 | 27.5 |
| 1941 | .96 | 11.0 |
| 1942 | .98 | 8.4 |
| 1943 | 1.65 | 10.7 |
| 1944 | 0.00 | 00.0 |
| 1945 | 1.54 | 7.2 |
| 1946 | 3.05 | 11.9 |
| 1947 | 3.57 | 13.4 |
| 1948 | 3.93 | 12.3 |
| 1949 | 3.38 | 11.3 |
| 1950 | 3.60 | 12.3 |

Source: *Statistical Abstracts* for 1947; 1950, p. 292; 1952, p. 258. U. N. Dept. of Economic Affairs, *Public Finance Information Papers: Iraq*, N. Y., 1951, pp. 34-35; Muzaffar H. Jamil, *Trade Policy of Iraq*, Cairo, 1949, p. 216 (in Arabic).

recover their prewar magnitude until 1951 when, with a new arrangement for the sharing of oil profits, Iraq entered a new era of development programs.

## Problems of Development

Between 1920 and 1950 the country registered appreciable progress, especially in its physical plant. On the whole, however, development was painfully slow, and the major part of the natural resources of the country remained idle. There were many reasons for this. Some of them were peculiar to Iraq, and others characteristic of most, if not all, under-developed countries.

1. *Political Problems.* A consistent policy of develop-ment requires a measure of public tranquility and national cohesion, both of which were absent. The period was one of turmoil during which the attention of both the public and the government was focused on political problems.

Internally, the central government was almost continually preoccupied with maintaining and consolidating its own position and in dealing with secessionist movements and dissident groups. For example, it had to deal with the Kurdish problem, the Assyrian problem, the Yezidi problem and, finally, the volatile Bedouin tribes, who regarded all organ-ized government as a nuisance and were ever ready to flout its authority at the least sign of weakness. They were particu-larly inclined to do so since the central authorities put a stop to their ancient sport of raiding, both of defenseless villages and among themselves.

Externally, there was always the ever-present question of relations with Britain and the Palestine question. Then came World War II, and soon after that the Arab-Israeli conflict.

2. *Frequency of Cabinets.* In theory, the Iraqi cabinet system is modeled after the British. In practice, it functions after the French system. Since 1921 there have been more than fifty cabinets, an average of one cabinet for each seven to eight months. This has affected the progress of the country considerably, since a continuing policy of development was not possible.

There is no responsible party system in Iraq. As in several
Arab countries, there are, instead, political groupings which
revolve around personal leadership. As a result, generally
speaking, each cabinet that came into power either materially
changed or discarded the program of its predecessor and
instituted its own, which in turn was discarded or changed
by the succeeding cabinet. This situation continued until
the establishment of the Development Board, which is by
law fairly insulated against political pressures and unaffected
by cabinet changes.

3. *Administration.* Another factor which affected development was the absence of a career civil service corps trained
in the efficient administration of government and the execution of policy. For centuries the Turks had ruled the country
with the aid of a few Arab officials. When they left, there were
only a few Iraqis adequately trained to replace them. This
problem is not peculiar to Iraq, but applies to many other
underdeveloped countries which have become independent
in recent years.

The organization and operation of the civil service in
Iraq was until recent years subject to patronage. The system
generally attracted the incompetent and discouraged the
able and resourceful. Many civil servants regarded government employment as a "business" and lacked the sense of
devotion to duty so necessary for an efficient administration. As
late as 1955, Lord Salter, in his report to the Development
Board, was moved to state:

> The chief limiting factor to the success of development in
> Iraq may prove to be neither the amount of money for invest-
> ment, nor even the limits of skilled labor and materials available,
> but the efficiency of the administrative machine.[10]

The corruption and inefficiency in the government machinery were officially recognized through a speech from the
Throne to Parliament on December 1, 1955. The King
stated in part:

> The Government is aware of the weak machinery of govern-
> ment due to the presence of inefficient individuals and persons

of ill-repute in the government service. It has therefore resolved to reform this machinery, making it reliable and effective, so that it can care for the interests of the country and fulfill its duty in the best possible manner. The Government, therefore, is seeking enactment of legislation which will guarantee the public interest and a full measure of justice.... [11]

In recent years the reform of the civil service has been the subject of several reports, the last of which was made in July, 1954 by Mr. William Brownrigg, an American public administration specialist. He recommended the establishment of a central personnel administration incorporating both the merit system and career service principles, the adjustment of and increase in salaries, and training in administrative methods.

In June of the same year a committee was set up to draft a new Unified Civil Service Law. Upon the recommendations of the committee which incorporated Mr. Brownrigg's suggestions, a new Civil Service Law was passed in May, 1956, providing for a considerable increase in salaries. [12]

4. *Conservatism.* The cabinets which have been in power so far are generally composed of members who belong to the "old generation." They have a paternalistic concept of government, tend to be quite conservative and wary of bold programs of development or radical economic reforms. With the exception of King Faisal I (1921-33), no dynamic personality has so far appeared in Iraq able to capture the public imagination and galvanize the energies of the nation behind him.

In addition, big landowners are the strongest social and political group. With but few exceptions they are reactionary in both orientation and outlook. They have resisted, and for the most part successfully so, any program of economic reform that might threaten their privileged position. Their effective opposition has been a serious limiting factor in the progress of the country, for, in the words of Lord Salter, the government's guiding principle in this respect has generally been not "what is most desirable" but rather "what is politically feasible."

5. *Shortage of Skilled Labor and Technicians.* The number of skilled workers even today is very small, and the number of those who could be imported was also restricted by a variety of considerations.

Moreover, the educational system instituted in the twenties followed the European tradition of emphasizing "classical" subjects at the cost of technical education. Consequently, today there is an oversupply of university and college men trained in the humanities and social sciences, as compared with the meager number of those trained in the natural sciences.

6. *Shortage of State Revenues.* Until 1951, the revenue of the state could not finance integrated large-scale development programs. Income from oil royalties was very small.

Alternatively, it was not possible for the state to use taxation as a means of financing development. As in all underdeveloped countries, indirect taxes are the largest source of regular revenue.

A graduated income tax was introduced in 1939 and amended in 1943, but it excluded agricultural income. The law established rates ranging from 6 per cent to a high of 15 per cent on income over 1,200 dinars; in addition there was a surtax ranging from 5 per cent (after exempting the first 1,500 dinars which are actually already taxed) to a high of 45 per cent on income over 9,500 dinars a year.

The major burden of the tax fell on the urban class, of whom a large number are employes of government and private establishments. In any case, revenue from this source has been comparatively small (*Table 5 below*). Since 1952 there has been a decline in the number of individuals subject to the tax because exemption limits were raised to 350 dinars for single persons and to 450 dinars for married persons, plus 30 dinars for each child.

In the agricultural sector, the *fallaheen* are too poor to be heavily taxed and it has not been politically possible to impose a tax on large landowners commensurate with their income. Consequently, revenue from taxes on agriculture has generally been very small (*Table 6 below*), especially when the fact that agriculture is the main source of national income is taken into consideration.

TABLE 5

INCOME TAX IN MILLIONS OF IRAQI DINARS

| Year | Individuals | | Companies | | Total |
| | Number | Tax & Surtax | Number | Tax & Surtax | |
|---|---|---|---|---|---|
| 1948/49 | 33,361 | 2.0 | 165 | .8 | 2.8 |
| 1949/50 | 30,405 | 1.6 | 463 | .7 | 2.3 |
| 1950/51 | 28,123 | 1.3 | 163 | .6 | 1.9 |
| 1951/52 | 27,307 | 1.3 | 154 | .6 | 1.9 |
| 1952/53 | 26,282 | 1.4 | 134 | 1.0 | 2.4 |
| 1953/54 | 24,319 | 1.2 | 195 | 1.0 | 2.2 |
| 1954/55 | 25,914 | 1.2 | 729 | 1.0 | 2.2 |
| 1955/56 | 23,735 | 2.5* | 332 | 1.1* | 3.6 |

Source: *Statistical Abstracts* for 1950, p. 284; 1952, p. 255; 1954, p. 124; 1955, p. 127; 1956, p. 203. Figures have been rounded.

*No surtax in 1956 figures.

State revenue from agriculture comes from two main taxes: (a) the *istihlaq* (consumption tax) which is collected when the produce is sold. At present the rate is 10 per cent of the value on such main products as cereals, dates, etc. In 1953 the tax was abolished on local consumption of several commodities such as meat, fats, vegetables, fruits, hides, wool, cotton, etc., but was raised to 20 per cent on the same products when exported. Probably the object is to encourage local consumption of such commodities and to combat inflation. (b) The Land Tax. This was originally conceived as a rental for the use of state land. The rate varies between 2.5 per cent and 10 per cent of the value of the produce. In operation the tax discriminates against those who regularly lease land from the state (usually small land-holders) and favors holders of *lazma* grants, usually big landlords (*see Chapter V*). Many of the latter, on the basis of tenuous claims, escaped the tax completely. Revenue from the land tax is meager, especially so since a large part of the land under cultivation is state land.

TABLE 6

STATE REVENUE FROM TAXES ON AGRICULTURE
IN MILLIONS OF IRAQI DINARS

| Year | Tax |
|------|-----|
| 1946/47 | 4.4 |
| 1947/48 | 3.6 |
| 1948/49 | 3.9 |
| 1949/50 | 4.0 |
| 1950/51 | 5.0 |
| 1951/52 | 4.7 |
| 1952/53 | 3.9 |
| 1953/54 | 3.6 |
| 1954/55 | 3.4 |
| 1955/56 | 2.7 |

Source: *Statistical Abstracts* for 1950, p. 291; 1952, p. 261; and 1955, p. 321; 1956, p. 241. Revenue is composed mostly of tax on produce, land tax, tax on livestock products, etc. Figures have been rounded.

7. *Lack of Private Capital.* Most, if not all, of the above-mentioned factors relate to state action. The past three decades, however, have also been characterized by lack of progress on the private level. No significant industrial development or basic change in the method of agricultural production took place until the late forties.

One of the obvious reasons is lack of capital. The Middle East economy has for many centuries been a hand-to-mouth one, with little or no savings for capital investment. In addition, the savings that were made were traditionally either hoarded in the form of jewelry (mostly gold and silver) or invested in real estate or trade where, it was believed, the capital would be safe and the returns high.

In the agricultural sector, those who had the means, the big landlords, lacked the initiative to improve their lands. With few exceptions, they were generally content to live in urban centers on the substantial income from their holdings.

8. *Religion and Tradition.* Religion (whether Islam or Christianity) in the Middle East is an all-embracing force which for many centuries has not only satisfied the spiritual yearnings of its adherents but also regulated their everyday

conduct and social life. Even today, it still remains the major medium of personal identification.

Institutional religion (both Christian and Muslim) in the Middle East has been, on the whole, detrimental to economic progress. It glorified as an ideal a life of contemplation and repose, de-emphasized the importance of time ("hurry is the devil's work" is a common proverb in the Middle East), and placed a very heavy emphasis on respect for tradition and authority. In such a tradition-bound society, initiative, innovation, enterprise, experimentation, and new creative ideas—all cornerstones of progress—are usually not only suspect, but reviled as dangerous to the public good and to time-honored institutions.

In addition, the emergence and development of modern banking and credit, insurance and the stock exchange, all necessary vehicles of economic expansion, were handicapped by the theories of Islam on "risk" and its ban on interest. It is only in recent years that these institutions have begun to make headway in Iraq.

On the whole, the three decades were a period during which the foundations were laid for future development. The end of World War II heralded a new era.

1. The attitude of the local population towards statistics in earlier years, which still finds an echo today, is illustrated by a letter of the Qadi (judge) of Mosul. In reply to an inquiry from an English traveler as to the size of Mosul, the number of its inhabitants, commerce, history, etc., he wrote: "My Illustrious Friend, and Joy of My Liver! The thing you ask of me is both difficult and useless. Although I have passed all my days in this place, I have neither counted the houses nor have I inquired into the number of the inhabitants; and as to what one person loads on his mules and the other stows away in the bottom of his ship, that is no business of mine. But, above all, as to the previous history of this city, God only knows the amount of dirt and confusion that the inhabitants may have eaten before the coming of the sword of Islam. It were unprofitable for us to inquire into it." Austen H. Layard, *Discoveries among the Ruins of Nineveh and Babylon* (New York: G. P. Putnam & Co., 1853, p. 663.)
2. Great Britain, Colonial Office, *Special Report . . . to the Council of The League of Nations on the Progress of Iraq During the Period 1920-31* (London: H. M. S. O., 1931), p. 224. Henceforth cited as *Special Report*, 1931.
3. *Ibid.*, pp. 65-67.
4. *Ibid.*, pp. 137-39, *passim*.
5. *Ibid.*, p. 137.
6. *Ibid.*, p. 142.

7. *Ibid.*, p. 157.
8. *Ibid.*, p. 171.
9. *Ibid,*, p. 141.
10. Lord Salter, *The Development of Iraq: A Plan of Action.* A Report submitted to the Iraq Development Board (London: The Caxton Press, 1955), p. 96.
11. Iraqi Embassy, Washington, D. C., *Bulletin,* January 1956, p. 3. Henceforth referred to as *Bulletin.*
12. *Iraq Times*, May 28, 1956.

# CHAPTER 3

## THE DEVELOPMENT BOARD

With the end of World War II, and particularly after 1951, Iraq entered an era of accelerated economic and social development which has had no parallel in the history of the country since the golden age of the Abbassid Caliphate some twelve centuries ago.

The primary factor which has brought about this change is the vast increase in oil revenues. Prior to 1951, the amount of oil revenue was comparatively small, though it averaged about 13 per cent of the total income of the state between 1934 and 1950. From 1951 on, however, it began to increase very rapidly, until by 1955 it accounted for over 30 and perhaps up to 40 per cent of the total national income (*see Table 7*). These funds, almost all in foreign exchange, made it possible for the state to initiate programs of development without the necessity of going through an austerity period or one of heavy taxation, either of which would probably have created considerable political unrest.

Another principal factor is that of a social awakening. Existing economic and social conditions are no longer acceptable to the masses. This is even more true of the urban middle class and the intelligentsia. This discontent resulted, in the years after the war, in almost universal social unrest and in widespread radical and extremist movements in the

cities. Most observers of a few years ago, if not all, believed
that Iraq was on the brink of a revolutionary upheaval which
would fundamentally change its political and social order.
As one writer recently put it, "The parallel with Czarist
Russia is uncomfortably obvious."[1] In short, the issue resolved itself into a race between reform and revolution.

TABLE 7

TOTAL GOVERNMENT REVENUE, GOVERNMENT OIL REVENUE, AND OIL
REVENUE AS PER CENT OF TOTAL GOVERNMENT REVENUE IN MILLIONS
OF IRAQI DINARS

1927-1955

| Year | Total Govt. Revenue | Oil Revenue | Per Cent |
|------|---------------------|-------------|----------|
| 1927-33 |                  | .64[a]      |          |
| 1934 | 5.02                | 1.02        | 20.3     |
| 1935 | 5.36                | .59         | 11.0     |
| 1936 | 6.03                | .60         | 9.9      |
| 1937 | 6.94                | .73         | 10.5     |
| 1938 | 7.84                | 1.98        | 25.2     |
| 1939 | 9.21                | 2.02        | 21.9     |
| 1940 | 9.72                | 1.58        | 16.2     |
| 1941 | 10.16               | 1.46        | 14.3     |
| 1942 | 13.83               | 1.56        | 11.4     |
| 1943 | 18.10               | 1.88        | 10.4     |
| 1944 | 18.89               | 2.22        | 11.4     |
| 1945 | 20.22               | 2.32        | 11.4     |
| 1946 | 25.10               | 2.33        | 9.3      |
| 1947 | 26.02               | 2.35        | 9.0      |
| 1948 | 26.72               | 2.01        | 7.5      |
| 1949 | 28.63               | 3.24        | 14.3     |
| 1950 | 33.49               | 5.28        | 15.8     |
| 1951 | 37.53[b]            | 13.93       |          |
| 1952 | 50.54               | 37.63[c]    |          |
| 1953 | 47.72               | 51.34       |          |
| 1954 | 52.17               | 68.37[d]    |          |
| 1955 | 65.28               | 73.74       |          |

Source: Jamil, *op. cit.*, p. 211; *Public Finance Papers: Iraq, op. cit.*, pp. 40-41;
*Statistical Abstracts* for 1947, 1950, 1952, 1955, 1956; Industrial Census, *op. cit.*,
p. 207.

   [a] Annual average for 1927-33 inclusive.

   [b] From 1951 on, only 30 per cent of the oil revenue was included in the
government budget. Seventy per cent was allotted to the Development Board.

   [c] Including 5 million dinars for settlement of previous claims.

   [d] Including readjustment for the retroactive 1954 settlement in conformity
with the March, 1955 agreement.

Thirdly, over the past three decades, Iraq was able to build a small skilled and semi-skilled labor force. In addition, a fairly large number of Iraqis, either on their own or through state support, received advanced training and education in the universities of the West. These persons are now making a valuable contribution to the development of their country.

Finally, a factor which began to play a positive role in recent years is technical assistance and the importation of personnel from abroad. These come from three main sources:

a)    The United States through its Point Four program. At present there are about 100 U. S. technicians and specialists assisting in the development of the country.

b)    United Nations agencies, such as WHO, UNESCO, UNICEF, the International Bank, etc., either conduct pilot projects or provide technical personnel or do both.

c)    Western business, at the expense of the Iraqi government, provides technicians and carries out most of the technical construction now taking place.

Unlike assistance in the past, the various technical assistance programs of today are also designed to train Iraqis to undertake the work themselves. This, for example, is one of the main objectives of the U. S. Point Four program and the programs of the U. N. agencies. In addition, all business concerns undertaking technical construction for the Iraqi government are required to train their Iraqi workers.

## *Organization of the Development Board*

It became clear to the government after the war that a much more energetic and consistent policy must be followed in developing the resources of the country. The two main questions in this respect were: (1) what was the most efficient method of administration, and (2) how was this development to be financed?

The pre-war experience of Iraq had clearly demonstrated that development programs suffered gravely from partisan politics and from frequent cabinet changes. Moreover, allocations for capital works were often raided to meet the ordinary expenses of government. The answer was clear. If development was to have a fair chance of success, then an

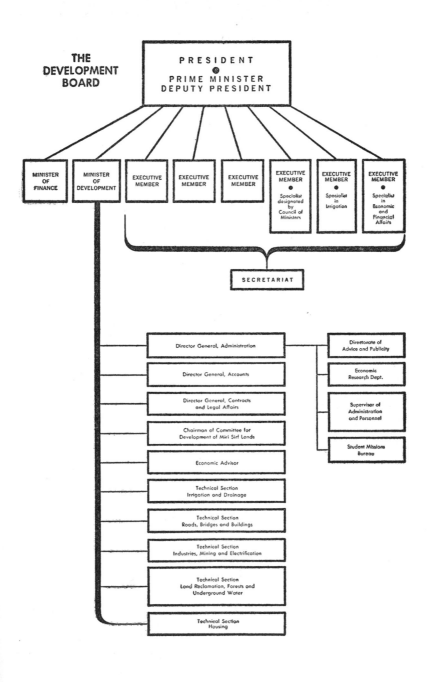

THE
DEVELOPMENT
BOARD

PRESIDENT
PRIME MINISTER
DEPUTY PRESIDENT

MINISTER OF FINANCE

MINISTER OF DEVELOPMENT

EXECUTIVE MEMBER

EXECUTIVE MEMBER

EXECUTIVE MEMBER

EXECUTIVE MEMBER
Specialist designated by Council of Ministers

EXECUTIVE MEMBER
Specialist in Irrigation

EXECUTIVE MEMBER
Specialist in Economic and Financial Affairs

SECRETARIAT

Director General, Administration

Director General, Accounts

Director General, Contracts and Legal Affairs

Chairman of Committee for Development of Miri Sirf Lands

Economic Advisor

Technical Section
Irrigation and Drainage

Technical Section
Roads, Bridges and Buildings

Technical Section
Industries, Mining and Electrification

Technical Section
Land Reclamation, Forests and Underground Water

Technical Section
Housing

Directorate of Advice and Publicity

Economic Research Dept.

Supervisor of Administration and Personnel

Student Missions Bureau

autonomous agency, protected from cabinet changes and partisan politics, must be created. Such an agency would have a budget completely separate from that of the government and would be run primarily by experts rather than by political appointees.

As to the second question, it soon became evident that development could be entirely financed from oil revenues which were expected to increase very rapidly, as in fact they did. At first it was thought that all the oil income should be diverted to development. Later, however, due to the increasing functions of government and the needs of the regular departments, the oil revenue was divided: 70 per cent to development and 30 per cent to the government budget.

In 1950, with the above objectives in mind, the government established, under Law No. 23 (1950), a Development Board and diverted to it 100 per cent of the oil revenues. Two years later, the above law was amended to restrict the income of the Board to 70 per cent. Under Law No. 6 (1952) the Board was constituted in the following manner:

The president of the Board is the Prime Minister. The members are: the Finance Minister and six other executive members, three of whom must be experts, one in finance and economics, another in irrigation, and the third in a field to be specified by the Council of Ministers. One of the expert members is to be the Secretary-General of the Board.

The executive members are to be appointed by the Council of Ministers and are to hold office for a term of five years each, which terms may be extended. No executive member may hold any other governmental, legislative, or judicial office, nor may he have private interests, during his membership, which may benefit from the activities and program of the Board. Two of the executive members are, by practice, foreigners—one British and one American. So far, two Americans and two British experts have been executive members.

### Powers and Duties

1. The Board shall have a juristic personality.
2. It is empowered to "contract loans, issue bonds, mortgage its assets or borrow funds. . . .etc., in its own right."

3. The Board shall present...a general economic and financial plan for the development of the resources of Iraq and the raising of the standard of living of her people."

4. "After the general programme has been approved by Parliament, the Board shall proceed to carry out the projects mentioned in the programme."

5. The Board shall make "a report on its operations for the preceding year indicating the extent to which the general program previously approved has been completed and the expenditures made in connection thereof."

## Finance

The Board shall have its own budget. Its revenues shall derive from "70 percent of the net revenues received from... the oil companies...and from such other sums as may from time to time be allotted to it by Parliament...and from the proceeds of any income domestic or foreign contracted by the Board under this law."

## Voting

Each member of the Board shall have one vote. Decisions are by majority vote, and in case of a tie, the president or vice-president may cast the deciding vote.[2]

## Administration

To assist the Board in formulating and executing policy, technicians and specialists were recruited and technical departments, called "sections," were created. Since the Board was not a regular government agency, its employees did not come under the Civil Service Law. In this manner, it was able to offer fairly high salaries and attract personnel of high caliber—Iraqis, other Arabs, and Europeans. The salaries of Americans working in the various sections, however, are usually paid by the U. S. government under its Point Four program.

## The 1953 Reorganization

As constituted in 1950, the Board was an autonomous agency, fairly protected from political pressures and pro-

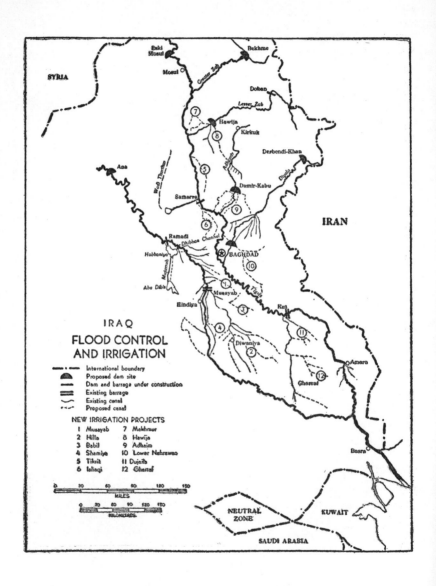

IRAQ

## FLOOD CONTROL
## AND IRRIGATION

| | International boundary |
|---|---|
| | Proposed dam site |
| | Dam and barrage under construction |
| | Existing barrage |
| | Existing canal |
| | Proposed canal |

NEW IRRIGATION PROJECTS

| | | | |
|---|---|---|---|
| 1 | Musayab | 7 | Makhmur |
| 2 | Hilla | 8 | Hawija |
| 3 | Babil | 9 | Adhaim |
| 4 | Shamiya | 10 | Lower Nahrawan |
| 5 | Tikrit | 11 | Dujaib |
| 6 | Ishaqi | 12 | Ghastaf |

SYRIA

Eski Mosul
Mosul
Bekhme
Dokan
*Greater Zab*
*Lesser Zab*
Hawija
Kirkuk
Derbendi-Khan
Ana
*Wadi Tharthar*
Samarra
Damir-Kabu
*Diyala*
*Adhaim*
IRAN
Ramadi
*Dhibbis Channel*
Habbaniya
*Makmiya*
BAGHDAD
Abu Dibis
Hindiya
Musayab
*Tigris*
Kut
Diwaniya
Amera
Ghastaf
Basra

MILES
0    30    60    90    120    150
KILOMETERS
0    30    60    90    120    150

NEUTRAL ZONE
KUWAIT
SAUDI ARABIA

vided with a continuity of policy. Liaison with the Government and Parliament was provided through its President, the Prime Minister, and the Finance Minister, a member.

Soon after its establishment, the Board began to run into difficulty. In the first place, its budget, under the control of only a few men, exceeded the total regular governmental budget. This caused resentment and even consternation in some political circles.

It was also argued that the Council of Ministers had hardly any authority over the Board and received too little information from it with which to answer intelligently questions and criticisms in Parliament.

The Board made the fatal mistake of failing to establish an adequate public relations program to inform and guide public opinion.

Finally, it made the further mistake of formulating a program which, as shall be explained later, could not but lead to disappointment. It promised a development-starved population what it could not possibly deliver within the time limits it had set for itself. This caused the Board to become, temporarily, very unpopular with the public, a situation which was exploited by some politicians to bring about its reorganization.

In 1953 the cabinet in power secured from Parliament the passage of a law (No. 27 of 1953) which in effect subverted the original intent for which the Board was created, restricted its powers, and made fundamental changes in its organizational structure.

The new law created a Ministry of Development and transferred all the staff (except the secretariat) and the technical sections of the Board to it. The Minister of Development became the ninth voting member of the Board.

Lord Salter describes the significance of the change in the following manner:

> This change fundamentally altered the character and authority of the Board. The new Minister, unlike the other ex-officio members, had no duties outside the same problems of development with which the Board is concerned and could therefore devote his whole time to their study. He alone had the technical

staff to advise on policy; he alone had the staff to implement it. The Board could only obtain the necessary technical advice and information on which to base their decisions from staff responsible to him, not to the Board itself, and could not execute them through him.

The original purpose of the Act of 1950 was thus frustrated and the Board made dependent for positive action upon agreement with Ministers changing with governments. All it could do otherwise was, by a majority, to veto the allocation of funds. There are limits even to this negative power, as has been shown more than once, both before and since the new law.[3]

The new law also created anomalies in the structure of the Board itself, which Salter pointed out. For example, the Minister of Development may be opposed to a certain policy or program but may be outvoted by the Board. On the one hand, being the representative of the Board on the Council of Ministers and its link with Parliament, he is required under the law to defend the policy to which he is opposed in Parliament; on the other hand, since he alone is vested with the power of execution, he can frustrate it and render it ineffective.

The new law also made important changes in the manner of execution of development plans and restricted the maneuverability of the Board.

Article 3(a) of the 1950 law, as amended, left a fairly wide margin of freedom for the Board. Moreover, when Parliament approved the Six-Year Plan in 1951, it allowed the Board to add unspent sums to the following year or years and to shift expenditures within major allocations.[4] Article 12 of the 1953 law restricts this freedom. First, it requires that each program be executed in a period of not more than seven years. Secondly, it requires the Board to carry out the works of each year during the year to which they relate. Thirdly, it requires that the program set forth in detail the forms of development it is designed to cover. "The Minister," Article 12 states, "shall present to the Council of Ministers the general programme of the Board accompanied by detailed studies showing its justification, its economic consequences, its effect on raising the standard of national income, method of execution for each year, total cost of the projects approved for each year, total cost of the programme, and actual or approximate cost of each project." Article 13, however, allows the Minister of Development to "present to the Council of Ministers any recommendations and proposals by the Board for such amendments to be made in the general programme as may appear to the latter necessary. . . provided that such amendments shall be within the policy laid down in Article 12."

Article 15 of the same law, probably with a view to decentralization, introduced another important change. It divided the Board's projects into two main categories: One, "capital development projects," which will continue to be executed by the Board; two, "small development projects" which, although conceived and financed by the Board, shall be entrusted by it to the appropriate government department for execution.

## Results of Reorganization

The immediate repercussions of the 1953 reorganization were the down-grading of the salaries of Iraqi employes as they were incorporated in the civil service and the consequent resignation of several members of the staff, resulting, it is reported, in some lowering of efficiency.

The long-term results cannot as yet be determined. The Board was created in 1950 by the Nuri as-Sa'id cabinet, which remained in power until 1952, thus becoming the longest in power since the establishment of the state. His resignation in 1952 was followed by a period of agitation, disorder, and violence, during which four cabinets rapidly succeeded each other. It was during this period, in 1953, that the Board was reorganized. In 1954, Nuri as-Sa'id returned to power and remained in control until July, 1957 when he was succeded by a political ally. Thus from 1954 to 1957 there was only one Minister of Development, a fact which lent stability to the operations of the Board. Now that a new Prime Minister and a new Minister of Development are in power, it is not certain how the Board will function. These men may or may not support the policies of their predecessors.*

* Nuri as-Sa'id returned to power in March, 1958.

In any case, the Board has, to all practical purposes, lost its independence. The only effective power it has left is a negative one: that of the veto by a majority vote. The smooth functioning of its operations has become dependent on the ability, goodwill, and cooperation of the Minister of Development, a politician who may change with each cabinet. Since cabinets have changed frequently, and since there is no responsible party system in Iraq but, rather, factional groupings, it is probable that the work of the Board will suffer from the revision of its structure described above.

On the other hand, it may be possible that the Board will become so entrenched and so popular with the public, because of its evident contributions, that no politician would dare to subject it to serious pressure, or seriously obstruct its work. This possibility is in the realm of political dynamics which are beyond organizational charts, legal authority, or an author's prescience. In the final analysis, Board members do have a minimum tenure of five years, while the life expectancy of a cabinet—if previous patterns will begin to operate again—is between seven and nine months. This fact, in itself, is one of the intangibles which can be a source of considerable strength to the Board.

## *The Operations of the Board*

Since its organization, the Board has presented to Parliament three programs: one in 1951, another in 1955, and a third in 1956. It will be noted that the second program was presented two years after the reorganization of the Board.

## The Six-Year Plan

In accordance with its terms of reference, the Development Board prepared a six-year program (1951-56) in May, 1951, which was approved by Parliament the following month. The program was presented in the form of six major allocations (votes), within which there were fifty-one subheadings, with financial provisions under these latter for specific projects for each of the six years (*see Table 8*.)

DEVELOPMENT BOARD PROGRAM FOR 1951-56

|  | Iraqi Dinars |
|---|---|
| Administration, Studies and Organization Expenses | 3,180,000 |
| Irrigation Projects | 53,374,000 |
| Main Roads and Bridges | 26,766,000 |
| Buildings | 18,018,000 |
| Reclamation of Land and Other Schemes | 22,986,000 |
| Industrial and Mining Schemes | 31,050,000 |
| TOTAL | 155,374,000 |

Source: Compilation of Laws Concerning the Development Board, *op. cit.*, p. 8, Schedule "A".

The proceeds of the Board during the same period were estimated at 168.74 million dinars—ID. 164.64 million to come from oil revenue, ID. 3.965 million from the International Bank loan,[5] and ID. 135 thousands from other sources.

The Board, in addition to its own operations, granted several loans to municipalities and other governmental and semi-governmental agencies, which amounted (up to the end of financial year 1953/54) to 14,113,000 dinars.

As can be readily seen from Table 9, the Board, during its first years of operation, failed to come anywhere near its projected targets. Planned expenditures from 1951 to 1954 were 58.2 million dinars. Actual expenditures, however, came only to 26.8 million, leaving a surplus of almost 32 million dinars. This result demonstrates in a spectacular manner that capital by itself is only one among many interlocking factors necessary for the success of a development program.

It is not surprising that expenditures lagged behind sanctioned amounts. Such a possibility was anticipated by the International Bank Mission to Iraq before the program was launched.[6] It is not easy to spend money in such magnitude, rapidly and efficiently, on a well-conceived development program. This has been the experience not only of Iraq, but of almost every country, including India, which embarked on a consistent policy of development. The International Bank, for example, "has noted that disbursements on its loans to underdeveloped countries seldom conform to original schedules."

The fact is that the government machinery was not geared to such large-scale spending. Such a program, involving comparatively large expenditures, requires a high level of administrative efficiency and careful planning and coordination. It requires a large number of technicians and an enormous amount of technical study. It is interesting to note in this respect that the building program, which does not require a great deal of technical work, was the most advanced; while the industrial and irrigation programs, which do, lagged far behind. Above all, perhaps, the program requires that the whole government administrative machinery be galvanized into action and imbued with a sense of mission and participation. All these factors were either absent or partly lacking when the program was launched. When the International Bank Mission visited Iraq in 1951, almost a year after the Board was organized, it noted that some government officials were not even aware of its existence, and where there was awareness, the tendency was to be cynical and to disparage possible results.[7]

The Development Board itself gave the following reasons for its failure to reach its targets during 1951/52:

(a) "Delay in sanctioning the budget."

(b) "The inability of the different ministries to execute the projects and works entrusted to them by the Board."

(c) "The necessity of providing adequate time for the preparation of estimates of costs and detailed specifications for inviting tenders for the various works. Sufficient time was also to be given to prospective tenderers to enable them to inspect the sites of the proposed works and to study the specifications prior to the submission of their tenders."[8]

The first two or three years of the program have to be regarded as essentially a period of preparation. It would have been folly to proceed with the program otherwise. It was one during which the government machinery was gradually geared to heavy spending, technicians and specialists recruited, technical studies of specific projects prepared, relations established with qualified foreign engineering firms, and technical assistance from abroad utilized. It is to be noted that, from 1953 on, the work began to proceed much more rapidly. For example, in 1955 actual expenditures came to 46,607,327 dinars—thus exceeding original planned expenditures for that year (32,335,000) by more than 14 million dinars.

TABLE 9

ALLOTMENTS (A) & ACTUAL EXPENDITURES (E) OF THE DEVELOPMENT
BOARD, 1951/52 TO 1953/54
(In Thousands of Iraqi Dinars)

|  | 1951/52 | | 1952/53 | | 1953/54 | | Total |
|  | A | E | A | E | A | E | Surplus |
|---|---|---|---|---|---|---|---|
| Administration | 170 | 110 | 460 | 260 | 600 | 300 | 560 |
| Irrigation | 3,024 | 1,733 | 7,100 | 1,064 | 10,840 | 4,000 | 14,167 |
| Roads & Bridges | 2,066 | 836 | 3,800 | 2,933 | 4,700 | 2,500 | 4,297 |
| Buildings | 2,368 | 1,368 | 2,650 | 2,650 | 3,100 | 2,900 | 1,200 |
| Reclamation, etc. | 1,736 | 953 | 3,450 | 2,076 | 4,150 | 2,150 | 4,157 |
| Industry, etc. |  | 6 | 3,000 | 5 | 5,000 | 500 | 7,489 |
|  | 9,364 | 5,006 | 20,460 | 8,988 | 28,390 | 12,350 | 31,870 |

Source: Iraq Government, Development Board, *Annual Reports for the Financial Years*, 1951, p. 11; 1952/53, p. 23; 1953/54, pp. 5, 9, 49.

## The Five-Year Plan: 1955-59

No new program was presented to Parliament until 1955. In April of that year, the Minister of Development presented and Parliament approved a new Five-Year Plan to supersede the first one. In the view of the Board, the new plan had become necessary for several reasons. In the first place, expected oil revenues far exceeded original estimates. The cost estimates of the first plan were also no longer realistic and the 1953 law had changed the basis of financing projects of other departments and agencies.

The plan called for the expenditure of 304,306,100 dinars ($852,057,000) from 1955 to 1959 inclusive. The revenue for the period was estimated at about 252,685,000 dinars, including 37 million dinars of unobligated balances from the previous program. The deficit, some 50 million dinars, was to be covered from expected increases in oil revenue and from anticipated savings on the estimated total cost of the program.

TABLE 10

THE FIVE-YEAR PLAN: 1955-59

*Iraqi Dinars*

Chapter I: Main Projects

| | Iraqi Dinars |
|---|---|
| Administration Expenses | 5,450,000 |
| Irrigation, Drainage & Flood Control | 107,935,000 |
| Roads & Bridges | 53,700,000 |
| Airfields | 5,000,000 |
| Railways | 15,500,000 |
| Main Buildings | 28,550,000 |
| Industry, Mining & Electrification | 43,571,000 |
| Development of Animal, Plant, and Underground Water Resources | 6,475,000 |
| TOTAL—Chapter I | 266,181,000 |

Chapter II: Small Projects

| | |
|---|---|
| Buildings & Institutes | 32,250,000 |
| Miscellaneous Projects | 5,875,000 |
| TOTAL—Chapter II | 38,125,000 |
| GRAND TOTAL | 304,306,100 |

Source: Law No. 43 (1955), Schedule (A).

## The Six-Year Plan: 1955-60

In May, 1956 the Minister of Development proposed a new supplementary Six-Year Program (1955-60) to Parliament to replace the one submitted the previous year. The new program was approved in June. Three main reasons prompted the Board to propose the new program: a sharp increase in oil revenues, the completion of several studies and surveys which now needed implementation, and, finally, the recommendations of Lord Salter, the economic adviser, in favor of a more flexible and inclusive program.

The new plan contemplates the expenditure of 500 million dinars ($1,400,000,000) between 1955 and 1960, including some ID. 46 million which had already been spent in 1955. The revenue for the same period is estimated at about ID. 400 million. The deficit, about ID. 100 million, is expected to be covered from unobligated balances of previous years amounting to more than ID. 50 million, and savings on the 1955-60 expenditures estimates—totaling about 15 per cent.

The new plan differs from previous ones in many respects. First, it is of much greater financial magnitude. It contemplates a rate of expenditure averaging about 85 million dinars a year, as against ID. 31 million for the first plan and ID. 61 million for the 1955 plan.

Then, unlike the first plan, execution is much more decentralized. The program is divided into "main" and "small" projects; the latter are to be executed by the appropriate government departments. This is a step in the right direction, since on the one hand it gives some relief to the administrative machinery of the Board and, on the other, it gives the regular government departments a sense of participation in the development of the country.

Finally, and also unlike the first plan, the program was presented to Parliament as a tentative proposal. Contemplated new projects may or may not be executed depending on whether, after careful study, they are found to be economical. Moreover, the Board may propose to Parliament, if necessary, a supplementary program either in the light of new studies or if oil revenues increase or decrease sharply. In other words, the program is much more flexible than its two predecessors.

The new plan differs also in content. Flood control, irrigation, and drainage in all three plans receive first priority in allocations. But where emphasis in the first plan was on the flood control aspect, the emphasis in the present one is on irrigation, drainage, and reclamation. This is because the flood menace has been brought under a reasonable measure of control through the completion of the major control projects. Attention can now be properly diverted to the constructive aspect of agriculture, i.e., improvement of existing areas and bringing new land under cultivation.

In both the 1955-59 and the present program, far more emphasis is placed on the transportation system, particularly roads and bridges. This new direction is probably due to two main factors: the greater realization that it would be

useless to develop agriculture, industry, etc., if there are no
adequate facilities to transport the products and, secondly,
because many of the technical road studies (location surveys,
design, etc.) have been completed and are now ready for
execution.

Industry in the present program rises to third place. More
than ID. 16 million are allocated for an asphalt refinery, a
cotton plant, two cement plants, and a sugar factory. All
of these, with the exception of the sugar factory, have
been completed as of this writing. The latter was due to be
completed in 1957. A new feature, absent from previous
plans, is the allocation of some ID. 11 million for the improvement and expansion of the construction, metal, and
agricultural industries—mainly in the private sector. ID
12 million are allocated for new plants, while ID. 10 million
more are set aside for plants still under study. ID. 12.6
million go for the construction of three electricity stations, in
the north, central, and southern parts of the country. The
industrialization program reflects the recommendations of
the *Little Report* (*See Chapter VIII*).

### TABLE 11
#### THE SIX-YEAR PLAN: 1955-60

| | | *Iraqi Dinars* |
|---|---|---|
| Chapter I:   Main Projects | | |
| 1. Administration | | 7,350,000 |
| 2. Irrigation, Drainage & Storage Schemes | | 153,754,600 |
| 3. Communications | | |
| Roads | 63,686,000 | |
| Bridges | 22,890,000 | |
| Airfields | 8,851,550 | |
| Railways | 24,940,142 | |
| Ports | 4,000,000 | 124,367,692 |
| 4. Main Buildings | | |
| Health Institutions | 9,975,000 | |
| Educational Institutions | 6,314,000 | |
| Public Buildings | 20,900,000 | 37,189,000 |
| 5. Resorts & Rest Houses | | 2,580,000 |
| 6. Housing | | 24,085,000 |
| 7. Industry, Mining & Electrification | | |

|  |  |  |
|---|---:|---:|
| Plants under Construction | 16,424,217 | |
| Mining Survey | 126,000 | |
| Electrification | 12,669,000 | |
| Improvement of Existing Industries and New Industries | 37,900,000 | 67,119,217 |

| 8. Development of Animal, Plant & Underground Water Resources | | |
|---|---:|---:|
| Research & Laboratories | 1,500,000 | |
| Plant Resources Development | 2,500,000 | |
| Animal Resources Development | 2,000,000 | |
| Forests | 1,000,000 | |
| 1955 Allocations for All Above | 1,036,818 | |
| State Land Reclamation | 1,125,000 | |
| Artesian Wells | 3,000,000 | |
| Main Water Projects | 1,125,000 | |
| Agricultural Machinery | 250,000 | |
| Agricultural Schools & Centers | 750,000 | 14,286,818 |
| TOTAL—Chapter I | | 430,732,327 |

Chapter II:  Small Projects

| 9. Buildings & Institutes | | |
|---|---:|---:|
| Health Institutions | 5,750,000 | |
| Elementary & Other Schools | 8,000,000 | |
| Housing for Labor | 1,800,000 | |
| Buildings for Government Departments | 28,825,000 | |
| Secondary Roads & Bridges | 8,500,000 | |
| Telephone, Telegraph & Wireless | 4,500,000 | |
| Eradication of Malaria | 2,000,000 | 59,375,000 |

| 10. Miscellaneous Projects | | |
|---|---:|---:|
| Minor Irrigation Works | 6,500,000 | |
| Improvement of Drinking Water | 1,500,000 | |
| Filling of Swamps | 300,000 | |
| Aerial & General Surveys | 850,000 | |
| Other | 750,000 | 9,900,000 |
| TOTAL—Chapter II | | 69,275,000 |
| GRAND TOTAL | | 500,007,327 |

Source: Law No. 54 (1956), Schedule (A).

The new program is by far more balanced and inclusive than the two preceding it. Unlike the others, it strikes a reasonable balance between long-term "brick and mortar" development projects and short-term projects geared to meet immediate human needs. Housing, which was almost completely ignored in previous plans, moved to fourth place and receives more than ID. 24 million. Expenditures on hospitals, clinics, drinking water, and other direct and indirect health measures receive a sharp boost. Allocations for education, including colleges, secondary, elementary, technical and agricultural schools and training centers are vastly increased.

Similarly, there is a much greater balance between expenditures on new projects and expenditures on the improvement of existing plant. The tendency in earlier plans, particularly the first one, was to allocate most of the available funds for launching new projects: new dams, new land, new roads, new factories, new schools, new hospitals, etc., with few allocations for improving those facilities already in existence. This was particularly true of irrigation projects. In the present program proper attention is paid to this aspect.

The main question concerning such a mammoth plan, involving the expenditure of an average of ID. 85 million a year in addition to some ID. 20 million spent annually by other departments, is whether the Board and the ministries are administratively capable of implementing it. The evidence indicates that they may be, or at least that the new plan will have a far greater success than the first one. Both the Board and the ministries have now had over five years of practical experience in intensive development problems and are probably far more administratively efficient than in 1950. Very heavy reliance in the execution of projects is now placed on competent foreign firms which have had wide experience in their respective fields. Too, many of the technical studies, the lack of which caused considerable delay in the past, are now completed and ready for implementation. Finally, Iraq has also drawn heavily upon the technical resources of the United Nations, the United States, European countries, particularly Britain, and those of neighboring countries.

### The Objectives of the Board

The Board was entrusted by Parliament to carry out programs for the "development of the resources of Iraq and the raising of the standard of living of her people."

As for the first part, "the development of the resources of Iraq," the Board in its first and second plans imposed a narrow construction on its mandate and concerned itself mainly with the physical type of development. By and large, its conception did not seem to include the "development of human resources." A glance at the first two plans shows clearly the heavy concentration on long-range projects such as dams, irrigation works, roads, bridges, industrial plants and so forth. Few projects related to the immediate human problem.

According to Lord Salter, the primary reasons why the Board was reluctant to enter heavily into the social welfare field was the question of departmental jurisdiction. It is wary of slipping into the habit of subsidizing current government operations under the umbrella of development. In some cases the lines of demarcation fade out and it becomes difficult to determine where "development" ends and an ordinary departmental operation begins. For example, is combatting malaria a development function or an ordinary government operation? Good arguments can be made for both views.

In any case, after the program gained momentum it became clear that an efficient plan of development has to be balanced and integrated. A new industrial plant needs skilled workers to run and maintain it, and efficient production requires a labor force free from debilitating diseases such as malaria and hookworm. Moreover, the Board's policy of emphasizing—almost exclusively—long-range projects soon made it unpopular with the public and was one of the main factors exploited to bring about its reorganization in 1953.

The present plan reflects the shift which has taken place in the development philosophy of the Board. This was brought about by the realization mentioned above, through popular discontent, and finally by the wise advice of Lord Salter in his report to the Board.

The pattern of the Board's expenditures leaves little doubt that one of its chief aims is the development of agriculture: to increase vastly the land under cultivation, increase pro-

ductivity per unit, diversify agricultural production, introduce intensive farming, and gradually to mechanize. Expenditures on agriculture (i.e., flood control, irrigation,
drainage, etc.) average, in all three plans, about 35 per cent
of total planned expenditures. This emphasis is understand-
able, since land and water are the country's most valuable
natural resources.

The second objective of the Board is to move Iraq from
its present stage, in which agricultural production dominates
the economy, into a second stage where agriculture, industry,
and other economic activities such as trade and services
are more or less on an equal footing. Among other things, this
will mean considerable investment in industry, siphoning
off part of the agricultural labor force from the land and a
geographical and occupational redistribution of the population.

Quantitatively, what do the programs of the Board mean
in terms of raising the standard of living—the second part
of the Board's mandate? The rise or decline in the standard
of living is governed by one basic factor: the relation between
the rate of population growth and the rate of increase in the
national income. Increase in the national income, however,
is also governed by two basic factors: the rate of productivity
and the rate of capital investment.

Net annual population growth has been estimated at
about 2.3 per cent. It may be that, as a result of the various
health measures now being undertaken by the government,
this rate may soon go up to 3 per cent.

The capital income ratio in Iraq has been recently estimated
at 6:1 (i.e., six units of invested capital produce one unit of
income). Thus, according to an Iraqi economist, taking into
consideration population growth, Iraq must, in order to
maintain the standard of living existing around 1950, make
an annual capital investment at the rate of 13.8 per cent of
the total national income $\left(\frac{2.3 \times 6}{1} = 13.8\right)$.[9]

In 1951 the IBRD Mission to Iraq estimated the national
income at about 150 million dinars ($424 million). Between
1951/52 and 1955/56, a five-year period, excluding other

government departments and the private sector, the Board alone made a total capital investment of over 150 million dinars (or 30 million dinars a year) equal to 20 per cent of the national income in 1951. This exceeds by 6.2 per cent the amount of investment necessary (13.8 per cent) to maintain the standard of living.

We have already stated that in Iraq each unit of capital investment produces one unit of product or income (capital productivity coefficient equals one-sixth). Hence the annual investments of the Board (20 per cent of the national income) increase the national income by 3..3 per cent annually $\frac{(20 \times 1}{6} = 3.3)$. But the population increases at the rate of 2.3 per cent a year, thus leaving a surplus of 1 per cent. In other words, the Board's rate of investment between 1951/52 and 1955/56 should have raised the standard of living by 1 per cent each year.

Under the present program, the Board plans to spend an average of 85 million dinars a year. Assuming, for theoretical purposes, that all other factors have remained constant (not a correct assumption), then this rate of investment equals about 56 per cent of the national income in 1951. Such a rate should theoretically produce 9.3 per cent increase in the national income annually (56 x $\frac{1}{6}$ = 9.3). If 2.3 per cent, the annual growth of population, is deducted, then this leaves a 7 per cent increase in the standard of living a year.

All the above data are, of course, based on theoretical formulations which, because of other variables, may not coincide with actual results. Despite probable wide margins of error, however, they do show rough approximations of trends.

It is quite obvious that the activities of the Board have on the one hand placed great quantities of money in circulation in the form of wages, and expenditures on services and materials. On the other hand, these activities were apt to cause shortages in certain materials, particularly in construction. Unless adequate measures are taken, this trend will tend to cause inflation and nullify an apparent rise in income.

The government wisely took various measures to forestall such an eventuality. It undertook the sale of some foods, particularly bread. It removed the *istihlaq* (consumption) tax on the local consumption of some commodities and raised it on the same if exported. It reduced import taxes on some consumer products and, finally, floated internal loans to siphon off some of the money in circulation. As a result of these and other measures, there has been no appreciable increase in prices, as table 12 indicates.

TABLE 12

WHOLESALE PRICE INDEX
(Monthly Average)
Base Year 1939 = 100

|  | 1945 | 1950 | 1951 | 1954 | 1955 | 1956 |
|---|---|---|---|---|---|---|
| Grain & Dates | 592.9 | 530.0 | 557.2 | 462.1 | 452.5 | 543.5 |
| Meat & Milk Products | 665.2 | 627.7 | 597.1 | 584.9 | 595.9 | 637.3 |
| Other Foods | 309.6 | 346.0 | 365.3 | 329.5 | 336.0 | 335.0 |
| Other Animal & Vegetable Products | 412.9 | 615.3 | 708.3 | 514.1 | 510.1 | 502.9 |
| Building Materials | 634.5 | 488.8 | 653.6 | 517.7 | 590.8 | 602.4 |
| Textiles | 944.0 | 792.5 | 890.5 | 620.7 | 597.8 | 597.7 |
| Fuels | 138.7 | 149.0 | 162.5 | 153.7 | 154.2 | 154.8 |
| Other Goods | 535.0 | 428.6 | 509.7 | 355.1 | 335.5 | 327.3 |
| General Price Index | 494.4 | 475.1 | 520.8 | 427.9 | 432.1 | 463.1 |

Source: *Statistical Abstract* for 1955, p. 137; 1956, p. 159.

## Other Government Agencies

Development work is by no means restricted to the Board and the Ministry of Development. Other state agencies carry out important major works which have averaged in recent years some 20 per cent of the total expenditures of the ordinary government budget.

1. There are "capital works" and "economic projects" in the general budget of the government. These have averaged more than four million dinars a year since 1951.

2. There are also expenditures for "administrative local councils and expenses of elementary education" and other projects carried out by the councils. These have also averaged over four million dinars a year (1953/54, ID. 4.5 million; 1954/55, ID. 6.1 million).

3. Various government banks such as the Industrial Bank, the Agricultural Bank, the Mortgage Bank, etc., carry out their own important projects.

4. Semi-governmental agencies such as the State Railways, the Port of Basrah, the Tobacco Monopoly, the Date Association, etc., finance many of their own projects in addition to any assistance they may receive from the Board.

5. There are also programs of the U. S. Point Four and United Nations agencies.

The chapters that follow will discuss in detail the transformation taking place in all sectors of Iraqi life, principally as a result of the activities of the Development Board and the Ministry of Development, but also of other government agencies and of private investment, both native and foreign.

1. Walter Z. Laqueur, *Communism and Nationalism in the Middle East* (New York: Praeger, 1956), p. 202.
2. Iraq Government, Development Board, *Compilation of Laws Concerning the Development Board*, (revised) (Baghdad: Government Press, 1952).
3. Salter, *op. cit.*, p. 97.
4. Articles 4 and 5 of Law No. 35 (1951).
5. In 1950 the Government of Iraq contracted a loan from the International Bank for 12.8 million dinars for the Tharthar project. Actually only a little over six million dollars of the loan were used. The loan was paid back in full by 1956.
6. *IBRD*, p. 76.
7. *Ibid.*, p. 79.
8. Annual Report for the Financial Year 1953-54, *op. cit.*, p. 5.
9. Abdul Sahib Alwan, "Population Increase and Economic Development in Iraq," *Majallat al-Zira'a al-Iraqiya*, (Special Issue), Vol. 12, No. 1, January-February-March, 1957, pp. 77-84. Published by the Ministry of Agriculture at Baghdad, in Arabic.

# PART II  *The Development of Agriculture*

CHAPTER 4

## CONTROL OVER THE WATER RESOURCES

Control and utilization of its water resources have been for generations—and indeed for centuries—the principal problem of Iraq. Although nature has endowed the country with abundant supplies sufficient to irrigate all the arable land, the desired amounts are not delivered when and where they are needed. Droughts scorch a thirsty land during the sowing season, and spring floods lay waste the crops when they are almost ready for the harvest, and devastate villages and even urban centers such as Baghdad.

Iraq is divided into two zones: a rainfall zone and an irrigation zone. Since the amount of rain is not controllable, agricultural expansion in the Mesopotamian valley must therefore depend on harnessing the waters of the Tigris-Euphrates river system.

### Regional Aspects of the System

Both the Tigris and Euphrates originate in Turkey. The Euphrates flows through Syria for some considerable distance before entering Iraq. Headwaters of the Lesser Zab and the Diyala, tributaries of the Tigris, are in the Iranian mountains and the east bank of the Shatt al-Arab forms one of the frontiers with Iran. Clearly then, both the Tigris and Euphrates are international rivers.

Iraq being a lower riparian country is in a very vulnerable position vis-a-vis Turkey, Syria, and Iran. Theoretically, there is very little that Iraq can do if any or all of these states embark on schemes for extensive exploitation and diversion of the waters of the two rivers and their tributaries. Moreover, anti-erosion measures, such as afforestation of the watershed areas of the system to protect the water storage works being built in Iraq from silting up, can be effective only with the cooperation of Turkey and Iran. A stable river development in Iraq is therefore contingent upon the execution of bilateral or multilateral agreements with the other riparian states concerned. The ideal would be one agreement to which Turkey, Iran, Syria, and Iraq would all be parties.

In the case of Iran, because of the mountainous terrain in which the watersheds of the Tigris tributaries are located, there is little likelihood that this country will divert any significant quantities of water. Its only objection could be concerning the possible deterioration of the Shatt al-Arab river for navigation. This eventuality seems remote.

Syria poses a different problem. Large areas there, adjacent to the Euphrates, are suitable for agricultural development. Actual large-scale projects, such as the proposed Yusuf Pasha dam, have been under consideration for some time. This would seriously reduce the amounts of water flow into Iraq from the Euphrates. Similarly, a proposed dam at Ana on the Euphrates in Iraq would back up the water into Syria over a distance of some sixty kilometers.

There is no agreement between Syria and Iraq concerning river control and allocation of water supply. A convention was signed in Paris on December 23, 1920, between France and Britain, as mandatory powers for Syria and Iraq, which called for the formation of a commission which would examine all proposed irrigation schemes in Syria which may seriously diminish "the waters of the Tigris and the Euphrates at the points where they enter the area of the British mandate in Mesopotamia." No such commission was set up. In any case, the convention is probably no longer binding. Iraq, upon the termination of the British mandate in 1932, declared herself bound by all the agreements made on its behalf by the Mandatory Administration. No such declaration was made by Syria when the French mandate was terminated in 1945.

The principle of cooperation (even though limited) between Iraq and Turkey over river control was established in the Treaty of Friendship and Neighborly Relations signed by the two governments on March 29, 1946. In Protocol I of the treaty Turkey allowed Iraq to establish meteorological stations in its territory, to conduct geological surveys for possible flood-control dam sites, and consented in principle, subject to confirmation in each case, to the construction by Iraq, in Turkey, of water works found to be necessary. Turkey also obligated itself to inform Iraq of any contemplated projects on the two rivers. Under the treaty, Iraq has so far established three meteorological stations in Turkish territory but no river works have been constructed there.

More recently, closer cooperation between Turkey, Iraq, and Iran over river control is being effected through the "Baghdad Pact." A Joint Irrigation Projects Committee has been established as a subdivision of the Pact's Economic Committee. There is also a subcommittee on cooperation in agricultural planning.

At a meeting of the Joint Irrigation Projects Committee held at Ankara in July, 1956, the Iranian and Turkish Governments undertook to establish meteorological and hydrological stations at the headwaters of the Euphrates, the Tigris, and their tributaries in their territories. The Committee also undertook to make a survey of joint irrigation projects which had been recommended by the Economic Committee at its meeting in Teheran earlier in the summer.

*Features of the Tigris-Euphrates System*

Sir William Willcocks, the great Anglo-Indian engineer, described the Nile as a "gentleman." In contrast, the Tigris and Euphrates can perhaps be described as two temperamental ladies who need considerable persuasion and control.

Unlike the Nile, the seasonal distribution of the water supplies of the system does not coincide with crop needs. Winter crops in Iraq need water from May onwards. The low-water season, however, lasts from July to December. During this period the mean water discharges of the Tigris and the Euphrates are 559 and 421 cubic meters per second (cumecs), respectively. The two rivers reach their lowest levels in September and October when water is badly needed.

When the crops are either half-grown or almost ready for the harvest and water is no longer badly needed, they are subject to the danger of inundation. Spring is the flood season. During this period the mean water discharges of the two rivers are 2,572 and 1,765 cumecs respectively.

In the case of summer crops which need water from April to September, the situation is reversed. At first they receive abundant supplies, then the supply declines gradually until it reaches a low point in September.

Again, unlike the Nile which flows gently, the Euphrates and the Tigris, particularly the latter, have very steep gradients in the upper and central parts of the valley, but very slight in the lower part. The bed of the Tigris slopes down at a ratio of 5.7:10,000 between the Turkish frontier and Baghdad, but from there on the ratio falls down to one in 20,000. The Euphrates, though not as steep (3.3:10,000), also flattens out from Ramadi on.

This feature has several important consequences. Erosive action in the upper reaches is extremely strong. Sediments are carried during all parts of the year. The effectiveness of water-storage and flood-control works and irrigation canals is therefore constantly endangered by silting. Moreover, the rivers during the flood season tend to be very violent (especially the Tigris). They thunder down the mountain slopes, sometimes sweeping away irrigation works, causing considerable damage to crops and carving themselves new courses.

On the other hand, the silt-laden waters have, during the past 5,000 years, built the southern part of the valley. At present, the delta on the shoreline of the gulf is being built entirely by the Karun river which flows from Iran, while the Tigris and Euphrates deposit their silt in the central marshes.

The waters of both the Tigris and Euphrates are somewhat saline. The proportion of salt in both rivers near Baghdad is thirty to thirty-three parts in 100,000. In the lower reaches of the Euphrates, however, salinity goes up to ninety per 100,000. This has resulted in progressive salination of the soil and declining crop yields. The Haigh Commission Report (*see below*) estimated that some 60 per cent of the irrigated areas have been affected by salination and that about 20-30 per cent of the cultivated land in the irrigation zone has been abandoned in recent decades because it was no longer suitable for cultivation.

Another feature of the system, which has had a favorable effect on agriculture, is that the bed of the Euphrates from north of Falluja southwards until the two rivers meet at Qurna, is slightly higher than that of the Tigris. In modern times, as in the past, this difference of elevation had been utilized to build a network of gravity flow canals from west to east to irrigate large areas of land.

Of the two rivers, the Euphrates is the more gentle and easier to control. During its course after leaving Turkey, only one main tributary, the Khabur in Syria, flows into it. Otherwise, in Iraq, it only receives the discharges of main *wadis* and seepages from the North Desert. Consequently, its water discharge fluctuates less widely than the Tigris.

In contrast, the Tigris is to a high degree unruly and difficult. It has a vast catchment area. As it flows from Turkey towards the Persian Gulf, it receives several tributaries: in Iraq, four: the Greater Zab, the Lesser Zab, the Udhaim and the Diyala. Both the Udhaim and the Diyala are difficult rivers. The floods of the former occur as a result of rain storms rather than melting snow, and, therefore, they fluctuate widely in volume and intensity. On the Diyala, floods occur suddenly with little warning. Hence, the Tigris is subject to periodic violent floods and is feared much more than the Euphrates.

*Reports on Water Control*

To appreciate the scope and significance of the vast water control program taking place now in Iraq, it is important to summarize here, in a few paragraphs, two global reports made on the subject in recent years. In fact, the present program is a modified version of their recommendations. They are the Haigh Commission Report[1] made in 1949 after some three years of field investigation, and the report of Knappen-Tippets-Abbett-McCarthy (KTAM), a New York engineering firm, made in 1952.[2]

## *The Haigh Report*

The report estimated the total gross area in the valley "available and suitable for cultivation" to be 27 million dunums (*see Table 13*). Only 12.7 million of this total are under cultivation, and only 5.2 million dunums are actually planted annually in winter crops, while most of the rest is left fallow.

With the installation of flood control works, water storage, drainage, land reclamation, new irrigation canals, improvement of existing canals, etc., the report states that 13 million dunums more can be irrigated, bringing the possible total to 25.7 million dunums.

The mean water supply of the Euphrates is 280 cumecs, of which 228 cumecs are used to irrigate inadequately some 4.7 million dunums. Of this area only 1.9 million dunums are planted in winter crops annually.

The report shows that by perennial live storage of some 17.2 billion cubic meters of water in Lake Habbaniya and the Abu Dibbis depression, it is possible to raise the water supply of the Euphrates to 510 cumecs, an amount sufficient both to irrigate four million dunums of new land and to improve the supplies of existing areas.

As for the Tigris and its tributaries, they have a mean water supply of 351 cumecs, which is used to irrigate a gross area of eight million dunums. Of this, only 3.3 million dunums, the report estimates, are annually planted in winter crops.

The report estimates that by perennial live storage of some 25 billion cubic meters of water in the Wadi Tharthar depression and other dams (such as the ones now being built), it is possible to raise the supply of the Tigris and its tributaries to 920 cumecs, making it possible to irrigate adequately the existing areas and also bring under cultivation 8.9 million dunums of new lands. Thus the total arable and irrigable areas in both basins would be 25.7 million dunums. The report assumes that the fallow system will continue to operate.

TABLE 13

THE HAIGH COMMISSION ESTIMATES: 1949
(in 1,000 dunums)

| | Estimated Total Area Suitable For Cultivation | Area Under Cultivation | | | | Gross New Land | Gross Total |
| --- | --- | --- | --- | --- | --- | --- | --- |
| | | Gross Flow | Gross Lift | Gross Total[a] | Annually Planted[b] | | |
| Euphrates | 9,110 | 3,109 | 1,562 | 4,671 | 1,897 | 4,029 | 8,700 |
| Tigris & Tributaries | 17,900 | 3,730 | 4,295 | 8,025 | 3,305 | 8,945 | 16,970 |
| Total | 27,010 | 6,839 | 5,857 | 12,696 | 5,202 | 12,974 | 25,670 |

Source: Haigh Report, op. cit., pp. 8-9, 88-100.

[a] Under the fallow system where land is allowed to rest in alternate years.
[b] Planted in winter crops. Most of the balance is left fallow.

## The KTAM Report

According to this report, the total arable and irrigable area in the Tigris-Euphrates Valley amounts to twenty-two million dunums, of which thirteen million are presently cultivated under the fallow system where the land is allowed to "rest" in alternate years. Nine million dunums more of arable land can be brought under irrigation.

The report proposes two alternative plans of development: Plan "A" and Plan "B" (see Table 14).

TABLE 14

KTAM REPORT ESTIMATES: 1952

Land Under Cultivation, New Land (Arable and Irrigable),
Plans of Development, and Water Requirements

| | Existing Areas Million Dunums | | New Land in Million Dunums | | | Annual Water Requirements in Billion Cubic Meters | | |
|---|---|---|---|---|---|---|---|---|
| | Fallow System | Intensive System | Intensive System | Total | Grand Total | Euphrates | Tigris | Total |
| Euphrates Basin | 4.9 | — | — | 2.8 | 7.7 | 6.1[a] | — | 6.1[a] |
| Tigris Basin | 8.1 | — | — | 6.2 | 14.3 | — | 11.3[a] | 11.3[a] |
| Total | 13.0 | — | — | 9.0 | 22.0 | 6.1[a] | 11.3[a] | 17.4[a] |
| Plan "A" | 13.0 | — | 9.0 | 9.0 | 22.0 | 12.1 | 26.1 | 38.2 |
| Plan "B" | 4.0 | 9.0 | 9.0 | 9.0 | 22.0 | 14.7 | 32.0 | 47.1 |

Source: KTAM Report, op. cit.

[a] Excluding new lands.

Under Plan "A", the 13 million dunums of existing land would continue to be cultivated under the fallow system with improved drainage. However, the nine million dunums of new land would be cultivated on the "basis of modern intensive methods including crop rotation, improved methods of cultivation and irrigation, livestock management, and other related modern practices." The annual water requirements under this plan would be 38.2 billion cubic meters of water.

Under Plan "B", four million dunums would continue to be cultivated under the fallow system (because of water supply limitations), and 18 million under the intensive system. The annual water requirements in this case would be 47.1 billion cubic meters.

The report argues that the water requirements of either plan "A" or "B" can be met from the available water supplies of the two rivers. In the case of the Tigris, measurements taken at Baghdad since 1906 show that its average annual discharge for the period has been 38.8 billion cubic meters. During 1930-34, a succession of dry years, the annual average discharge for the period was 32.5 billion cubic meters.

Similarly, measurements taken of the Euphrates since 1924 at Hit show an average annual flow for the period of 26.4 billion cubic meters. During the dry five-year period (1930-34), the average annual flow was 17.2 billion cubic meters.

The above figures show that the water supply is assured in both cases. The problem reduces itself to one of perennial storage. "If storage reservoirs are built, it will be possible to store water during a wet year and use it during a succeeding dry year; therefore, the flow during a single dry year is not necessarily critical."

The report estimates the total population of the valley as 3.3 million persons (against 5.1 for the whole country) of whom 1.2 million are urban and 2.1 million are rural. On the basis of these population estimates, the farm income of the inhabitants of the valley would rise in the following manner:

|  | Present (13 mil. dunums Fallow System) Dinars | Plan "A" Dinars | Plan "B" Dinars |
|---|---|---|---|
| Gross Farm Income (Includes Production Cost, Labor Cost & Surplus) | 118,000,000 | 542,000,000 | 764,000,000 |
| Net Farm Income, (Includes Labor Cost & Surplus) | 62,000,000 | 295,000,000 | 416,000,000 |
| Average Net Farm Income Per Head of Inhabitants (3.3 million) | 19 | 89 | 126 |

This vast increase in farm income, which would make the farm population of Iraq the most prosperous in the Middle East, is made contingent by the report on meeting certain basic requirements:

  (a)  Construction of new facilities
     1.  Drainage
     2.  Water storage facilities

    3. Irrigation canals and control works
    4. Flood control facilities

(b) Management
    1. Improved farm practices
    2. Organization and training
    3. Maintenance of completed works

The program of development would depend primarily on flow irrigation. Lift irrigation by comparison is very costly. The total cost of the program, excluding cost of flood and storage reservoirs, would be 198 million dinars ($555.4 million) with expenditures spaced over a period of twenty-five years.

At present, the target of the Development Board is—and correctly so—more modest than the KTAM proposals. During the past five years the Board has concentrated mainly on building basic facilities such as flood control and water storage works. In the recent program the emphasis has begun to shift to drainage and irrigation. The rest of this chapter will be devoted to the accomplishments of the Board in the fields of flood control, storage, irrigation, and drainage.

## Flood Control and Water Storage

Until 1952 very little was done to control the flood menace. Minor works, mostly embankments called "bunds," were constructed, and Lake Habbaniya was utilized to some extent for overflow from the Euphrates. These measures could cope with the danger of moderate floods only. No wonder, then, that the Development Board gave first priority in its program to flood control projects.

In 1956, the two major flood control works were completed, bringing a good measure of safety to Iraq for the first time in its long history. Others which are now under construction will bring the flood menace under full control, making it a memory of a dreaded past.

### The Euphrates

The worst recorded flood on the Euphrates, that of May 5, 1929, had a maximum discharge of 5,200 cubic meters per second at Hit. Flood control and storage on the Euphrates centers around the Lake Habbaniya water complex reduce the maximum possible flood danger from 5,200 to 2,000 cumecs. With the use of the Abu Dibbis depression, it can be reduced still further to 1,500 cumecs, thus giving full protection against flood from the Euphrates.

The complex is composed of six major components:

1. *Lake Habbaniya itself*, which serves the dual purpose of a flood escape and a storage reservoir. Until 1956, its storage capacity was 1.3 billion cubic meters. In that year, however, work on raising its dykes from 49.5 to 51 meters above sea level was completed, giving it a storage capacity of 2.3 billion cubic meters. This has now reduced the flood danger from 5,200 to 4,000 cumecs.

2. *The Ramadi Barrage.* Work on this barrage started in 1953. Its total cost came to 1.4 million dinars. It is located across the Euphrates and is 209 meters long and fourteen meters high. It has a fish ladder and a navigation lock to allow the passage of river craft.

The barrage arrests the upstream waters of the river and thus reduces the flood danger further to 2,000 cumecs, and makes it possible to fill the lake to a higher level. The excess flood water is diverted to the lake through the Warrar regulator.

3. *Warrar Inlet Canal and regulator.* Both the canal and the regulator were completed in 1952. The canal is 8.5 kilometers long and connects the river with the lake. During floods, its regulator can divert water through the canal at the rate of 2,800 cumecs.

4. *The Dhibban Outlet Canal and regulator.* Both were completed in 1951. The canal is thirteen kilometers long and connects the lake with the Euphrates. Its purpose is to feed the river from water stored in Lake Habbaniya during the dry season. Its regulator has a discharge capacity of 250 cumecs.

5. *The Majjara Escape Canal.* This was completed in 1945. It is 8.2 kms. long and connects the lake with the Abu Dibbis depression. Should floods exceed the storage

capacity of the lake, the regulator on the canal can discharge water to the depression at the rate of 850 cumecs. At present another escape canal to the depression, with a discharge capacity of 2,800 cumecs, is under study.

6. *The Abu Dibbis Depression.* This is a natural depression with no outlet canal. At present it is used only for flood control purposes: that is, to receive the water overflow from Lake Habbaniya through the Majjara Escape Canal.

The new storage provided by the Habbaniya complex has now raised the available water supplies of the Euphrates from 280 to 440 cumecs. This amount can now provide sufficient water supplies to existing cultivated areas and in addition bring under cultivation some 2.4 million *dunums* gross of new land.

It is possible to increase the water supplies of the Euphrates and provide for additional flood protection by using the Abu Dibbis for storage (*see preceding summary of Haigh Report*). The depression would have a storage capacity of 21 billion cubic meters gross or 14.5 billion net. This would reduce the flood danger still further to 1,500 cumecs and increase the water supply of the Euphrates to a total of 510 cumecs.

The IBRD Mission, however, had very serious reservations about the usefulness of the depression for irrigation storage because of its high salt content, which would render water stored there useless for irrigation purposes.[3]

The above question is now under study. If it is proved that the water stored in the depression is usable for irrigation, then the full potential development of the Euphrates basin, insofar as water supplies are concerned, has already been achieved. Otherwise, an alternative storage site will have to be found.

## The Tigris and Its Tributaries

Many studies have been made to determine the best sites for flood control and storage works on the Tigris and its tributaries. Several proposed sites are now under investigation by engineers; some are under construction and one has been completed.

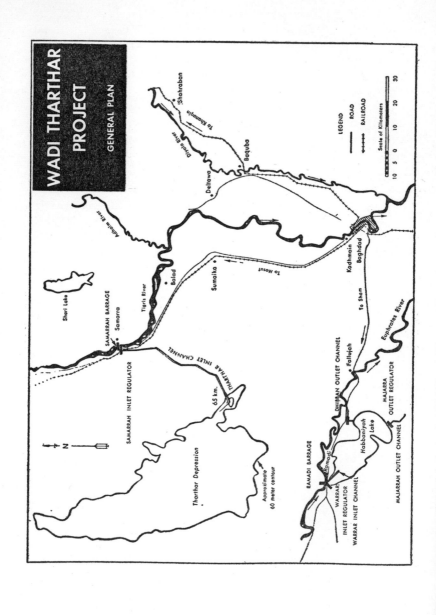

*The Wadi Tharthar Project.* The major flood control
work on the Tigris and, for that matter, in the whole of
Iraq is the Tharthar project. It was officially inaugurated by
the king on April 2, 1956 in an imposing ceremony attended
by foreign diplomats, government leaders, and most of the
prominent personalities in the country.

Work on the project started in 1952 with an average labor
force, until completion, of about 3,000 workers and 140
engineers. The earthwork removal came to about 60 per
cent of that carried out for the construction of the Suez
Canal. The cost, up to March 1956, amounted to 12.1
million dinars ($33.88 million); 4.5 million dinars more are
expected to be spent before completion.

The maximum recorded flood discharge of the Tigris
at Samarra where the barrage of the project is located, was
12,000 cumecs (in February 1941). The project reduces
this maximum danger to 3,500 cumecs, thus giving Baghdad
and downstream areas a considerable margin of safety.
The project consists of three main parts.:

1. *The Wadi Tharthar.* This is a vast natural depression
which lies between the Tigris and Euphrates about forty
miles northwest of Baghdad. Its lowest point is three meters
below sea level, but its edges rise to a height of 60 meters above.
The wadi is 100 kilometers long and some forty kilometers
wide with an area of 2,025 square kilometers. When filled to
a height of sixty meters, it forms a lake with a gross capacity
of sixty-eight billion cubic meters, comparable in size to the
Dead Sea in Palestine. Its live (net) storage, however, depends on how high the depression is filled and on how low
an outlet irrigation canal is drawn. For instance, if the depression is filled to a height of fifty-eight meters, and the
outlet canal is drawn at a height of thirty-eight meters, then
the dead storage would be 33 billion cubic meters, and the
live storage, thirty billion cubic meters.

2. *The Inlet Canal and regulator.* The canal is sixty-
five kilometers long and connects the Tigris with the depression. Its regulator can discharge water at the rate of
9,000 cumecs. Consideration is now being given to enlarging
the canal and the discharge capacity of the regulator.

3. *The Barrage.* This lies across the Tigris near the town of Samarra. It backs up the upstream waters of the Tigris and diverts the excess flow to the depression through the canal. The barrage has an estimated potential capacity of generating 112,000 kilowatts of electric power.

As in the case of the Abu Dibbis depression, there are doubts that the Wadi Tharthar depression is sufficiently water-tight for irrigation storage. The Haigh Commission was certain that it is. Other experts and consulting engineers who have studied the project since are not so certain. In the view of Lord Salter, its usefulness, according to the criteria of salinity and seepage, cannot be determined before 1961 and, in any case, it will take ten years for the depression to fill to the level at which water can be used.

Should the depression be found suitable for irrigation storage, there will be very little need for any further storage works, for, along with the dams under construction, it will be able to meet all the water requirements of existing and new lands in the Tigris Basin. An interesting project, which is under study now, is a canal connecting the Habbaniya complex with the depression.

*The Dokan Dam.* This project is located on the Lesser Zab river at the Dokan gorge some 60 kilometers northwest of the town of Sulaimaniya near the Iranian border in the northeast of Iraq. Work on the dam started in 1954 and is scheduled to be completed in 1958. The budgeted cost of the dam proper is 13 million dinars ($36.4 million).

The dam, when completed, will be the largest of its kind in the Middle East. It consists of a massive concrete arch-shaped wall across the gorge, 325 meters long and 108 meters high. The thickness of the wall at the bottom will be fifty meters and at the top nine meters. It will create a mountain lake fifty square kilometers in area with a storage capacity of 6.8 billion cubic meters.

The structure will also have two diversion tunnels, 12.5 and 11 meters in diameter respectively, to be used as spillways for flood water. In addition, it will have five outlets, each 3.65 meters in diameter, for future generation of electric power.

The dam is a multi-purpose structure. Its primary purpose is to store water for irrigating an estimated area of 1.3 million dunums. Its second important purpose is flood control. It will reduce further the flood danger on the Tigris and protect the downstream areas on the Lesser Zab. Thirdly, it is estimated that the dam can generate 170,000 kilowatts of power. Finally, the lake created can be used as a resort area.

*The Darband-i-Khan Dam.* This structure is located on a gorge of the Diyala river in the northeast of Iraq near the Iranian border. Work on the dam began in 1955 and is scheduled to be completed in 1959. The budgeted cost is 17 million dinars ($47.6 million).

The project calls for the construction of a dam across the gorge 35 meters long and 130 meters high which will create a lake with an estimated storage capacity of 3.2 billion cubic meters. Like the Dokan, it is a multi-purpose structure for water storage, flood control and potential generation of hydroelectric power. It is expected to irrigate some 1.5 million dunums.

*The Batma Dam.* Specifications for this dam are now ready and work is scheduled to start late in 1957 and to be completed in 1958. The amount budgeted for this project is two million dinars.

The dam will be located on the Lesser Zab and is considered as part of the Dokan dam complex. It will consist of a barrage across the river which will store water supplied by the Dokan Dam for irrigation of the Makhmur land and the Hawija project. The dam will also divert the surplus water, through a feeder canal to be constructed, to the Udhaim River.

*The Udhaim Dam.* Like the Batma Dam, this will also be part of the Dokan complex. Work is scheduled to begin in 1957 and is expected to be completed in 1958. 1.5 million dinars have been budgeted for this project.

The structure will be located on the Udhaim river. It will consist of a barrage across the river which will store the water of the river itself and that conveyed by the feeder canal from the Batma dam. The structure is expected to irrigate an estimated area of 214,000 dunums on its right bank, and 662,000 dunums on the left bank.

*Other Proposed Dams.* Two more dams have been under study and investigation for some time: The Bekhme on the Greater Zab river, and Eski Mosul on the Tigris north of Mosul. Their suitability as dam sites has been established. Studies indicate that if a dam is erected on the Bekhme gorge to a height of 165 meters, it would have a storage capacity of 8.3 billion cubic meters of water in addition to generating 600,000 kilowatts of electric power. It is estimated that the Eski Mosul dam would have a storage capacity of eight billion cubic meters. Funds have been allocated for these two dams in the 1955-60 program. However, construction will take place only when and if it is determined that there is need for further water storage. Such a decision may be reached towards the end of 1959.

## *Irrigation*

Canal building in Iraq was brought to the level of a fine art by the ancient Babylonians and was further developed by the peoples that followed them. Historical evidence indicates that, up to the thirteenth century A. D., there was a much larger area of land under cultivation than at present. The canals of today follow to a surprising degree the ruins of those built centuries ago.

When the Development Board was organized, there was already in existence an intricate system of canals, a large number of which were built during the past three decades. The Board's task in this respect is twofold: first, to improve the efficiency of the existing system by the installation of barrages, regulators, pumping plants, and desilting works; by reclamation of canals which had silted up; and by remodeling, expanding and extending others; second, to build new canals where needed. Through such measures, water supplies to areas under cultivation can be improved, large areas of land can be reclaimed, and finally, the danger from floods can be reduced further by diverting excess waters to where they can do no harm.

As pointed out above, the emphasis during the past six years has been more on building dams and less on improving existing facilities. In recent programs far more emphasis is being placed on irrigation and drainage than before. For instance, in the first Six-Year Plan (1951-56), the amount allotted to irrigation was ten million dinars, most of which was not spent. In the second Six-Year Plan (1955-56), irrigation was allotted more than 30 million dinars under various expenditure categories. What is more important is that the allotments are actually being spent. In the following few pages some of the main irrigation projects either under study or construction will be discussed.

*The Euphrates*

1. The Hilla Canal System.

This canal is commanded by the Hindiyah barrage built in 1913. It is the largest canal in Iraq served by a single intake. With its four main branches, it serves some 2.7 million dunums of land in the Euphrates basin. One of its branches, the Dagharra, has deteriorated to the point of becoming useless.

Investigations by the engineering firm KTAM show that if the Hilla system is expanded, remodeled, and desilting works installed, it can be made to serve 1.8 million dunums more of government land. This land can be divided into small holdings and cultivated under the intensive system. The estimated total cost of improving the canal is 25 million dinars. Ten million have been allocated for it during the 1956-60 program.

As a first step the Board has already approved the expansion of the Hilla Canal from its head down to its first branch, the Babil Canal, together with the expansion of the Babil Canal itself, to provide water for 400,000 dunums of government land. Aside from enlargement, the work also includes earth embankments, one cross regulator on the Hilla Canal, two cross and one inlet regulator on the Babil Canal.

2. The Greater Musayyib Project.

Work on this project began in 1953 and was completed in the fall of 1956. It brought under irrigation 250,000 dunums of new land, the distribution of which began in November 1956 (and brought reassured supplies of water to 85,000 dunums which were already under irrigation and privately owned).

The work consisted of two parts. First, enlarging, re-modeling, and extending the old canal. It is now 50 kilo-meters long, has twelve lateral canals, and a 500-kilometer network of small canals. Second, providing full drainage facilities to the areas to be irrigated. In addition to excava-tion, the work also involved installing cross, main, and small regulators, pumping stations, etc.

3. Euphrates Tail Regulators.

In the rice-growing area just above Lake Hammar in the south, constant erosion has made the bed of the Euphrates there so low in relation to the silted land that water distribu-tion in the dry season has become almost impossible. To control erosive action, and to raise the water level in the river when needed, work on the installation of five regulators on the tails of the Euphrates before Lake Hammar, began in 1954 and is due to be completed in the early part of 1957. Expenditures on this project amounted to some 700,000 dinars.

4. The Shamiyah Canal Project.

The Shamiyah is actually a branch of the Euphrates which has been canalized. It needs extensive improvements, including remodeling and expansion. This, however, is still under study. In the meantime, erosive action, a phe-nomenon known in Iraq as *naggarat*, lowers the bed of the canal and its subsidiaries in the dry season, making the distribution of water in this rice land very difficult. As partial measures, a main regulator was installed at the tail of the canal (250,000 dinars), and the Directorate of Irrigation on behalf of the Board is at present installing eleven small regulators (total cost 37,000 dinars) on both sides of Mish-Khab, in addition to constructing bunds, a cross regulator, a side regulator, and a navigation lock (total cost 33,000 dinars).

## The Tigris

1.  The Gharraf Canal Project.

The Gharraf is the main canal system on the Tigris. It is commanded by the Kut barrage built in 1939. With its two branches, the Shatrah and the Bad'a, the Gharraf serves an area roughly estimated at about 2.3 million dunums. Studies show that with remodeling, enlargement, and extension, water supplies to existing areas can be improved and 600,000 dunums of new government land can be brought under irrigation. The consulting engineers, KTAM, recommended the construction of the following works:

    a.   Drainage: The Western and Eastern outfalls, also the Dujailah outfall.

    b.   Four regulators on the Gharraf with bunds and lateral gates.

    c.   Seven regulators on the Bad'a canal.

    d.   A new canal extension to irrigate new government land in the Jazirat area.

Some eight million dinars have been allocated for this project. Construction of the regulators is scheduled for completion in 1958, and construction of the new canal is expected to begin in 1957 with the hope that by 1960 some 10 per cent of the new land will be served with water.

## The Lesser Zab and Udhaim Basin

The construction of the two dams on the Lesser Zab and the Udhaim to utilize the waters of the Dokan dam will necessitate the enlargement of one canal, and the construction of one feeder canal to irrigate some 1.3 million *dunums* of land. The areas that will benefit are as follows:

| | | |
|---|---:|---|
| Makhmur | 162,000 | dunums |
| Hawija | 253,000 | " |
| Udhaim right bank | 214,000 | " |
| Udhaim left bank (Ghurfa) | 663,000 | " |
| | 1,291,000 | |

The Hawija canal is at present being enlarged. Construction of canals and related works was scheduled to begin in 1957 and to be completed in 1958. Construction of other structures and canals was also to begin in 1957. It is expected that 15 per cent of the area will be served by 1960.

*Other Projects*

1.   Reclamation of Nahrawan Lands

These lands are located on the eastern bank of the Tigris south of the Diyala river. They constitute about 1.2 million dunums. Study of their reclamation is under way and construction of canals and related works is scheduled to begin in 1958. Very little land, if any, however, will be ready to be served with water by 1960 when the present program terminates.

2.   The Ishaqi Area

Irrigation of the Ishaqi area on the Tigris south of the Tharthar barrage is now under study. Construction of canals and drainage is expected to begin in 1958 and it is hoped that about 15 per cent of the area will be served with water by 1960.

3.   Basrah Lands

Improvement of irrigation, flood control on the Shatt al-Arab and Lake Hammar, and land reclamation in the Basrah area have been under study for some time. Four million dinars have been allocated to this project between 1955-60 and construction is expected to begin in 1957.

4.   Northern Districts Project

Studies of small irrigation projects in Mosul, Arbil, and Kirkuk and Sulaimaniya *liwas* for relocation of persons displaced by the Dokan and Darband-i-Khan reservoirs are now under way. Construction in each case will commence when plans are ready. Eleven million dinars have been allocated for these and other irrigation projects in the north.

5.   Diyala Basin Project

The Diyala barrage built in 1939 commands six canals which irrigate an area of some 1.3 million dunums. Water from the Darband-i-Khan Dam is expected to irrigate 1.5 million more dunums of new land. Studies are now under way to enlarge and remodel some of the existing canals and build new ones to irrigate the new land to be brought under cultivation. Five million dinars have been allocated for the Diyala lands project.

*Drainage*

Salination of the soil is a deadly enemy of the Iraqi *fallah*. The Haigh Commission estimated that 60 per cent of the flow-irrigated area has been affected and 20 to 30 per cent abandoned in the past three decades because it became either not profitable or impossible to cultivate it. Crop yield, it was also estimated, declined by 20 to 50 per cent.

The high concentration of salt in the soil, especially in the flow-irrigated areas, is due primarily to continuous irrigation and flooding combined with the high rate of evaporation that obtains in these climatic conditions. Irrigation keeps the sub-soil water table high, just below the ground surface, exposed to the hot summer sun. When evaporation takes place, it leaves salt deposits in the plant root zone. As the years go by, the salt accumulation becomes toxic in quantity, gradually causes a decline in crop yield, and finally makes further cultivation impossible.

Fortunately, the chemical composition of the salt in most of Iraq is such that it can be "washed out" of the land by drainage. With deep drains, the sub-soil water table is lowered; accumulated salts are flushed and further accumulation prevented. Moreover, in this manner, as the KTAM Report states, "The root zone of the plant will be deepened, more minerals that are available in the soil will become available to the plants, stagnant waters will be removed, the growing season will be lengthened...crop rotation...will become possible; in general, the health and yields of crops will be greatly improved."

Hardly any measures were taken to combat salination during the past thirty years. Even new settlement projects such as Dujailah (1945), in which the government invested considerable amounts of money, were not provided with drainage facilities, so that after ten years of cultivation salt began to appear and the land began to deteriorate.

The "drainage movement" began in earnest when the Development Board was organized. Since its creation, the

Board has become more and more drainage-conscious. In its first program, the total allocation for drainage amounted to 4.1 million dinars. In its second program, it rose to 13.9 million, and in the last program, the allocation jumped to 28.3 million dinars. Drainage of cultivated areas is now taking place on a fairly large scale. Excavation of new canals and reclamation of new land go hand in hand with installation of drainage facilities. In the following few pages, the main drainage schemes that have been completed or are under construction or study will be discussed.

The drainage program consists of three main parts. First is the excavation of drainage outfalls. These are very large channels. Because of the vast areas they serve, they will be almost small rivers when completed. To protect them from silt- and sand-laden winds, especially in undeveloped areas, windbreaks consisting of trees and other vegetation are also planned as part of the program. Secondly, deep main drains and their subsidiaries are being excavated. These are designed to lower the underground water table. They will empty into rivers and natural depressions or into outfalls. Finally, some of the drains will flow by gravity. In the case of a large number, pumping will be required.

The KTAM Report mentioned previously estimated the total cost of a full drainage program at 79 million dinars ($221 million), divided as follows:

a)  7 drainage outfalls        —     26,700,000  dinars

b)  main drains
    21 in Euphrates Basin—      19,648,000     "
    12 in Tigris Basin      —      32,508,000     "

                               78,856,000     "

Some 30 million dinars have been allocated for the period up to 1960. Assuming this sum is fully spent, then at the termination of the present program in 1960, only 38 per cent of the drainage work needed will have been completed.

1.  *The Musayyib Project Drains.*  This is the first project to be fully completed providing drainage for some 335,000

dunums of land. Work on excavating both the Musayyib-Babil outfall and the main drains began in 1954 and was brought to completion in the closing days of 1956.

TABLE 15

DEVELOPMENT BOARD ALLOCATIONS FOR DRAINAGE
(in 1,000 Iraqi Dinars)

|  | Actually spent up to March 31, 1956 | 56 | 57 | 58 | 59 | 60 | Total |
|---|---|---|---|---|---|---|---|
| Left Bank of Euphrates & Hilla Canal including Rumeitha | 825 | 1,100 | 1,000 | 650 | 500 | 750 | 4,825 |
| Right Bank of Euphrates & Hilla Canal | 245 | 300 | 700 | 1,350 | 1,300 | 1,350 | 5,245 |
| Land on the Gharraf Canal Project |  | 200 | 500 | 1,600 | 4,000 | 5,700 | 12,000 |
| Diyala Land Project | 180 | 200 | 500 | 1,000 | 1,700 | 1,600 | 5,180 |
| Others | 450 | 500 | 300 | 400 | 500 | 600 | 2,750 |
| Total | 1,700 | 2,300 | 3,000 | 4,980 | 8,000 | 10,000 | 30,100 |

Source: Law No. 54 (1956), p. 19.

2. *The Dujailah Project.* As a pilot project, 25,000 dunums of the Dujailah settlement were provided with drainage facilities. Work began in 1954 and was completed the following year. Work on drainage for the whole area continues. The excavation of the Dujailah outfall was scheduled to start in 1956 with the expectation that the greater part of it will be completed by 1960.

3. *The Saqlawiyah Drain.* Through this project some 166,000 dunums of land on the Saqlawiyah and Abu Ghraib canals will be provided with drainage facilities. Work began in 1954 and is due to be completed in 1957.

4. *The Tuwairij Drain.* Work on providing drainage for some 31,000 dunums in the Hindiyah area began in 1954, and will be completed in 1957.

5. *The Ba'quba Drain.* This provides drainage for 11,800 dunums of land on the Khoraisan canal on the Diyala river. The work has now been completed.

6. *The Hawija Settlement.* Work on providing drainage for the Hawija settlement on the Lesser Zab began in 1955 and still continues.

7. *The Shamiya Drain.* Work on the eastern drain of the Shamiya canal area began in 1954 and still continues.

8. *Construction of Outfalls.* Construction of the Euphrates-Tigris outfall began in 1950. Only a small part of it however will be completed by 1960. Work on the Shamiya and Gharraf outfalls was scheduled to begin in 1956.

9. *Scheduled Projects.* Work will begin soon in earnest to provide drainage to the areas served by the following canals: left and right banks of the Euphrates and Hilla canal; the Gharraf, Abu Ghraib, Yusafiyah, Bani Hasan, and Husseiniyah. All these, with the exception of the Gharraf, are on the Euphrates.

*Conclusion*

Iraq is well under way in its agricultural development program. Within the short span of six years, it has forged ahead of every country in the Middle East. By 1960, most if not all the water reservoirs and flood-control structures will have been built. The effort will then shift almost exclusively to the improvement of the irrigation system, drainage and land reclamation.

The total cost of the agricultural development program was estimated by the Minister of Development in 1955 at 282 million dinars. By 1960, if the program keeps on schedule, some 180 million will have been invested. This means that over 60 per cent of the program will have been completed. About a million and a half dunums of new land will also have been reclaimed and developed by then.

Tangible effects of the agricultural development program have just begun to be felt. The floods of 1956 were completely

averted; crop yields are beginning to improve in both quality
and quantity; landless peasants are being settled on new
lands in increasing numbers and lands which remained
desert wastes for centuries are beginning to bloom again.

Agricultural development in Iraq is of significance not
only for the country itself, but also for the Middle East. Iraq
can become the main supplier of agricultural products,
particularly of cereals, to the area. This would be far less costly
to the Middle East than importing these commodities from
distant areas such as Canada and Australia. In times of war,
the Middle East would not have to suffer food shortages because of lack of transportation facilities on the high seas. During World War II, such shortages did occur and it was necessary for the British and American Governments, which controlled the shipping in the area, to organize the Middle East
Supply Center to control distribution of basic commodities.
Moreover, this new development would encourage intraregional trade, the lack of which has been one of the chief
economic problems of the area during the past three decades.

1. Iraq Government, Directorate General of Irrigation, *Report on the Control
of the Rivers of Iraq and the Utilization of Their Waters.* Submitted by the Irrigation Development Commission, F. F. Haigh, president. (Baghdad: The
Baghdad Press, 1951.) Hereafter referred to as Haigh Report.
2. Knappen-Tippetts-Abbett-McCarthy, Engineers, *Report on the Development
of the Tigris and Euphrates River Systems.* A report submitted to the Iraq Development Board, (mimeographed) (New York: 1952.) Hereafter referred to
as KTAM Report.
3. *IBRD,* p. 186.

CHAPTER **5**

# THE PROBLEM OF LAND TENURE AND AGRARIAN REFORM

*Forms of Land Tenure*

For all practical purposes, a class of independent farmers who own the lands they farm does not exist in Iraq. The land is owned, largely, under various forms of land tenure by a very small group of tribal shaikhs, *aghas*, and city landlords. The great majority of the farming population is composed of what would be called in the United States sharecroppers. Since over 70 per cent of the population is employed in agriculture or allied industries, land tenure is the human problem *par excellence* in Iraq. In one way or another, it lies behind most, if not all, of the social, economic, and political problems of the country.

In theory, the state has ultimate ownership of almost all lands and the underground water and mineral resources pertaining to them. Within this framework, four main forms of tenure are recognized:

1. *Mulk.* Land held in absolute private ownership. In most cases, this is restricted to urban property.
2. *Matruka* (literally, "What is left"). Land reserved for public purposes. In actual practice this is treated as state land.

3. *Waqf.* Property or land in trust. There are two types of waqf.

    (a) True *waqf.* Property or land administered for the benefit of religious institutions by the government Awqaf Administration, or for the benefit of private persons by individuals appointed by religious courts.

    (b) "Untrue" *waqf.* Property or land from which taxes or revenues were assigned in the past to religious institutions.

4. *Miri* land. State land, of which there are three kinds:

    (a) *Miri Tapu.* Land held in permanent tenure from the state amounting to absolute private ownership. Documentary proof of registration is required for such tenure. Otherwise, factual evidence that the land has been productively used by the holder or his predecessors for at least ten years during which no rent was paid, or that it was planted with trees. *Tapu* land can be mortgaged, sold, or inherited.

    (b) *Miri Lazma.* Land held under the same general conditions as *tapu* lands. The holder must prove that he has made productive use of the land during the preceding fifteen years. In contrast to *tapu*, however, the government may veto the transfer of *lazma*.

    (c) *Miri Sirf.* Land which definitely and exclusively belongs to the state.

Although *tapu* and *lazma* lands are still officially regarded as state or *miri* lands, in actual practice they can hardly be distinguished from full private ownership. *Tapu* land, as mentioned above, may be mortgaged, sold, or inherited. The same applies to *lazma* with certain reservations which are now very seldom employed. Legally, ownership of both *lazma* and *tapu* lands may lapse if they are not productively used for three and four successive years respectively but this rarely, if ever, happens. Before 1939, holders of both *lazma* and *tapu* lands were assessed an annual payment for "rent" and water rights, which was a little higher for *lazma* than for *tapu*. In that year these assessments were abolished. With this furtherance, very little distinction remained between *tapu* and *lazma* lands and between *tapu* and *lazma* and full ownership.

## History of Land Tenure

The land tenure system is the result of historical forces, legal concepts, and tribal traditions which go back to ancient times. When the Arabs first occupied Iraq (641 A.D.), land was classified into two kinds: *kharaj* (tax-land) and *'ushr* (tithe-land). During the Abbassid Caliphate (750-1257) these two were expanded into five classifications: the King's lands, feudal lands, *mulk* (private property), *masha'a* (common land) and *wafq* (religious trust land).

The period between 1258, when the Mongol hordes invaded Iraq, and 1534, when the Ottomans established their rule, was one of general retrogression. The great irrigation canals were destroyed, the blooming gardens and green fields gradually became wasteland, the desert encroached on the farmland, the population decreased rapidly, and nomadism spread. Internecine tribal warfare became the order of the day. Only in the twentieth century did Iraq begin to recover from the havoc and devastation wrought by the Mongols and subsequent war lords.

From this period until the nineteenth century laws were loosely enforced. Both individuals and tribes, in most cases, claimed title to the land by the simple expedient of occupying it without making any special effort to seek or obtain legal sanction. Tribal land was regarded as the common property of the tribe.

As the tribes changed their nomadic mode of existence and began a settled life, their shaikhs, being powerful, were able to assert their claim to tribal land as their personal property. Their free warrior tribesmen gradually became their subservient sharecroppers. In addition, large land grants were made by the state to tribal chieftains either to bribe them into good behavior or to reward them for services rendered.

In 1858 the Ottoman government attempted to bring some order into the chaos. Through the Land Code which it promulgated in that year and the Land Registration Law of the year after, it sought to establish one system of tenure, the *tapu*. The attempt was not only a failure but also added to the general confusion.

For one thing, because of the existing system of shifting agriculture, it was difficult in many cases to determine what land belonged to whom. Grants were made in most cases without examination of conflicting claims and were used as a means of rewarding some and punishing others. Influential notables and tribal chiefs with the help of corrupt officials were also able to register huge tracts of lands in their names.

In the northern districts whole villages and their lands were registered as the personal property of local notables and *aghas*. These had previously served as intermediaries between the state and the cultivators, collecting taxes and performing other functions.

Land-grabbing by the powerful few was assisted to some extent by the cultivators themselves. Many of them were apprehensive that registration might mean more taxes and/or military service (not a farfetched assumption). Moreover, they were powerless against the periodic raids of nomadic tribes, or against the ubiquitous money-lender. With promise of protection against all these dangers, many of them were willing to register their lands in the names of neighboring influential notables and tribal chieftains. Later, as was to be expected, these latter claimed the lands as their own and the original owners became their tenants.

During the British mandate (1920-32) the Ottoman Land Code continued to operate. The administration's policy tended to use the land for political purposes, to win supporters and punish troublemakers. By special decrees some large holdings were given to shaikhs, some land sold and the ownership of some transferred to others.

A new complication appeared during this period with the introduction of fuel-pump irrigation. Many financially able city merchants entered into agreements with holders of *miri* land whereby they supplied the pumps and in return received a specified share of the crop. This added one more claim to the many unresolved existing claims.

By the time the national government assumed full power, the land problem had become extremely serious. When the Turks left the country, they either took with them or destroyed all the land registry records so that there was very little documentary proof of ownership left. Almost invariably, ownership was contested among various parties, which many times led to tribal warfare. Very few, if any, felt legally secure in their claims to the land which they held. In his report to the government on the subject, Sir Ernest Dawson, a British land expert, wrote:

> No man engaged in the management and cultivation of a landholding, large or small, can be expected to sink his capital in the land and devote his energies unreservedly to its development, if he is uncertain whether he and his heirs will benefit by his husbandry. . . .
> The injurious effect of the existing welter of uncertainty and dispute upon both the agricultural prosperity of the country and public order, can hardly be exaggerated. . . . Indeed the most diligent enquiry would be unlikely to reveal anywhere any appreciable number of holdings, large or small, held in undisputed possession and free from hampering and conflicting claims. It needs no great effort of the imagination to appreciate the blighting effect of these unhappy conditions prevailing throughout the country, upon the prosperity of the main national industry and the welfare and contentment of the people as a whole.[1]

In line with the recommendations of Sir Ernest Dawson, the government took concrete steps. In 1932 it passed the Land Settlement Law (replaced in 1938), which recognized the four forms of tenure discussed at the beginning of this chapter and inaugurated a cadastral survey to be conducted by settlement committees. The task of these committees was to survey the whole country, to investigate conflicting claims and to adjudicate ownership under the forms of tenure recognized by the law. The survey has been going on since 1933 and is at present almost complete in most of the provinces.

A feature of the law, which was absent before, is the introduction of *lazma* tenure. This was designed to recognize prescriptive rights to tribal lands. In application, however, the shaikhs and other persons with sufficient influence managed to have a considerable part of these lands registered in their own names. Settlement officers, many of whom were either inexperienced or subject to influence, accepted from such persons the most flimsy proofs. Cultivation of the land for any one year, or even more tenuous evidence, was regarded as sufficient to establish prescriptive rights. In this manner many tribesmen were dispossessed of their property, and large areas of state land alienated to shaikhs and notables.

## Land Distribution

Table 16 shows the areas of land under the various systems of tenure classified up to 1956 by the cadastral survey. Of the land classified, over 61 per cent is *miri sirf* or state land. The Government's newly inaugurated agrarian policy of land reform depends on this *miri sirf* land reserve for the creation of a new farmer class of independent, small peasant proprietors.

Full data on the distribution of ownership by size of holdings are not available since the cadastral survey is not yet completed. However, partial data up to February 8, 1951, when the survey was about half-completed for the fourteen provinces, show that the total area classified in private ownership (*mulk*, *tapu*, and *lazma*) was divided then in size of holdings as follows:[2]

*Per cent of Area in*
*Private Holdings*

  1.1 in holdings of  100,001-200,000 dunums
23.2 in holdings of   10,001-100,000 dunums
42.8 in holdings of    1,001- 10,000 dunums
  6.2 in holdings of     501- 1,000 dunums
11.0 in holdings of     101- 500 dunums
15.7 in holdings of       1- 100 dunums

Although these figures do not cover the whole country, they are representative. Of the privately owned land classified, only 15.7 per cent belongs to small peasant proprietors. Over 67 per cent is owned in holdings of over 1,000 dunums. These are national averages and do not reflect the full picture. For instance, of the private land classified in six provinces, up to 1951, holdings of 10,000-100,000 dunums accounted for the following percentages: Amara, 75.8; Kut, 47.5; Karbala, 31.3; Mosul, 27.2; Baghdad, 20.9; Diwaniya, 20.6.

TABLE 16

TYPE OF LAND OWNERSHIP
CLASSIFIED BY THE CADASTRAL SURVEY
1933-1956

| | In Thousand Dunums | Per Cent |
|---|---|---|
| Mulk | 239 | 0.3 |
| Matruka | 5,136 | 6.5 |
| Waqf | 840 | 1.1 |
| Tapu | 12,348 | 15.6 |
| Lazma | 11,649 | 14.8 |
| Miri Sirf | 8,701 | 61.7 |
| Total | 78,913 | 100.0 |

Source: *Statistical Abstract for 1956*, p. 70.

It is true that some of these holdings are owned by more than one person. This is more than counterbalanced by the fact that many persons own a number of holdings in several administrative areas. These have been registered as separate units. For instance, the survey lists only one holding over 100,000 dunums in the Kut province. It is a well-known fact, however, that there are several holdings there, each of which is over 300,000 dunums. These figures illustrate the central point, namely, that the country to all practical purposes is devoid of small peasant proprietors and that the land is mostly owned by large landholders, most of whom are tribal shaikhs and city notables. Data available since 1951 support the above picture. Table 17 shows the number of *lazma* grants in holdings of over 10,000 dunums and their total areas, made between 1933 and 1954 in nine of the provinces. Sixty-six of these holdings are owned by single individuals. It should be noted that several of these holdings may be owned by one person.

*Condition of the Fallah*

As has been shown, the greater part of the private agricultural holdings are owned by a very small landed aristocracy. Conversely, the large majority of the *fallaheen* are tenant sharecroppers.

Until recent years, the lot of the *fallah* in Iraq has been a very sad one. His income barely served to keep body and soul together. In 1948, Doreen Warriner reported the following distribution of the crop as being typical in southern Iraq:

|  | *Per Cent of Crop* |
|---|---|
| Government | 10.0 |
| Landowner (shaikh or notable) | 40.0 |
| First tenant (shaikh) | 7.5 |
| Shaikh's bailiff | 2.5 |
| *Fallah* (sharecropper who works the land) | 40.0 |
| Total | 100.0 |

In 1945 an Iraqi writer estimated the income of the *fallah* including his family of five or six dependents to be, in prewar prices, ten to twelve dinars in the south and fifteen to twenty dinars in the north.[3] In the same year, Alfred Bonné estimated income on the same basis as six to ten dinars in the northern provinces and in the order of nine to fifteen dinars in the south.[4]

In 1951, the Bank Mission after noting that "conditions [were] extremely varied and information virtually nonexistent," suggested that "a hypothetical example of the condition of a *fallah* in the irrigation zone, where barley is the principal crop, may serve as a rough guide." It calculated his share of the crop (two-fifths) as three tons which he could

sell at the prevailing 1951 local prices of ten dinars a ton. His
share of the summer crops was estimated at about ten dinars.[5]

TABLE 17

LAZMA GRANTS IN HOLDINGS
OF OVER 10,000 DUNUMS
1933-54

| Liwa | No. of Lazma Grants Over 10,000 dunums | Total Area of Lazma Grants Over 10,000 dunums |
|---|---|---|
| Kut | 37 | 755,964 |
| Mosul | 28 | 521,252 |
| Diwaniya | 14 | 240,244 |
| Hilla | 6 | 143,930 |
| Amara | 3 | 86,483 |
| Baghdad | 2 | 38,627 |
| Diyala | 2 | 37,275 |
| Erbil | 2 | 21,331 |
| Kirkuk | 1 | 15,442 |
| Total | 95 | 1,860,578 |

Source: Agricultural Reform and Land Development, *op. cit.*, pp. 146-50.

Now let us add up the gross income in 1951 of this "hypothetical" *fallah* with five or six dependents in the irrigation
zone. His income from winter and summer crops is forty
dinars. If we add a maximum of thirty dinars to cover casual
work during the off season, home consumption, and income from other sources, then his total annual income would
be at maximum, about seventy dinars a year. If we divide
this by five, the number in the family, this would bring the
income per head of a *fallah's* family to a maximum of fourteen
dinars a year.

Until recently, the government provided the *fallaheen* with
extremely limited economic or social services. Negatively,
the legal and social system reduced them into a state of
virtual servitude.

The law "Governing the Rights and Duties of Cultivators,"
enacted in 1933 and still operative though apparently ineffective, prescribes in one of its debt clauses that when
a sharecropper is dismissed or moves from a plantation, he
must pay his agricultural debt to the landlord immediately,

and that pending such payment, unless he receives a certificate of release from the landlord, he is prohibited employment on any other plantation, in any government office, or in any private business establishment of any kind including domestic service in private homes. Since the *fallah* is perpetually in debt to his landlord or to the money-lender, the law, at least theoretically, makes him and his children virtually serfs attached to the land.

Aside from the human problem involved, the economic effects of the depressed condition of the *fallah* and the present sharecropping system are obvious. The *fallah* has no incentive to improve the land beyond the year in which he is cultivating it. He has no assurance that the same plot will be leased to him the following year, or for that matter, that he will be given a lease at all. If he manages to save some money beyond his needs and the needs of his family, he may buy a cow, a donkey, or a mule, but he is hardly likely to invest in the land. Nor is he interested in improving his methods of production such as terracing, crop rotation, drainage, etc., for all these relate to "results" after the year's harvest.

As for the landlords, some of them have proved surprisingly progressive and have introduced many improvements to their benefit and the benefit of their tenants. The large majority of them, however, have had little interest in the land beyond receiving huge incomes from it and spending them in the city. In the case of some, there is hardly any link between them and the land. Many huge estates belong to a family or a number of families, with each member usually living in the city, receiving his *pro rata* share of the estate's revenue.

Neither the sharecropping system nor large land-holdings as such are necessarily bad. Both of them, with an enlightened approach on the part of the owners, can be of benefit to all the individuals concerned and to the country as a whole. The topography of Iraq is ideally suited to large-scale agriculture. There are holdings of comparable size, or even larger, in progressive countries such as the United States, Canada, and Australia. It is the anachronistic economic and social system on which they are based that makes them bad or even evil.

As has been pointed out previously, the depressed condition of the *fallah* has resulted in recent years in a migration movement from rural areas to the city, particularly from the provinces of Amara, Hilla, Kut, and Muntafiq where conditions are considered to be very bad indeed. This movement, particularly in the case of Amara province, has assumed such proportions that it causes considerable concern among the authorities.

For the present, the movement constitutes no serious danger and, in fact, it is good. In this way, surplus agricultural labor is being siphoned off the land and deployed to where it is needed. In addition, if agricultural labor becomes scarce, this condition may force the landlords either to mechanize (which has happened in some cases) or to grant better conditions to their tenants in order to induce them to stay.

*Land Reform*

A movement for amelioration of the conditions of the *fallah* and the initiation of agricultural reform has been in the making in the Middle East for some time. Basically, however, it began and gathered momentum only after World War II.

At first the movement expressed itself on the intellectual level. Prior to the war, literary production concerned itself mainly with political problems. Only a few scattered articles could be found dealing with social and economic issues and particularly with agricultural reform. In contrast, in the postwar era there has been a deluge of studies and scholarly articles in Arabic and Western languages dealing with various aspects of the latter subject.

Whereas, in some countries, land reform struck at the root by reforming the existing structure of land-tenancy and other related questions, in Iraq it outflanked the problem and took the line of least resistance, namely, the distribution of government land with assisted development and a variety of other governmental aids.

There are two main reasons for this. Fortunately, over 61

per cent of the land in Iraq still belongs to the state. This is a vast reserve upon which the government can draw to resettle all the landless peasants, without in the meantime disturbing the status quo. In the long run, resettlement of a large number of *fallaheen* would reduce the power and the hold of big landowners.

Then too, the big landowners are the most politically powerful social unit in the country. Any reform legislation that might infringe on their privileged status or interests can be blocked. Lord Salter, in his report to the Development Board, expressed the problem very graphically when he wrote: "It may be that some among the great landowners will accept or welcome some changes on the principle of 'reform that you may preserve.' In the meantime, however, successive Governments have usually felt that new legislation on land tenancy must be kept within the bounds of what will not be actively resisted by landowners."[6]

Although the government is making some progress in its resettlement program, as shall be pointed out later, its approach to the problem of land reform has its dangers. Resettlement, by its nature, is slow of results. Land has to be reclaimed and developed, irrigation and drainage works have to be installed and so forth. In the meantime, the time element has become very important. As in all Arab areas, there is considerable social discontent in Iraq which may express itself as violently as has been the case in neighboring countries. Although the masses have little power in legislative halls, they command, as Salter correctly stated, "an ultimate power which is altogether out of proportion to their present representation in Parliament and their ability to influence legislation by constitutional means."[7]

*The Land Settlement Law*

In Law No. 23 (1945), entitled "The Dujailah Land Development Law," the first planned scheme of resettlement was initiated. In 1951 it was replaced by Law No. 43 (1951), entitled "The Land Development and Settlement Law." This was further supplemented by Ordinance No. 52 (1952) and amended by Ordinance No. 4 (1952).

According to official sources, the law has six main objectives:[8]

1. Improvement in the techniques of production and the expansion of agriculture.
2. Assistance and encouragement of the Iraqi *fallah*, and the creation of a class of small peasant proprietors.
3. Full employment of the agricultural labor force.
4. The orderly settlement of nomadic tribes.
5. The creation of a modern rural society.
6. Reclamation and exploitation of all state land.

*Main Provisions of the Law*

1. *Coverage.* All the land which has been or will be adjudged state land by the cadastral survey, and cultivable must be developed and distributed within the provisions of this law. Otherwise, it is prohibited to sell, alienate, rent, or grant in *lazma* any kind of state cultivable land.

2. *Size of Settlement Project.* Development projects shall be in units, the sizes of which shall not be less than:

    a.   2,000 dunums in mountain areas
    b.   20,000 dunums in flow- and pump-irrigated areas
    c.   80,000 dunums in rain-fed areas.

3. *Size of Plot.* The land shall be distributed in plots, each of which is not to exceed in size:

    a.   20 dunums in mountain areas
    b.   100 dunums in flow-irrigated areas
    c.   200 dunums in low-pump areas
    d.   400 dunums in rain-fed areas
    e.   500 dunums in high-pump irrigated areas.

4. *Beneficiaries.*

    a.  The plots shall be distributed among those who have no land.

    b.  The beneficiary must be at least eighteen years of age. No person may receive more than one plot. Priority in distribution shall be given to the inhabitants of the area, followed by the inhabitants of neighboring areas. Other factors being equal, preference shall be given to persons with families.

c. Graduates of agricultural schools, retired army and police officers; and servicemen and policemen who have been in active service not less than four years, shall be allowed not more than a total of 20 per cent of any one settlement project, provided the authorities are satisfied with the individual's agricultural abilities.

d. Government employees who served not less than eight years or are retired; persons with not less than elementary education; and graduates of recognized religious institutions, who are unemployed, shall be allowed a total of not more than 25 per cent of any one settlement project, provided the authorities concerned are satisfied with the individual's agricultural abilities and with his sincere intent to work the land.

5. *Benefits.*

a. The land is to be given free.

b. The settler receives full *tapu* title to his plot after ten years of continued occupation and development.

c. Upon the death of the settler before the expiration of the ten-year period, his rights and obligations are inherited in common by his successors. If death occurs after the ten-year period, the land may be divided among the successors provided that each share is not less than one-fourth of the area of the plot. Otherwise, the plot must remain in common ownership.

d. Upon allocation of the plot to him, the settler may borrow, on a supervised basis, from the appropriate government authorities up to 100 dinars at 3 per cent interest to be paid back in yearly installments over a period of five years. In the event of flood or crop failure, payment may be deferred for one year.

6. *Obligations.*

a. During the ten-year period, the settler may not alienate, rent, or allow anyone else the right to cultivate part or all of his plot, nor may he enter into any contractual arrangements whatsoever concerning the plot or the crop without the knowledge and approval of government authorities.

      b.   For ten years after receiving full title, the farmer may not alienate his land in any way, or mortgage it except to the State Agricultural Bank.

      c.   During the ten-year period, the settler must follow the instructions of the authorities regarding the methods of production, the types and quantities of crops to be planted, and the size of the areas to be planted of each kind.

      d.   The settler undertakes to follow the cooperative system in the sale of his crops and in his consumption, and to belong to and abide by the regulations of the cooperative society established in his settlement for this purpose. (This provision is part of the contract and not the law.)

      e.   The settler must build a house according to the plans and specifications of government authorities. Government authorities will plan the whole settlement including houses and public buildings.

      f.   The settler must plant an orchard on a plot of land specified by the authorities. The trees must be issued by the authorities, and planted under their supervision and the guidance of the officer concerned. (The latter part of this provision is an administrative regulation.)

      g.   The settler undertakes to devote all his time and the time of men in his family to the land (part of the contract). Nor may he leave his land for more than five days without the knowledge of the government officer in charge (administrative regulation).

   7.   *Water Distribution.*

      a.   Distribution of water shall be restricted to lands of the settlement project at no cost to the settlers. However, it may also be distributed to *tapu, lazma,* and *mulk* lands by a decision of the Council of Ministers, provided the owner of such lands either (1) transfers to the government, in one bloc to be selected by the authorities, the ownership of one-fourth of the land to be irrigated, or (2) pays the state treasury his *pro rata* share of the moneys spent by the government on the construction of irrigation works from which he desires his land to benefit.

      b. In pump-irrigation projects, the settler shall pay over a number of years his *pro rata* share of the money the government spent on the installation of pumps and other related works. He shall also pay his share of the annual costs of maintaining and operating these pumps.

      8. *Administration.* When the law was first enacted in 1945, a special *Miri Sirf* Department managed by a Central Committee was created to administer the law. It was first attached to the Ministry of Economics, then transferred to the Ministry of Agriculture when the latter was established. In 1954 it was transferred to the Ministry of Development as a technical section.

The Committee, apart from its administrative and executive staff, is composed of an irrigation engineer, an agricultural specialist, a doctor, and an agricultural economist. These are assisted by experts in various fields from Iraq, U. S. Point Four, and the various United Nations Agencies. Among foreigners, however, particular mention should be made of Point Four specialists, of whom there were ten attached to the Committee in 1956.

## Criticisms

Several criticisms have been made of the law and its operations. A government committee which was recently organized to study the questions of land distribution and water rights made the following recommendations:

      1. The settlers should pay for the land they receive over a long period of time. It was argued that it is morally wrong to give away the land and that the settlers would be more appreciative of its value if they paid for it.

      2. The costs of irrigation works, drainage, and other related structures are very great. New settlers and others who benefit should at least pay part, if not all, of the cost. The settler's share can be incorporated in the cost of the land and paid in a similar manner over a long number of years.

3. Ownership of ground and surface waters should remain vested in the state but water rights should be predicated on continued usage. Non-settlers may use any excess water supply under a special agreement with the government, provided the latter reserves its right to the use of this oversupply in its future projects when they are established.

4. Another question, which was not touched upon by the committee, is the provision of the law which allows up to 45 per cent of settlement projects to go to army personnel, civil servants, and school graduates. This provision has been severely criticized from various quarters. First, it cuts down the amount of land available to the *fallaheen*, whom the law is supposed to help. Secondly, with the Arab social background in mind, it is doubtful that army officers, civil servants, and school graduates would be sincerely interested in tilling the soil themselves. They are more likely to hire others to do the work for them. This would frustrate the whole intent of the law.

## Distribution of State Land

According to official sources, between 1945, when the first law was enacted, and 1955, over 2.7 million *dunums* (1.7 million acres) of state land were distributed (*see Table 18*). Of this, about half a million were developed in settlements under close government supervision and planning. Most of the rest was distributed without reclamation or assisted development. Some of the settlements that have been established are discussed below.

## The Dujailah Settlement

Dujailah, established in 1945, was the first and is still the largest government experiment in planned and supervised settlement of peasants. It has proven itself conspicuously successful. The income of the farmers has risen to three and four times its former level.

When the scheme was first inaugurated it met with strong opposition from the shaikhs, and the government had considerable difficulty in inducing the *fallaheen* to accept land grants. Since then the idea has caught on like wildfire

TURKEY

SYRIA

JORDAN

SAUDI ARABIA

IRAN

Mosul
Sanjar
Shoura
Makmur
Dokan
Howija
Kirkuk
Suleimaniya
Shahrzoor
Dujail
Khurasan
Tarmiya
Kazimiya
Yaquba
Ramadi
Baghdad
Nahrawan
Karma
Musayeb
Kerbala
Kut
Hilla
Hilla
Babil
Dujaila
Diwaniya
Ghawar
Nasiriya
Fao

Greater Zab
Lesser Zab
Tigris
Adhaim
Diyala
Euphrates

### IRAQ

State-Land Reclamation
and
Distribution Program

Projects Completed

Projects to be Completed soon

Projects to be Completed by 1960

TABLE 18

DISTRIBUTION OF MIRI SIRF LAND
Number of Persons on Settlement;
Number of Holdings;
Total Area of Holdings in Dunums up to the End of 1955

| Settlement | No. of Persons | No. of Holdings | Total Area of Holdings |
|---|---|---|---|
| Dujailah | 14,320 | 2,864 | 373,990[a] |
| Shahrzoor | 2,545 | 509 | 33,830 |
| Hawija | 1,595 | 319 | 23,300 |
| Latifiya | 2,325 | 765 | 23,250 |
| Musayyib | 875 | 175 | 10,500 |
| Makhmur | 930 | 186 | 17,700 |
| Sub-total | 22,590 | 4,818 | 482,570 |
| Karma | 3,590 | 718 | 70,671 |
| Saddah | 325 | 65 | 5,200 |
| Sanjar | 39,350 | 7,870 | 1,568,750 |
| Lands in other areas | 14,680 | 2,936 | 169,870 |
| Sub-total | 57,945 | 11,589 | 1,814,491 |
| Total | 80,535 | 16,407 | 2,297,061 |
| Land Distributed but Unidentified | n.a. | n.a. | 424,210 |
| Grand Total | | | 2,721,271[b] |

Source: Agricultural Reform and Land Development, op. cit., pp. 7, 141. See, however, conflicting date in *Statistical Abstract* for 1956, p. 98; also Salter, *op. cit.*, p. 204.

[a]This figure seems suspect. Up to the end of 1953 only 131,700 dunums had been distributed. Other data indicate that land distributed and actually irrigated in the project amounts to 165,650 dunums. The explanation may be that the 373,990 figure shows the land actually distributed, not all of which however is yet settled or under cultivation. Also the number of holdings seems suspect (i.e., 2,864). Other data indicate that they numbered 1,523 in 1955.

[b]This total seems suspect. The Minister of Development stated that up to March 1956, 2,416,254 dunums had been distributed. (*Iraq Times*, March 29, 1956).

and the authorities are unable to keep up with the thousands of requests they receive. By 1955, the Dujailah settlement had grown into a prosperous community of 2,820 families comprising 14,320 persons.

The settlement is located on the Dujailah Canal (fifty-one kilometers long) which is commanded by the Kut Barrage on the Tigris. The canal, with its thirteen branches, irrigates a total area of over 395,000 dunums, of which 261,000 are irrigated by flow and 134,000 by pump. Land is distributed as it is reclaimed.

Cultivation is prescribed by the government and follows the fallow system: out of one hundred dunums belonging to each cultivator, thirty-five are devoted to winter crops (wheat and barley); five to fruit-trees; two to cotton; two to winter vegetables, and five for pasture. The rest is left fallow.

It is interesting to note the introduction of crop diversification and vegetables and fruit-tree farming. Animal husbandry as part and not as an adjunct of agriculture was also introduced. Settlers have begun to raise chickens, turkeys, goats, sheep and cows in addition to their draft animals.

The government has three experimental nurseries and a few demonstration farms. The idea of an extension service is still in the embryonic stage. Although the primary purpose of the nurseries and the farms is supposed to be demonstration, they serve largely to supply young trees for planting in the orchards.

A new adventure in Iraqi agriculture and indeed in Iraqi life began in the Dujailah settlement, with the initiation of the cooperative system. The settlers, with government aid, were organized into a general-purpose cooperative which in 1951 owned ten tractors, two trucks, a small flour mill, a club house, and some shops. The cooperative failed in later years, mostly owing to inexperience, bad bookkeeping, and lack of adequate guidance. Between 1952 and 1955 one consumer and eight credit cooperatives, with a total combined membership of 274 persons, were established.

By 1955, there were 1,523 houses in the settlement with an average of four rooms each. Although the large majority of the houses does not come up to planned standards and specifications, it is much more sanitary and far superior to the houses the settlers were used to in former times.

The authorities planned the settlement on the basis of the independent "homestead" system with the houses located on the farms and distant from each other. This proved to be a mistake. First, with the lack of good transportation facilities, it made movement within the settlement difficult. It also made the provision of drinking water and other facilities and services both expensive and cumbersome. Furthermore, it does not fit the traditional pattern of gregarious Arab village life, in which housing is concentrated in one village area from which agricultural land radiates outwards in widening segments.

Health services include two clinics, a mobile clinic, and a doctor who makes regular weekly visits from the nearby town of Kut. A bilharzia center was also established to combat that disease in the settlement. In 1955 the various clinics treated 16,514 outpatient cases.

Primary education facilities, though not adequate, are larger in number and far superior to other farming areas. By 1954-55 six schools for boys were operating, with 605 students and seventeen teachers, and one school for girls with forty-eight students and three teachers. One of the boys' schools and the girls' school were established and are run by UNESCO under its program for "Fundamental Education."

UNESCO's program of fundamental education in Iraq is centered in the Dujailah settlement. It is composed of a health center and the two schools mentioned above. The health center, in addition to treating patients, serves as a demonstration unit to teach peasant women sewing, weaving, child care, sterilization of drinking water, habits of cleanliness, etc.

In the two UNESCO schools, advanced educational techniques and concepts are used. The emphasis is more on creating human beings fitted to live in their environment than on classroom work where students are taught by rote subjects that have little relation to their daily life.

In the boys' school, students' time is divided between classroom work and practical application. They plant vegetable gardens, crops of wheat and barley, and raise chickens. They have built their own football and basketball fields. In 1954-55 they established a cooperative shop.

In the girls' school the same advanced methods are employed. Girls are taught not only the "three R's," but also sewing, ironing, needlework, cooking, hygiene, and sports, in addition to practical training in agriculture.

Several modern light industries were established by the government on the project. They consist of a small spinning and weaving plant, a carpentry shop, a machine shop, and two brick kilns. There are several objectives in establishing these industries: to absorb concealed unemployment; to train farmers and their children in complementary industries; to provide them with supplementary income and to supply them with essential, cheap, locally-produced articles and services. Settlement farmers are also employed in the construction of houses and public buildings, repair shops, and in the construction of irrigation and drainage works in the project.

From the preceding description, it can be seen that the government has spent considerable time, effort, and money to insure the beginning of a good life to the settlers and the scheme has been, without question, very successful. An index of the scheme is that in Iraq it is said, "You can tell a Dujailah man from the way he walks."

And yet, several serious mistakes were made. First and perhaps the most serious, no drainage facilities were installed, so that within a relatively short time the land began to deteriorate on account of salt accumulation. The authorities are now installing the necessary drainage facilities at considerably higher cost than if they had been installed when irrigation works were excavated. Secondly, locating the houses at such distances from each other in a sparsely populated area created many hardships.

Encouraged by the success and popularity of the Dujailah scheme and armed with the practical experience gained from it, the government has since established several other settlements. However, Dujailah still remains "the pet" of the authorities.

### The Latifiya Settlement

Some of the experience gained in the Dujailah project was applied in the Latifiya settlement, which was established in 1953 on the Latifiya Canal. The present water supply irrigates an area of 24,285 dunums.

In 1955 there were 765 holdings averaging in size about fifty dunums each. There were then 2,325 persons living on the settlement, with an average of six persons to a family. The income of the settler averaged 200 dinars a year, which is almost three times higher than the maximum income of other Iraqi farmers.

Cultivation is supervised and follows the fallow system: 20 dunums are planted in winter crops (fourteen wheat, six barley); four in summer and winter vegetables; two with jute; one with cotton, and the rest is devoted to a house plot, an orchard, and a pasture.

There are a nursery and an experimental and demonstration field on the settlement. Agricultural extension work is carried out among the farmers by government specialists. Better wheat, cotton, and vegetable seeds are also distributed. Extensive experiments are carried out to determine the effects of various kinds of fertilizers on crop yields, and new crops such as jute, clover, and sugar beets are gradually being introduced.

The steel moldboard plow was introduced on the settlement. The introduction of this comparatively simple device and its replacement of the centuries-old wooden plow are perhaps more valuable and more significant to the small farmer than the introduction of heavy and expensive agricultural machinery.

There is one primary coeducational school in the settlement. In 1954-55 it had 142 students of whom 24 were girls. Both electricity and treated-and-piped drinking water are supplied to all parts of the project.

Supervised loans were extended to sixty-nine settlers, and in 1955 arrangements were being made for sixty more loans. With the loans made, 725 sheep, seventy-two work horses, and forty-seven cows were bought, in addition to other needs.

As in the case of Dujailah, modern light industries began to be introduced by the government. At present they consist of a small spinning plant and a carpentry shop. Others are now under construction.

*The Greater Musayyib Settlement*

This is the greatest reclamation and land settlement project of its kind in the Middle East. It combines both irrigation and drainage. The project will certainly revolutionize agricultural concepts in Iraq since, for the first time, intensive cultivation has been introduced into a large area of land.

The settlement is located on the Greater Musayyib Canal (*see Chapter IV*), and covers 335,000 dunums of land, of which 250,000 dunums are reclaimed state land and 85,000 dunums are privately owned and presently cultivated. Construction of irrigation and drainage works for the whole area was completed in 1956 after four years of intensive work.

Official sources estimate that 15,000 persons will be settled directly on the project in addition to some 35,000 persons who will indirectly benefit from it. Two modern towns are planned on the settlement, one to be located about thirty-three kilometers east of the town of Musayyib, and another at the end of the project area some fifty kilometers east of Musayyib. In addition, fifty villages will be built on the settlement, with fifty to ninety families each. The land will be distributed in plots of sixty-seven dunums, of which fifty dunums are to be devoted to winter and summer crops, five for an orchard and twelve for a pasture, a house plot, roads, irrigation, and drainage canals.

Actual distribution of land was officially begun on November 17, 18, 19, and 24, 1956, in the Biblical town of Cutha. Press dispatches tell an interesting and human story. It is reported that thousands of landless peasants poured into the town to attend the four-day lottery. They came on foot, on horseback, on donkeys, in truck loads, and in hired taxis.

They watched as the names of the winners were drawn by government officials from a cardboard box containing the names of approved applicants (some 30,000 had applied for 2,000 plots). As the public drawing came to an end, 431 landless peasants were selected to settle on sixty-six dunum plots comprising the land that was then ready.

*Other Projects*

There are several other settlement projects, both supervised and unsupervised (*see Table 18*). They include Hawija, Makhmur, and Shahrzoor. These are supervised in a similar fashion as the ones discussed. Others include the vast Sanjar area, lands in the provinces of Hilla, Dulaim, Diyala, Diwaniya, and others.

*Conclusion*

The government has made a good start in its land distribution program. It is hoped that, by 1960, 500,000 more dunums will have been reclaimed and distributed in supervised settlements. With the completion of several flood control and storage works a major obstacle has been overcome. The land distribution program can now proceed at an accelerated rate. Through land distribution the government is helping solve the major social and human problem of the country. This should lead to both political stability and economic prosperity.

1. Sir Ernest Dawson, *An Inquiry into Land Tenure and Related Questions.* Printed for the Iraqi Government by the Garden City Press. (Letchworth, England: 1931), pp. 32-33.
2. IBRD, *op. cit.*, p. 142.
3. Hashim Jawad, *The Social Structure of Iraq,* Baghdad, New Publishers Press, 1945, p. 21.
4. Alfred Bonné, *The Economic Development of the Middle East.* (London: Kegan Paul, etc., 1945), p. 36.
5. IRBD, *op. cit.*, pp. 132-133.
6. Salter, *op. cit.*, p. 54.
7. *Ibid.*, p. 55.
8. Iraq Government, Ministry of Development, Miri Sirf Central Committee, *Agricultural Reform and Land Development,* Baghdad, 1956, p. 34 (in Arabic).

# CHAPTER 6

## AGRICULTURAL TECHNIQUES, FACILITIES, AND SERVICES

Prior to World War II, the government was not vitally interested in agriculture, the mainstay of the majority of the population. This is reflected in the fact that a Ministry of Agriculture was created only after a recommendation by a mission of the International Bank to Iraq in 1951. Until then only a small directorate had existed.

The creation of a Ministry of Agriculture is symbolic of the conceptual change which has taken place concerning the function of government in public life. Gradually at first, but then more rapidly, the government began to play a positive role by providing services and creating institutions and facilities which hitherto had been absent.

The preceding chapters discussed the efforts being made to develop the agricultural sector through harnessing the forces of nature and converting them into constructive use. This chapter will deal with the introduction of new techniques and the development of new services and institutions designed to increase the quantity and quality of agricultural production and to lift the peasant from his present impecunious state. Many of these innovations are taken for granted in the United States and other technologically advanced countries, but in Iraq they are new. Despite their elementary character, they represent a significant step forward on the path of progress.

Administratively, unlike the building of dams, land reclamation, bridges, etc., these new services do not come under the jurisdiction of the Development Board, but are regarded as routine government operations. Moreover, they arose, not as a result of a coordinated plan, but gradually in the different departments, with the expansion of government functions. All these "innovations" are still in an embryonic stage. Their significance lies not so much in their immediate contribution, but rather in their cumulative effect and in the role they will play in changing the socio-economic base of agriculture in Iraq.

## Farm Mechanization

It is perhaps of historical interest to note that the drive for farm mechanization in Iraq was given its first impetus by the United States Lend-Lease Program during the war. Until then hardly any modern agricultural implements were used. The wooden plow of ancient form reigned supreme.

With the war experience behind it, the government embarked on a policy of introducing and generating demand for farm equipment among farmers. Several devices have been used to put government policy into effect:

1. The Agricultural Machinery Administration was created. It became a Directorate in 1956. This agency performs several functions. At present it controls the importation and licensing of all agricultural machinery. Originally, the agency also held a complete monopoly on the sale of such equipment. Following the recommendation of the International Bank mission, however, it now licenses private importers with the stipulation that they also must import adequate stocks of spare parts and erect service stations.

The agency itself owns a fairly large number of tractors, combines, and other farm equipment which it rents out to farmers. Until 1952, the rental rates were so low that the agency operated at a considerable annual loss. Finally, the agency provided technical help and service stations in various parts of the country.

2.  Settlers on state land are implicitly required to use modern machinery.

3.  Loans are advanced to independent farmers by the State Agricultural Bank for the purchase of farm equipment. Such loans may amount to as much as fifty per cent of the purchase price.

Table 19 illustrates the results of government policy. From 1945 to 1956 inclusive, 2,097 tractors and 1,368 combines were sold. The Agricultural Census mentioned previously reported that, in 1953, there were 2,091 tractors on agricultural holdings with a total of 88,000 horsepower. If the number of tractors sold in 1954, 1955, and 1956 is added, then at the end of 1956 there were some 3,061 tractors in the country.

The flatlands of Iraq are ideally suited for the use of heavy machinery. The main obstacle to their use is the numerous irrigation canals. While there is little question about the advisability of universal mechanization in the future, there are arguments both for and against its speedy adoption.

First, there is the question of relative costs. It is a known principle that where labor is cheap and abundant, it is, generally speaking, more economical in certain sectors to use human labor. A reasonable argument can be made that this is the case in Iraq. In addition, experience over the past ten years has shown that the life expectancy of agricultural machinery in Iraq is about half what it is in the United States and other advanced countries. This is because of the lack both of adequate training and maintenance facilities. Hence, in many cases, the use of heavy equipment is not economical, especially when the comparatively large initial investment is taken into consideration.

Secondly, mechanization may create a social problem. There has been a growing concern in Iraq that while speedy mechanization may be economically desirable, it may also aggravate further the rural problem through wholesale displacement of tenant peasants and their consequent emigration to the cities.

There are two arguments in favor of controlled mechanization. At present mechanization is not of such proportions as to constitute a serious problem. In fact, the contrary may be true. Mechanization by landlords and as a government policy is, at least in part, the result of considerable migration of peasants to urban centers and the need for their replacement. This was the main argument advanced in 1956 by the director of the Agricultural Machinery Administration.[1]

Mechanization as a state policy can be used to serve three interrelated functions: to increase and improve the quality of production; to distribute and exploit the labor potential more efficiently. It is widely known, for instance, that there is considerable concealed unemployment in agriculture. Mechanization would force surplus labor out and transfer it to other sectors of the economy where it is needed. Then, too, it can indirectly aid in the breakdown of the present land tenure system and other archaic traditions and social institutions in rural areas.

The government realized that mechanization, for some time to come, will remain beyond the financial reach of the majority of farmers. For the time being, the path of improvement lies in the direction of introducing, on a universal basis, simple modern implements which farmers can afford, which need little servicing, and the use of which can be taught in a short time. With the advice of American specialists, the government has been increasingly active in this field. The most significant development in this respect is the recent introduction of the steel moldboard plow.

### Agricultural Credit

The establishment and development of the state Agricultural Bank is another illustration of the expansion of government activity in the agricultural sector. In Iraq, as in most underdeveloped countries, one of the chief impediments to economic expansion is the lack of modern credit institutions. Until recently, the few banks that operated in Iraq were all foreign, and were primarily concerned with commercial transactions. Moreover, to this day, banks continue to be urban institutions of which the majority of the Iraqi population are only vaguely aware. Credit, therefore, could only be obtained from the traditional money-lender at rates of interest varying between 30 and 300 per cent. Both landlord and peasant were perpetually in debt. A story quoted by an Iraqi writer and alleged to be true is illustrative: "A farmer borrowed the price of three chickens which he served to a visiting guest. Interest compounded at such a rate that the farmer was forced to sell two cows to liquidate his debt."[2]

TABLE 19

MAIN AGRICULTURAL MACHINES SOLD IN IRAQ 1945-55

| | 1945 | 1946 | 1947 | 1948 | 1949 | 1950 | 1951 | 1952 | 1953 | 1954 | 1955 | 1956 | Total |
|---|---|---|---|---|---|---|---|---|---|---|---|---|---|
| Tractors | 134 | 69 | 94 | 84 | 73 | 167 | 54 | 105 | 343 | 333 | 260 | 381 | 2,097 |
| Combines | 12 | 30 | 35 | 53 | 87 | 98 | 98 | 96 | 421 | 154 | 70 | 214 | 1,368 |
| Cultivators | 31 | 65 | 8 | 36 | 39 | 46 | 43 | 45 | 109 | 184 | 96 | 107 | 809 |
| Threshers | 8 | 6 | 2 | 3 | 5 | 1 | 14 | 2 | 1 | | | 6 | 48 |
| Binders | | | | 2 | 1 | | | | 2 | | | n.a. | 5 |
| Automatic Trailers | | | | 2 | | 3 | | | 21 | 17 | 30 | 31 | 104 |
| Ditchers | | | 2 | | 3 | 3 | | 3 | 6 | 6 | 15 | 15 | 53 |
| Plows | 115 | 40 | 110 | 65 | 119 | 146 | 78 | 74 | 187 | 185 | 179 | 282 | 1,580 |
| Grain Drills | 10 | 4 | 1 | 9 | 15 | 21 | 3 | 9 | 8 | 2 | | 10 | 92 |
| Disk Harrows | 30 | 18 | 7 | 30 | 14 | 14 | 21 | 31 | 48 | 58 | 27 | 76 | 373 |
| Farm Jeeps | | | | 62 | | | 32 | 44 | 17 | | | | 155 |

Source: *Statistical Abstract* for 1952, p. 222; 1955, p. 88; 1956, p. 105.

The Agricultural Bank began operating after the war with a moderate capital of one million dinars. In 1952 its paid-up capital was raised to two million and, in 1957, to three. The experiences of the bank illustrate the problems of a new experiment. Despite many pitfalls, the bank steadily expanded in size and in the scope of its operations. Initially its loans went mostly to farmers of substantial means since they could provide the necessary securities required. This meant that the majority of small farmers were automatically excluded from its services. Moreover, most of its loans were of short duration.

Gradually the Bank began to enter new, less orthodox fields. For instance, it now makes loans at five per cent for the purchase of agricultural machinery. During 1953 and 1954, it made 581 such loans with a total value of 444,853 dinars. The loans made possible the purchase of 673 agricultural machines including tractors, harvesters, and water pumps. It now also makes loans to agricultural cooperatives at 3 per cent interest.

In 1955 the Bank launched a pilot project to provide credit to small farmers under expert supervision and guidance. The scheme was initiated for the Bank by a Point Four specialist in Hilla province where, during 1955-56, some thirty farmers in three villages received supervised loans totalling about 800 dinars ($2,240) at 3 per cent interest. In December, 1956, after the limited experiment proved successful and popular, the scheme was expanded to cover the whole country and its administration was transferred from the Bank to the directorate of agricultural economy in the Ministry of Agriculture.

Table 20 shows the loans made by the Bank from 1948 to 1954. It indicates two trends. First, an increase in the role of the Bank in the agricultural development of Iraq and, secondly, a growing awareness on the part of the farmers of the facilities with which such an institution can provide them.

There is a growing awareness that the Bank also has an educational function in addition to its regular duties. As indicated previously, banking is a new phenomenon in

Iraqi economic life. Hence, by going out to the people, by opening branches in rural areas, the Bank can also function as an educational institution, in addition to providing badly needed services. Its lack of initiative in this respect has been one of the chief criticisms leveled against it.

It is quite obvious that the Bank still falls far short of meeting the vast needs of the farmer for credit facilities. It has taken initial steps on a long road that has yet to be traveled. Its primary function is to lead the way, to act as a pioneer, but it cannot in itself be the final solution. In the first place, no matter how active the Bank can be, its facilities will still remain inadequate in relation to the need. Secondly, as business organizations, state agencies of this type everywhere suffer from a crusading spirit and are apt to be comparatively inefficient since their primary function is to serve rather than to make money. The solution lies rather in the development of private banking and private credit institutions. A beginning in this respect has already been made, but until such time as these are more numerous the state will continue to play the major role in this field.

TABLE 20

LOANS OF THE AGRICULTURAL BANK:  1948-54

| Year | No. of Loans | Total Value in Dinars |
|------|------|------|
| 1948 | 264 | 121,247 |
| 1949 | n. a. | n. a. |
| 1950 | 524 | 144,621 |
| 1951 | 789 | 263,693 |
| 1952 | 1,256 | 660,010 |
| 1953 | 2,186 | 1,353,639 |
| 1954 | 1,894 | 882,952 |

Source: Agricultural Bank, *17th, 18th, and 19th Annual Reports* for 1952-53, 1953-54 and 1954-55. (All in Arabic.)

*The Agricultural Cooperative Movement*

In 1944, with the passage of Law No. 27 (1944), the cooperative movement reached Iraq, nearly a century after it was first introduced in Europe. Unlike its European counterparts, however, the movement is not doctrinaire and has no

philosophical history. It was borrowed from Europe and
America without its intellectual paraphernalia, and it arose
primarily through state action—purely as a utilitarian instrument to meet particular needs. Most of its members
belong to one of two groups: salaried employees and farmers.

Among farmers the cooperative movement made little
headway during the 1940's. Only a few cooperatives were
organized, most of which failed. This was mainly due to
lack of experience and adequate guidance, and because
cooperatives are alien institutions, many aspects of which
conflict with certain traditions and patterns of behavior
among Iraq's rural society.

The initiation of the land distribution program gave the
government an opportunity to introduce the cooperative
system under its guidance among farmers on state land. In
the first place, new settlers are people who have been up-
rooted from their traditional environment and, therefore,
are more likely to be receptive to new ideas and practices.
Secondly, until the advantages of the system become apparent through successful examples, it is only possible to
introduce it among the settlers as one of the conditions for
granting the land. Hence, nearly all receivers of state land
are obligated, under their grant contracts with the government, to join settlement cooperatives if and when they are
organized.

The state encourages the growth of the cooperative movement in two main ways: through sponsorship and guidance
as in the case of agricultural cooperatives and through low-
interest (3 per cent) loans on a long-term basis. According
to official data, in 1955 there were fifty-one consumer, credit
and housing cooperatives in various parts of the country.
Nearly all of them received state aid in one form or another.
About half were agricultural cooperatives (consumer and
credit) which were organized under state sponsorship and
guidance.

Despite its apparent advantages, the growth of the cooperative movement among farmers will probably be very
slow and subject to many pitfalls and initial disappointments.
Its significance is not so much in its present-day contribution,

but in its great potential as a means of social change and as a powerful instrument through which farmers can band together for self-help. It is the antithesis of the growing dependence on the state.

*Agricultural Extension*

The concept of extension work is very new in Iraq. The counterpart of the American county agent was conspicuous by his absence. An extension service worthy of the name was organized only some four years ago. At the end of 1956 it had fifty-nine agents, six supervisors and five American Point Four specialists.

Although the service is very limited in its scope, it has shown quite healthy signs of growth. Perhaps what is most significant at this stage is that it has taken roots, that it is popular among the farmers, and that at this initial period in its development, it has the guidance and advice of specialists from the United States, a country where this field is most highly developed.

In addition to its direct functions, the extension service, if and when it is fairly developed, may indirectly serve as an important link of confidence between the government and the peasant farmer. The schism between the two is centuries old, and the latter almost instinctively distrusts the government. The two main points of contact between them have traditionally been the ubiquitous tax-collector and military conscription. The extension agent, by working with the farmers as their trusted friend, may provide part of the link missing for many centuries.

*Research and Training*

Another facet of agriculture which has registered considerable progress in recent years is research and training. Whereas in the past only token attention was paid to this field, it has now become a regular governmental function.

Agricultural research is carried out primarily by the various departments of the Ministry of Agriculture. Other ministries also participate in areas of their particular interest. The Ministry has five experimental stations. Here, and in laboratories, research is conducted for weed and pest control, the use of fertilizers and insecticides, the introduction of new plants, crops, and trees, the improvement of others, etc.

For instance, the plant pathology division, which has a Point Four adviser, launched in September, 1956 a five-year program to survey, study, and catalogue all plant pests including diseases and insects. For this purpose it received a grant of about a million dollars from the Development Board (ID. 335,000). In the summer of 1955, it launched a wheat-smut control campaign. Approximately 620,000 acres were protected by treating seeds before planting. The program was renewed in 1956 and the government allotted to it 86,000 dinars. After the experiment proved successful, seed treatment has now become available to farmers at the very low rate of six fils (1.5 cents) per dunum. Research campaigns have also been conducted against tomato diseases and fruit pests (apples, peaches, pears, plums, grapes, almonds, and quince). The spray for apple trees has now been in use for two and a half years on demonstration farms, and the use of other sprays has recently been begun by extension workers. Malnutrition in plants, very common in Iraq, is also receiving considerable attention. A development related to research is the establishment in 1956 by the Ministry of Agriculture, with Point Four assistance, of an agricultural reporting service which publishes information useful to farmers.

Like research, the training program is of very recent origin. It includes regular college education, in-service training, and vocational agriculture in rural schools. In 1950 a college of agriculture, the first and only one in the country, was established. It has now the largest and most fully developed experiment station in the country and includes laboratory facilities. In 1956 its student body numbered 220 with a staff of twenty-eight instructors, including six American professors from the University of Arizona under contract with the International Cooperation Administration.

Training programs are also conducted by the various departments of the Ministry of Agriculture. For instance, the Extension Service has a program for training agents; the Agricultural Machinery Administration (which became a Directorate in 1956) has a program in the use and maintenance of machinery; the Soils Laboratory, recently established jointly by the Irrigation Department, the College of Engineering, and Point Four, has a training program in soil classification and analysis.

Finally, the rural school syllabus is being revamped in favor of far greater emphasis on practical training in vocational agriculture. This includes teaching children to raise vegetables in garden plots, planting, taking care of and harvesting field crops such as wheat and barley, and organizing the counterpart of 4-H clubs. An Arbor Day has also been set.

*Crop Diversification*

Agricultural production in Iraq is restricted to five principal products: two winter crops, wheat and barley; two summer crops, cotton and rice; one fruit, dates. These constitute the bulk of Iraq's exports in addition to animals (on the hoof), raw wool and hides. Other fruits and crops are grown only in limited quantities. Poultry and dairy farming are almost non-existent. Animal husbandry is an adjunct to, but not a part of, agriculture.

A number of economic and social factors must have brought about this traditional pattern of production. Some of them may only be guessed at. The salinity of the soil in the Mesopotamian Valley dictated the choice of hardy crops which have a comparatively high resistance to salt. Hence the choice of wheat and barley. Then the economy of Iraq was, and still is, basically a subsistence rather than a money economy. Production was primarily geared to meeting consumption needs. There was, therefore, not sufficient incentive to raise cash crops. Too, dietary habits and lack of good communications and storage facilities operate in favor of the production of some foods and against others. For instance, the staple foods of the Iraqi farmer are wheat and barley (for bread). He eats very few vegetables and fruits with the exception of onions and dates. Production of fruits and vegetables is, therefore, necessary only for supply to urban markets and for export. But this supply is hindered by lack of good transportation and storage facilities, since fruits and vegetables spoil quickly and require either immediate delivery or refrigeration. Finally, the fallow system which requires the land to "rest" in alternate years probably operated to limit crop variation. For generations this system was treated as sacred. All plans for agricultural expansion were based on the assumption that it would continue to be followed. Only in recent years has it begun to occur to planners that there is nothing particularly sacrosanct about the system and that, surely, after the advantages of other systems have been demonstrated to the farmer he will not be too reluctant to adopt them.

In recent years the state has begun to take an active interest in the diversification of agricultural products. The drive has several objectives: first, to increase the number and variety of fruit trees. For instance, certain parts of central-southern Iraq are suitable for the development of a citrus industry, and others, to the north, for growing a variety of fruits and nuts. Second, to increase the variety of crops. In the 1920's cotton was introduced by the British as a cash crop, and later tobacco was introduced for local consumption. After several years of experimentation with sugar-producing crops, the state has, in the last few years, introduced sugar beet cultivation to provide raw material for the emergent refining industry. More recently, jute cultivation began on an experimental basis. Several other crops and legumes have also been introduced. Third, to encourage vegetable cultivation on a much larger scale. Finally, to improve animal husbandry and gradually to integrate it with agriculture.

## Conclusions

The period beginning after World War II may be described as a formative one in the history of agricultural development in Iraq. Agricultural expansion (including flood control, irrigation, reclamation, and drainage) became almost overnight the most important activity of the government. This stems from the recognition that agriculture is the most important sector of the economy and that it is the springboard to economic expansion in all other sectors.

Initially the program of agricultural development suffered from lack of adequate detailed planning and technical studies. Consequently, the pace at which it moved was slow indeed and the program was unable to meet its targets.

The first five-year program emphasized the construction of flood-control and water-storage structures for protection and for bringing more land under cultivation. Basically, this objective has been achieved. The dams and reservoirs that have been completed or are under construction are more than adequate for Iraq's immediate needs.

In recent programs the emphasis has shifted to irrigation, drainage, and improvement of areas already under cultivation. This is a field which requires vast expenditures and years of coordinated intensive efforts. Only a beginning has so far been made.

Almost all the institutions and services necessary for a modern agricultural system have either been created or are in the process of being organized. They are all, however, still in their formative stages. Their value is not so much in the magnitude of their present contribution, for this is limited, but in their potential, if and when they are fully developed.

No studies have been made to measure and quantify the impact of the program. *Prima facie* evidence indicates that it is beginning to have its effects. In all probability its impact will not be greatly felt before 1960. By then, a large number of the works under construction will have been completed and their cumulative effects should become visible. Also, the agricultural institutions which have been recently created will have had time to grow into somewhat more effective instruments.

The agricultural expansion program in Iraq is the only one of this magnitude in the Middle East. Despite many criticisms that may be made of its details, all the evidence shows that, on the whole, it is well planned and effective. If uninterrupted, it will probably be able to lift the standard of living in Iraq to three and four times its present level by 1970.

The program has several characteristics:

1. It has some of the attributes of socialism in the sense that it is being undertaken almost exclusively by state agencies, principally by the Development Board, with hardly any participation by private capital. Its benefits are designed to go primarily to the small farmer. For instance, state land, after being reclaimed and developed, is given away, but only to landless persons, principally farmers. Irrigation and drainage works are in many cases planned in such a manner as to avoid having big landowners derive any benefits from them, sometimes even at the cost of greater efficiency. In effect this amounts to a redistribution of public wealth in favor of the masses. This is of great significance since more than 61 per cent of the land in Iraq is owned by the state.

Side by side with this pronounced orientation of the program, the government has avoided introducing any agricultural reform, particularly in the land tenure system, which might antagonize or be resisted by the big landlords. These latter are very heavily represented in Parliament and are able to block any reform legislation which might seriously threaten their privileged position and interests. Thus the tendency of the program is to outflank the problem rather than to attack it directly. The big landlords are left in peace, but the peasant, through land distribution and other benefits, is given the opportunity to shed his economic and social shackles, and to begin a new life.

2. Generally speaking, the program is fairly isolated from politics and protected from the vicissitudes of changing cabinets and the raids of party politicians. It has continuity and is controlled and directed to a considerable degree by experts. This arrangement is unique in the history of Iraq and the other countries of the Middle East.

3. Due to personnel shortages in Iraq, the program depends very heavily on the services of qualified foreign technicians, consulting firms and construction companies, in addition to technical aid from the United States and United Nations agencies. For instance, nearly all heavy construction (dams, drainage, etc.) is carried out under contract by British, German, French, American, and Italian

firms. American technicians and specialists are particularly active as advisers in setting up new government agricultural services and institutions, and in improving others.

1. *Iraq Times*, May 2, 1956.
2. Ja far Khayyat, *The Iraqi Village*. (Beirut: 1950), f. n., p. 66. (in Arabic).

CHAPTER 7

## BENEFICIARIES OF REFORM—LANDLORD OR PEASANT?

Since the majority of the population in Iraq is engaged in agriculture or associated enterprises, landlordism may be said to be at the root of almost all the ills that have plagued the country for several centuries. There is hardly any problem, whether political, social, or economic, which in one way or another is not related to this central fact. It follows, therefore, that no development program in agriculture can be really effective if it is not accompanied by a program of agrarian reform.

Large land holdings, as such, are not necessarily bad. In the United States, Canada, and Australia there are holdings comparable in size to those of Iraq. In Iraq, however, landlordism is a way of life with rigid lines of demarcation denoting economic, social, and political status with little or no mobility. Such a system means that the peasant leads a marginal existence with no hope for a better life, while the landlord receives most of the income from agricultural production and retains effective control of the political institutions of the country.

The devastating effects of such a system are obvious. Economically, it results in very low productivity. While most of the landlords take little interest in the land beyond enjoying its income, the peasants have no special concern for improving it since they have little or no stake in it. Socially, the system leaves the peasant in virtual economic bondage, deprives him of his dignity as a human being, and limits his capacity to develop his potentialities or to contribute to the community. Politically, such a system in a twentieth-century world can only lead to instability and to the emergence of subversive movements. There is increasing realization that such a system is not an immutable law of nature, and that each individual has a right to a more equitable share of the goods of this earth and to a voice in the determination of his own destiny.

Iraq today stands at the threshold of a new era. If there is to be economic and social progress, if the transition is to be effected peacefully without revolutions, then ways and means must be found to solve this problem effectively and with dispatch.

What are the possible basic objectives of a program of agrarian reform in Iraq? First, to increase the productivity of the agricultural sector of the economy; secondly, to provide the peasant with economic security and a higher standard of living; and thirdly, to restore to him his dignity as a human being by liberating him from ignorance and disease, and at the same time allowing him to develop his potentialities.

There are two alternatives open to the Iraqi government in dealing with the matter of land distribution. One approach would be to expropriate, in one way or another, large land holdings and redistribute them among landless peasants. Such a move, even if politically feasible, would be unsound. The land is ideally suited for large-scale agricultural techniques, including the use of heavy machinery. If the landlords can be induced to use modern techniques, this would result in far greater increase in productivity than if the land were to be broken into small units.

The second approach, the one which has been taken by the Government of Iraq thus far, is to leave the big landlords alone and to distribute the vast state-owned land reserve among the landless peasants. In addition to the land grant, the government extends to the new owner various types of aid: supervised loans, technical assistance, and extension work; it sponsors agricultural cooperatives, provides water either at little or no cost, encourages him to use new machinery and techniques, and protects him against raids from money-lenders and other would-be profiteers. Such a policy accomplishes a number of objectives.

1.   It puts into productive use large areas of land which hitherto have been idle, thus increasing the productivity of the country.

2.   It provides the peasant with a measure of economic security, raises his standard of living through the consequent increase in his income, and gives him an incentive to improve the land.

3.   The policy of land distribution is a flank attack on the big landlords and the economic and social practices for which they stand. The acquisition of land by the peasant, in itself, destroys the age-old relationship of master to servant. The peasant becomes economically independent. His welfare and his livelihood are no longer at the mercy or the caprice of the landlord. He is no longer in a position of subservience but becomes free to exercise his judgment and act in accordance with his own interests. This psychological change in the attitude of the peasant, his new pride and confidence, was immediately visible among the peasants of Dujailah, the first settlement established by the government.

The granting of state lands to peasants will also result in the withdrawal of part of the agricultural labor force available for hire from the labor market. A labor shortage already exists in certain rural areas. Until the recent past, the peasant has had almost no choice but to work for the landlord. Today his bargaining position has been strengthened. The implications are obvious: the existing social and economic relationships will gradually break down, for the peasant is no longer dependent on the landlord; in order to induce the peasant to stay, the landlord will have to pay him either higher wages or give him a better share of the crops; the scarcity of labor or its relatively high price may force the landlord to mechanize or to sell. In effect, a wider ownership of land, together with industrial development, will gradually destroy the foundations of landlordism as practiced in Iraq, leaving the landlord in virtually the same position as that of his counterparts in more advanced economies.

One important question remains to be answered: how persistent and how speedy has the government been in implementing this program? It is in this area that criticism can justly be made. Although the plan was initiated in 1945, the number of landless peasants who have actually been settled is still comparatively small. Successive conservative administrations have been charged with failure to give adequate attention to the program. But these charges, although largely true, should be examined in the light of certain considerations. The program, in its initial stages, was a new venture for which the existing administrative machinery was not prepared. The natural tendency was to proceed slowly. Secondly, it was only after 1951 that funds became available on a sufficiently large scale to finance the program on more than a skeleton basis. Finally, preparatory work had to be carried out before distribution; plans had to be drawn, land surveyed, classified, and reclaimed and irrigation and drainage works had to be constructed. In the last few years the program has picked up considerable momentum and is proceeding at a more rapid rate.

The efforts of the government during the last few years to give the peasant a measure of economic security and independence have not been insignificant, especially if judged in the light of the millions of dollars that have been invested in improving land and water resources. The legislation authorizing this investment provides that only landless peasants shall benefit from such improvements. Landlords are prohibited from participating in benefits. The Development Board has gone to considerable lengths to insure that no landlord will benefit from its activities. In some irrigation and drainage projects efficiency has been sacrificed in order to live up to the letter of the law.

Now let us turn to the human aspects of agrarian reform, namely the activities of the government in the fields of education, health, rural welfare, and community development. So much needs to be done in each of these fields that, no matter how extensive the efforts of the government, they can never be considered adequate. Over 95 per cent of the peasant population is illiterate. Almost every peasant is the victim of one endemic disease or another. As of 1956, 80 per cent of all houses in the country were either mud or reed huts, or tents; 79 per cent had no piped water supplies; 83 per cent had no electricity; 67 per cent had no toilets; and 90 per cent had no baths. The national average of occupancy per room was 2.73. Conditions in rural areas are generally much worse than in urban districts.

Each year in the postwar period the government of Iraq has intensified its efforts to improve the basic conditions of the masses. Expenditures of the Ministry of Education rose from 1.6 million to 10.5 million dinars a year in the period from 1946 to 1957. This excludes expenditures of the Development Board and of other ministries and the costs of most college education. The number of elementary, intermediate, and secondary schools during the same period rose from 1,003 to 2,070; the number of students from 130,000 to 430,000; the number of teachers, from 5,371 to 14,679. In recent years the number of elementary schools has been increasing at the rate of about 150 schools per year. College facilities have been considerably expanded, and a number of new colleges and technical schools have been opened. In 1956/57, over 3,000 Iraqis were studying at universities abroad—about a thousand of them at state expense.

Elementary school facilities in the rural areas are being expanded quite rapidly. Whereas the children of peasants a few years ago had few or no opportunities for education, today it is possible for a peasant's son to go all the way through a university at state expense. Thus, the benefits which used to be restricted to a privileged few are now being more widely extended. The gap which separates the peasant from the upper class is being gradually closed, and the possibility that his children may move up the social ladder, although still limited, has nevertheless become a reality. Such basic changes constitute a state-sponsored socio-economic revolution more significant than the political developments usually headlined in the press. These changes herald the gradual destruction of class lines, the rejection and replacement of existing social and economic institutions and traditions, and the adoption of a rational view of the universe and of man's place and functions in society. In the wake of such a revolution, a readjustment, either peaceful or violent, in the distribution of political power is sooner or later inevitable.

Similar progress has taken place in public health. Rural hospital and clinic facilities are being increased rapidly. The shortage of trained personnel is the main problem in this program. Perhaps the most encouraging progress has been made in the recent extensive campaigns to wipe out the endemic diseases which have long ravaged Iraq, particularly the countryside. Malaria, which used to kill some 50,000 persons each year, most of them peasants, has now been brought under reasonable control. In 1946, over 742,000 malaria cases were treated. Ten years later, in 1956, the figure was brought down to 217,000 cases. The facilities and functions of the Endemic Diseases Institute have undergone considerable expansion in the last few years, and a Malaria Board was established in 1957.

Until the past three years the government has not been active in rural community development in the fields of housing, water purification, and sanitation. In 1956, however, a Rural Community Development Council on the ministerial level was under consideration. During the same year a housing census was completed. At the same time, the Development Board in its 1955-60 plan allocated some 25 million dinars to housing throughout the country. Ultimately, it plans to construct some 125,000 housing units in rural areas. Work on providing clean water supplies in rural communities has been intensified.

The activities of the government designed to improve the living conditions of the poorest classes of the population reveal a basic interest in the general welfare. The government is, in effect, sponsoring changes which in the Western world required a long time to take hold. It should be pointed out that most of these state activities represent new concepts which, in contrast with the conservative environment of the country, are revolutionary in character. In view of the fact that state responsibility for safeguarding human welfare was virtually unrecognized until after World War II, progress in this respect may be considered significant.

The question of whether the state effort is "adequate" involves a difficult value judgment. The human needs in Iraq are virtually limitless, and vastly greater sums could be absorbed in programs attempting to meet them. A scale of priorities must be established, however, which will provide for the most judicious expenditure of the considerable, but limited, capital for investment.

When both are badly needed, which should take precedence, a dam or a hospital? Should priority be given to the physical plant or to human resources? Or should there be some balance in expenditures? The expenditures of the Development Board provide the best index as to policy.

During the first years of operations the Board gave a decisive priority to the physical plant. This policy was based on the theory that to raise the standard of living there must be an increase in production which, in turn, required improvement and expansion of the physical plant. A study of the 1950-55 plan, however, reveals that over 45 per cent of all planned expenditures went to the construction of flood control works, water storage schemes, irrigation, drainage, and land reclamation. As noted previously, the main beneficiary of these works is the peasant and not the big landlord. In other words, although the peasant was not receiving any immediate benefits from the activities of the Board, the land distribution program assured that, when the government's investment began to pay dividends, the peasant was to be the main recipient.

The 1955-60 plan reflects a decisive shift in the policy of the Board. The physical plant still receives the major share of expenditures. However, comparatively large sums, a total of about 70 million dinars, are also allotted to education, health, housing, and water purification. Agricultural works, from which the peasant is the principal beneficiary, constitute the largest single allocation.

It is sometimes said that the development of the physical

plant has not been accompanied by a "concurrent program of social and agrarian reform," that the government is not "doing enough quickly enough" to win the support of the people, and that, despite painstaking precautions against profiteering, the vast expenditures of the Development Board are "benefiting the contractors and entrepreneurs far more than the great sharecropping mass of the populace."[1]

As to the first point, the previous discussion demonstrates that this is not the case and that a program of social and agrarian reform does exist. It is true that, in its initial stages, it was slow in taking hold. But in the last few years reform has gathered considerable momentum.

The second point raises a completely different issue. Should the Development Board, originally organized so as to be isolated from political pressures, become the handmaiden of political expediency? Should the Development Program, planned and executed by capable and presumably honest specialists, be oriented toward winning popular appeal at the expense of the welfare of the country? If this is to be the case, would the capital made available from oil revenues not be wasted on elaborate social welfare schemes? Would the country not eventually find itself economically more or less in the same position in which it started in 1950? Would it not be the better part of wisdom and political strategy to withstand pressures for immediate benefits in order to assure greater benefits later? This is not to say that the development program is perfect or that more funds should not be allocated to meet immediate human needs. It does mean that, if the program is to be effective, it cannot be subordinated to political expediency or oriented to satisfying the whims of popular fancy.

As to the third point, it is true that contractors absorb a considerable part of the expenditures of the Board. Unfortunately, this is a necessary evil. The government administrative machinery is not capable (nor should it be) of carrying out the construction work itself. Part of the reason for the failure of the 1950-55 plan to reach its objectives was the inability of the various government departments to carry out the work entrusted to them by the Board. Experience in Iraq has shown that the most efficient and economical method of executing the development program is to entrust firms of international repute in their respective fields with major construction work. Contracts are awarded on the basis of competitive bidding. It is reported that some companies, particularly German and French, contract at a loss in the hope of capturing the Iraqi market.

In summation, it can be stated that while the peasant's share of immediate benefits is comparatively small, he is, however, receiving a larger share each succeeding year, and that he will be the major future beneficiary of the agricultural development program.

[1] *Reporter* Magazine, May 17, 1956, p. 18

# PART III *The Development of Industry*

# 8

## THE OIL INDUSTRY

*Ownership*

There are two oil industries in Iraq: one extractive, producing only crude oil, essentially a foreign enterprise financed and developed by foreign capital and skill; the other, very recent, principally engaged in refining, financed and owned by the state. The state industry will be treated in the next chapter along with other new industries. This will be devoted to the extractive industry.

The development of the oil reserves of Iraq represents the largest industrial enterprise in the country. The complex political history of its evolution and its political significance will not be discussed except where necessary to make clearer the economic design.

There are four international companies exploiting the oil resources of Iraq: the Khanaqin Oil Company, a subsidiary of the British Petroleum Company (previously Anglo-Iranian Oil Co.); the Iraq Petroleum Company (I.P.C.), the Mosul Petroleum Company (M.P.C.), and the Basrah Petroleum Company (B.P.C.). The last three are actually one, and are owned by the same interests. Stock participation in each of them is as follows:

                                                            *Percent*
Near East Development Co. (American)[1]                      23.75
Cie. Française des Pétroles (French)                         23.75
Royal Dutch Shell Group (British-Dutch)                      23.75
Anglo-Iranian Oil Co. (British)                              23.75
Estate of C.S. Gulbenkian (Armenian, British national)       5.00

The Khanaqin Oil Company is the smallest. Its production is small, and its concession covers only the "transferred territories," a small area of about 648 square miles on the Iraqi-Iranian frontier.

The company's first concession was signed on August 30, 1925, and was revised in 1926. In accordance with the agreement, the company produces oil from the Naft Khaneh field and operates a small refinery at Alawand for the supply of refined products to Iraq. In 1932 it organized a marketing subsidiary, the Rafidain Oil Company, for the distribution of oil and oil products in the country. In 1927, a twenty-five-mile pipeline was completed, connecting the refinery with the oil field.

On December 25, 1951, the government reached an agreement with the company and its subsidiary, whereby the government took over, as of January 1, 1952, the Alawand refinery and the distributing facilities of the two companies. However, it was agreed that the Rafidain Oil Company will continue to operate the refinery for the account of the government until otherwise requested and, for the ten years from 1952, will continue to be the distributor of oil products in Iraq on behalf and for the account of the government. It was agreed further, that the Khanaqin Oil Company shall, within seven years from date of agreement, commence regular exports of crude oil at a rate of not less than two million tons a year, or will surrender its concession. Profits from exports shall be shared equally between the company and the government.[2] In 1954 the crude oil production of the company amounted to a little more than half a million long tons.

The Iraq Petroleum Company operates in north central Iraq. Its first concession agreement with the Iraqi government was signed on March 14, 1925. It was revised on March 24,

1931, giving the company exclusive rights to exploit all lands situated east of the Tigris river, covering an area of about 32,000 square miles.

The Mosul Petroleum Company has exclusive rights to exploit all lands in the Mosul and Baghdad provinces west of the Tigris river and north of the thirty-third parallel, an area of about 46,000 square miles. The company now operates only in the north around Ain Zala. Actually, the company inherited this concession. The first concession agreement was signed on April 20, 1932 with the British Development Co. During the same year, the Mosul Oil Fields, Ltd., with British, German, Italian, Dutch, French-Swiss, and Iraqi participation, was organized to buy up the share capital of the British Oil Development Company. By 1935, the Italians were the majority shareholders with 52 percent stock interest.

In 1936, the Iraq Petroleum Company organized a subsidiary, Mosul Holdings, Ltd., for the purpose of acquiring the stock shares of the Mosul Oil Fields, Ltd. By 1937, the I.P.C. was in effective control. In 1941, the British Oil Development Company assigned its 1932 concession to Mosul Holdings, renamed Mosul Petroleum Company. Both B.O.D. and Mosul Oil Fields, Ltd., retired from the scene.

The Basrah Petroleum Company, which operates in the south near Basrah, obtained its concession on December 4, 1938. The concession covers all areas not included under previous concessions, including the Iraqi part of the Iraqi-Saudi Neutral Zone—a total area of about 93,000 square miles.

Thus, by 1938, the Iraq Petroleum Company and its affiliates had exclusive control on the production of oil in all Iraq with the exception of the small "transferred territories" concession. This final settlement was achieved after over thirty years of struggle, beginning in 1904, among many interests for the control of Mesopotamian oil.

### The "Fifty-Fifty" Formula

The agreements signed with the oil companies were basically identical. The principal provision, so far as we are here concerned, was that the companies were to pay the government a royalty of four gold shillings per metric ton of oil produced. This rate prevailed until 1950, when it was raised to six shillings per ton.

Early in 1951 the Saudi Arabian government signed an agreement with Aramco introducing for the first time in the Middle East the "fifty-fifty" profit-sharing formula. In April of the same year, Iran nationalized the Anglo-Iranian Oil Company.

With the formula already introduced in one country, and threats of nationalization in others, there was no alternative to the oil companies in the Middle East but to apply the formula universally.[3] In Iraq, after lengthy negotiations, a new agreement was signed on February 3, 1952 with the I.P.C. and its affiliates. The major provisions of the agreement are as follows:[4]

1. It was retroactive to January 1, 1951.

2. The government and the companies to share the profits on an equal basis before the deduction of foreign taxes. In addition, the companies are to pay, in lieu of taxes, 20,000 pounds a year each. (Articles 2 & 9.)

3. The government has the right to take in kind, as part of its share in the profits, 12.5 per cent of the net production of each of the companies. It can sell the oil on the open market, or resell it to the companies at current world prices. (Article 3.)

4. The companies guarantee the government's share in each calendar year not to be less than 25 per cent of the net production value at posted prices, as to I.P.C. and M.P.C., and $33\frac{1}{3}$ percent as to B.P.C. (Article 4.)

5. The companies jointly and severally guaranteed that the government's share of the profits will not be less than 20 million pounds annually for the years 1953 and 1954 and not less than 25 million for 1955 and every year thereafter. (Article 6.)

6. The companies guaranteed annual production minima as follows (Article 5):

I.P.C.: 20.75 million tons beginning January 1, 1954.
M.P.C.: 1.25 million tons beginning January 1, 1954.
B.P.C.: 3.00 million tons beginning January 1, 1956.

7. The I.P.C. is to supply the government refineries all the necessary crude oil for local consumption at 5.5 shillings (current sterling) per ton. [First Schedule, Point 5 (2).]

8. If production is halted, due to *force majeure* or an act of God, the companies are to loan the government a minimum of five million pounds a year, provided the amount loaned and unpaid does not exceed ten million pounds at any one time. (Article 8.)

9. If, in the future, higher royalty levels obtain in neighboring countries, the government has the right to ask for similar increases, and the company shall be willing to discuss the matter with the government.[5]

10. Each of the companies is to appoint two Iraqis on its Board of Directors. (Schedules 1, 2, and 3.)

11. Payments of the companies to the government are to be in pounds sterling.

*Discovery*

Exploratory drilling by the I.P.C. began on April 5, 1927. Two months later, on June 27, 1927, oil was struck at Baba Gurgur on the Kirkuk structure. By the end of 1930, twenty-eight producing wells had been completed, and in 1934 production began on a commercial basis.

In the Mosul concession farther north, drilling began in 1933 and continued with heavy expenditures until 1939 without success. A few days before the outbreak of the war (1939) deposits of light oil were discovered at a depth of five to six thousand feet at Ain Zala.

In the Basrah concession actual drilling did not begin until after the war. In 1948 oil was discovered in commercial quantities at Zubair at depths of ten to eleven thousand feet.

*The Pipeline System*

Due to the inland location of most of the oil fields, the production of oil in Iraq is governed to a considerable extent by the availability of transport. Hence, the industry depends on an intricate pipeline system which carries its crude oil to sea terminals for export to the world markets.

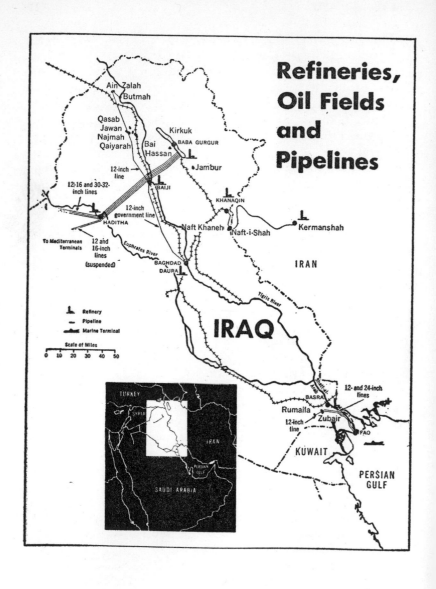

The first international pipelines to be constructed were two twelve-inch lines, with an annual capacity of two million metric tons each, from Kirkuk to Haditha, a distance of 150 miles. From there they branched off; one taking a southern route and terminating at Haifa, a distance of 470 miles, and the other taking a northern route and terminating in Tripoli, Lebanon, a distance of 380 miles. They were completed in the last weeks of 1934 and officially inaugurated in January, 1935. Due to the Arab-Israeli hostilities, the pumping of oil to Haifa ceased on April 17, 1948, and has not been resumed since.

In October, 1946, the construction of a sixteen-inch parallel pipeline, to follow the same route of the twelve-inch pipeline and to have an annual capacity of eight million tons (four million each) was begun. Again due to the Arab-Israeli hostilities, the work on the Haifa branch was suspended in 1948 after the completion of 575 miles of line—then only forty-two miles short of its destination. The Tripoli branch, 531 miles in length, was completed in the latter part of 1949.

Work on a thirty- to thirty-two-inch single pipeline linking the Kirkuk and Mosul fields with Banyas on the Mediterranean in Syria, a distance of 556 miles, began in April, 1950, and was completed in April, 1952, at a cost of forty-one million pounds. The line has a capacity of 13.5 million tons a year. In July of the same year (1952), a single 135-mile, twelve-inch pipeline connecting Ain Zala (Mosul oil fields) with Baiji (K-2 station) on the main Kirkuk pipeline system was completed.

After the development of the oil industry in southern Iraq, a new pipeline system was begun, connecting the southern oil fields with the Persian Gulf at the Fao sea terminal on the Shatt al-Arab. In 1948 work began on a single seventy-five mile, twelve-inch pipeline to connect the Zubair oil fields with Fao. It was completed in October 1951. Due to the expansion in production, another seventy-five-mile, twenty-four-inch parallel pipeline was found necessary and completed on January 1, 1954. After the discovery of a new oil field at Rumaila, southeast of Zubair, a twenty-mile, twelve-inch pipeline was constructed connecting Rumaila with Zubair and the B.P.C. pipeline system.

An interesting development is the entry of the Iraqi Government into the refining business, and it will be discussed in greater detail later. For this purpose a government 135-mile, twelve-inch pipeline was completed in 1954, connecting Baiji on the I.P.C. pipeline system with its newly-built refinery at Dawrah near Baghdad.

At present there are various plans for expanding the pipeline system. Putting these into effect is complicated by political factors. A new twenty-four-inch pipeline from Kirkuk to Banyas on the Mediterranean in Syria will soon, it is hoped, be completed. The pipeline has an annual capacity of nine million tons. It was originally scheduled to terminate at Tripoli in Lebanon, but a recent decision switched the terminal point to Banyas. The line has been completed as far as Homs in northern Syria. Another plan calls for the diversion of the idle Kirkuk-Haifa pipelines (annual capacity 7.5 million tons) from Mafraq in Jordan to Sidon in Lebanon, across Syrian territory. In 1956 extensive discussions took place in this connection, and in late September 1956 final agreement was reached with the Lebanese government.[6]

Similar negotiations between Iraq and Kuwait were conducted for the construction of a pipeline from the Basrah oil fields to Mina al-Ahmadi oil terminal on the Persian Gulf in Kuwait. The pipeline would have an annual capacity of four million tons. Its purpose is to make possible the shipment of oil on larger tankers which are unable to enter the shallow waters of the Shatt al-Arab. Agreement in principle is said to have been reached.[7]

A plan which has received considerable publicity in the world press calls for the construction of a forty- to forty-two-inch pipeline system commencing at Kuwait, going through Iraq, and terminating in Alexandretta on the Mediterranean in Turkey, just north of Syria. Several international oil companies would underwrite its cost, and it would serve Kuwait, Iraq, and Iran.[8] The plan is still in the speculative stage. A more recent plan was sponsored by the Saudi-Arabian government in late 1957. The plan calls for the formation of a corporation which would own and construct all future pipelines. The Arab governments in the area would be the stockholders.

*Reserves and Production*

The estimated proved oil reserves of the Middle East at the end of 1956 were some 144.4 billion barrels. Iraq held a little over fifteen per cent of this total (*see table 21*).

TABLE 21

ESTIMATED PROVED OIL RESERVES IN THE MIDDLE EAST
(End of 1956)

*Million U. S. Barrels*

| | |
|---|---|
| Kuwait | 50,000 |
| Saudi Arabia | 40,000 |
| Iran | 30,000 |
| Iraq | 22,000 |
| Qatar | 1,500 |
| Neutral Zone (Kuwait-S. Arabia) | 650 |
| Bahrain | 205 |
| Israel | 50 |
| | 144,405 |

Source: U. S. Senate, *Hearings Before the Committee on Foreign Relations and the Committee on Armed Services*, 85th Cong., 1st Sess. on S. J. Res. 19 and H. J. Res. 117. (Washington: U. S. Government Printing Office, 1957), Part I, p. 32.

Iraq's production remained comparatively low until after World War II. This was due to several factors. First, in the initial stages, the I. P. C. was reluctant to begin production until a settlement had been reached on concessions and its position was secure. Secondly, because of the location of the Kirkuk oil fields, the only producers at that time, production depended on the availability of transport facilities. Until pipelines had been constructed, production had to remain low. Thirdly, oil production in Iraq is extremely sensitive to international political tensions. For instance, during the war a good number of the producing wells of the Kirkuk and Ain Zala areas were destroyed by the British military command in Iraq in anticipation of a possible southward advance by German forces. Similarly, two pipelines with a total annual capacity of over six million tons have been idle since 1948.

The Suez conflict of 1956 caused a temporary suspension of pumping to the Mediterranean with an estimated revenue loss to Iraq of some seventy million dollars.

Table 22 shows crude oil production in Iraq. From 1927 to 1933 production was insignificant. In 1934, with the commissioning of the Kirkuk-Haifa-Tripoli pipelines, it jumped to over a million tons, and in each of the years 1937 and 1938, it was over four million.

With the outbreak of the war in 1939 production began to decline, reaching a low of over 1.5 million tons in 1941. In 1942 it began to pick up, rising in 1944 to its pre-war levels. In 1949, with the completion of the sixteen-inch pipeline to Tripoli, it made an uninterrupted rise. In 1951, production jumped to 8.5 million, and since then, with the completion of a variety of pipelines, the temporary shutdown of the Iranian oil industry, and the demands in the world markets, the rise has been in leaps and bounds. In 1952 it rose to over eighteen million and by 1955 reached over thirty-three million.

TABLE 22

CRUDE OIL PRODUCTION IN IRAQ
(in thousand long tons)

| Year | Thousand Tons | Year | Thousand Tons |
|------|------|------|------|
| 1927 | 110 | 1942 | 3,555 |
| 1928 | 120 | 1943 | 3,804 |
| 1929 | 120 | 1944 | 4,300 |
| 1930 | 120 | 1945 | 4,621 |
| 1931 | 110 | 1946 | 4,698 |
| 1932 | 100 | 1947 | 4,746 |
| 1933 | 100 | 1948 | 3,470 |
|      |     |      |       |
| 1934 | 1,060 | 1949 | 4,168 |
| 1935 | 3,677 | 1950 | 6,545 |
| 1936 | 4,013 | 1951 | 8,561 |
| 1937 | 4,257 | 1952 | 18,549 |
| 1938 | 4,288 | 1953 | 27,740 |
| 1939 | 3,954 | 1954 | 30,141 |
| 1940 | 2,621 | 1955 | 32,188 |
| 1941 | 1,609 | 1956 | 29,469 |

Source: Iraq Government, Principal Bureau of Statistics, *Report on the Industrial Census of Iraq, 1954*. (Baghdad: al-Noor Press, 1956), p. 203; *Statistical Abstracts* for 1956, p. 192.

The demand for Middle East oil in Europe and Asia is expected to be at least twice its present level within ten years. Production in Iraq will, therefore, in all probability continue in a steep upward trend. There are, however, two necessary conditions: the construction of more pipelines and regional peace. Because of dependence on foreign markets and the international character of the pipeline system, production is also governed to a considerable degree by international tensions that affect the Middle East.

### The "Integration" of the Industry

The year 1951, when the new agreement was signed, can be taken for the sake of convenience as the turning point in the history of the oil industry in Iraq.

In the first place, unlike the oil industry in Saudi Arabia for instance, the industry in Iraq was born under a cloud of international political suspicion. The vast amount of literature that has been written on the subject, and the numerous allegations and counter-allegations attest to this fact. Consequently by the very nature of its birth the industry was at a disadvantage in its relations with the Iraqi public. Regardless of its intentions and contributions, it was *ipso facto* looked upon as a "colonial" and "imperialist" venture designed to "steal away" the main resource of the country.

In the second place, until the late 1940's, the company made little effort to improve its relations with the public. Following in the footsteps of the British government, it relied very heavily on the support and friendship of the ruling class.

The waning of British prestige and influence, the rising tide of nationalism and extreme movements, the increasing power of the masses, the stormlike eruption in Iran, and, finally, a more positive attitude on the part of management, were factors which brought about a radical change in the orientation of the industry in favor of what is called "integration."

Since 1950, there has been a determined drive to integrate the industry into the social and economic life of the country, and to change it from a symbol of Western superiority into a cooperative enterprise of which the Iraqi can also be proud, and where both Iraqi and foreigner alike work on equal terms for the common good.

The outward manifestations of this change are many. Among others, they are reflected in the profit-sharing formula. Westerners in top positions are being replaced at an increasing rate by Iraqi nationals. Workers receive much higher wages than before. Working conditions, health, housing, and recreation benefits have been vastly improved. The industry takes an active part in public life and community affairs. These include fairs, fire-fighting, charities, city and village campaigns, athletic contests, and so forth.

*The Role of the Industry*

The petroleum industry has now become the central factor affecting the economic and, indirectly, the political stability of the country. Its influence, directly or indirectly, permeates every aspect of economic and social development. An idea of its strategic position may be gained from the fact that it alone accounts for over one-third of the total national income. Any extended interruption of the flow of oil would bring in its wake chaos, poverty, and political unrest.

## Oil Revenue

Between 1934 and 1950, revenue from the industry averaged about 14 per cent of the total revenue of the state. From there on it began to rise steadily until in 1955 it reached 73.74 million dinars (*see Table 8*), thus exceeding government receipts from all other sources by some forty-five million dinars. Oil revenue has been directly significant in three respects:

a. It exclusively underwrites the program of the Development Board. Not only that, but such a program would otherwise have been impossible, since no alternative sources of income of the same magnitude are available.

b. Between 1927 and 1950, oil revenue paid a minor part of the costs of government. From 1950 on, in addition to supporting the development program, it has been partly responsible for the expansion that has taken place in government services in the fields of health, education, credit, agriculture, social welfare, etc. Thirty per cent of the oil revenue goes to the regular government budget to defray the cost of ordinary operations.

c. It supplies Iraq with the necessary foreign exchange for her international trade. Iraq's perennial problem in her trade relations with other countries has been the great gap between the value of imports and the value of exports. The foreign exchange deficit over the years has usually been covered by income from the transit trade; expenditures by pilgrims and tourists; expenditures by foreign vessels and recently airlines; expenditures by British forces for goods and services prior to, during, and after the war; oil royalties which represent income from the export of petroleum, and foreign exchange disbursements by the oil companies and expenditures of their foreign employes in the country.

It is important to note that the oil industry after 1927 became an important factor influencing Iraq's balance of trade. On the one hand, the heavy imports of the oil industry became one of the factors contributing to the import surplus, and on the other, foreign exchange payments by the oil industry in royalties, local disbursements, and expenditures of its foreign employes, have been the major source from which Iraq covered its trade deficit.

From 1947 to 1949, payments of the oil industry failed to cover the trade deficit and Iraq drew heavily on its sterling balances and other assets which had accumulated during the war. Since 1940, owing primarily to income from the oil industry, there has been an increase in Iraq's foreign assets. The foreign assets of the National Bank of Iraq (which acts as a central bank), almost all in sterling, stood at 77.6 million dinars in September 1954.[9]

## Labor

The oil industry is the largest industrial enterprise in the country and the largest employer after the government. Its character and location are the two main determinants of the size of the labor force and the role employment plays in the national economy.

The industry produces only crude oil. Unlike the case in

Iran, it does not engage in any refining operations for commercial purposes. Once a well is drilled and connected, it needs little attention. The labor force is therefore comparatively small compared to the size of the industry, and is mainly concerned with drilling, maintenance, and pumping operations. For instance, the labor force in the Iranian oil industry was about 60,000 in 1948; the industry's labor force in Iraq during the same year was only 14,200.

The second feature of the industry in Iraq is the dispersion of its operations in various parts of the country. Therefore, he recruitment of the labor force is not concentrated in one area. Because of the size of the labor force and its dispersion the oil industry in terms of employment occupies no commanding position, as is the case in Iran, Bahrain, and Saudi Arabia.

Nor does the industry have an exclusive monopoly on labor but—especially today—has to compete for it under progressively adverse conditions because of competition from the Development Board and industrial expansion. While the industry is required to employ only Iraqi labor, unless otherwise absolutely necessary, Iraqi labor is free to move to other areas, such as Kuwait, in search of better opportunities. During the last few years there has been an acute shortage of industrial labor in Iraq.

Table 23 shows the number of workers in the oil industry in 1938 and from 1943 to 1956 and local disbursements of the industry during the same period. From 1927 to 1938 (not indicated in the table) the number of workers ranged between three and four thousand. During the early years of the war the number dropped considerably, but in 1943 it returned to its pre-war level. In 1946, the year in which expansion began in earnest, the number jumped to 11,000 and in 1956 it reached close to 16,000.

As shown by the table, the labor force is composed mostly of Iraqis, with a sprinkling of Jordanians, Syrians, Lebanese, and Palestinian refugees. Hardly any other nationality, with the exception of Europeans, is represented. The difficult question of employment of foreigners does not, therefore, arise as it does in Bahrain and Kuwait.

In terms of rank, position, privileges, facilities, and salaries, the labor force is divided into three main groups.

1. *The Covenanted Staff.* This group constitutes the executive, administrative, and higher technical labor force. The salaries of this group are calculated on an annual basis.

The "staff" is divided into two categories. "London covenanted" are mostly Europeans—and primarily British—who sign a contract with the London office. Their salaries and allowances are geared to the European wage scale.

TABLE 23

NUMBER OF IRAQI AND FOREIGN WORKERS; AND
LOCAL DISBURSEMENTS OF OIL COMPANIES
IN MILLIONS OF IRAQI DINARS

| Year | Iraqis | Foreigners | Total | Local Disbursements |
|---|---|---|---|---|
| 1938 | n.a. | n.a. | 3,600 | 0.58 |
| 1943 | 3,804 | 158 | 3,962 | n.a. |
| 1944 | 4,311 | 232 | 4,543 | n.a. |
| 1945 | 5,486 | 256 | 5,742 | n.a. |
| 1946 | 10,756 | 504 | 11,260 | 2.14 |
| 1947 | 13,900 | 656 | 14,556 | 5.60 |
| 1948 | 13,463 | 778 | 14,241 | 7.03 |
| 1949 | 12,069 | 814 | 12,883 | 6.49 |
| 1950 | 10,578 | 796 | 11,374 | 4.39 |
| 1951 | 10,385 | 659 | 11,044 | 5.69 |
| 1952 | 12,317 | 997 | 13,314 | 7.18 |
| 1953 | 12,279 | 906 | 13,185 | 8.76 |
| 1954 | 11,949 | 821 | 12,770 | 8.91 |
| 1955 | 14,468 | 860 | 15,328 | n.a. |
| 1956 | 14,914 | 918 | 15,832 | n.a. |

Source: *Statistical Abstracts* for 1950, p. 170, 1952, p. 235, 1955, p. 236, and 1956, p. 193; *EDME*, 45-54, p. 97; Iraqi Embassy, Washington, D. C., *Bulletin*, March, 1956.

The second group is called "local covenanted staff." These sign a contract with the Baghdad office and their salaries are geared to wage levels in the Middle East. The great majority of this group are Iraqi nationals, many of whom are paid at higher rates than those prevailing in the area as a whole.

Other than differences in salary scale, the two groups enjoy the same privileges and facilities (clubs, cinemas, mess halls, housing, etc.) The local staff comprises only a small percentage of the total staff. Since 1950, however, a drastic change in policy has taken place. Local staff, increasingly and wherever possible, is replacing foreigners.

2. *The Monthly Rate.* The salaries of this group are calculated on a monthly basis. It consists mostly of clerical and skilled workers. Usually the members of this group are high school and local college graduates, skilled artisans, foremen, and the like. It comprises about 15-20 per cent of the total labor force and probably represents its more stable elements. This group is second in importance to the first mentioned, although the gulf between them is very wide. It has many privileges not enjoyed by others.

3. *The Daily Rate.* The salaries of this group are calculated on a daily basis. It represents the lowest rung in the employment ladder. It consists of unskilled, semi-skilled, and skilled workers. On the whole the workers are either new with the industry, or do not have sufficient skill to be placed on the monthly payroll. A large majority of this group is illiterate.

The above three groups constitute the regular labor force. In addition, during heavy construction periods the industry makes arrangements with contractors to supply labor at specified rates for definite periods of time.

From the preceding discussion, it is evident that the importance of the industry as an employer in the industrial sector of the economy is steadily increasing. Between 1945 and 1955, the number of workers increased nearly three times. It is also significant in another respect. There is an increasing trend among workers to regard their employment as a lifetime occupation rather than a temporary measure. For instance, at Kirkuk (I.P.C.) in January, 1953, the total monthly and daily labor force was divided in length of service as follows:[10]

|  | Daily | Monthly | Total | Percent |
|---|---|---|---|---|
| 1 year and above | 2,254 | 304 | 2,558 | 47.4 |
| 5 years and above | 1,664 | 362 | 2,026 | |
| 10 years and above | 339 | 80 | 419 | 45.6 |
| 15 years and above | 171 | 91 | 262 | |
| 20 years and above | 34 | 38 | 72 | |
| 25 years and above | 6 | 13 | 19 | 7.0 |
| | 4,468 | 888 | 5,356 | 100.00 |

*Wages*

The legal minimum wage rate for unskilled workers in Iraq is 250 fils (seventy cents) per day. The oil industry generally tries to stay close to the legal minimum. Its wages are therefore divided into two parts—basic wage geared to legal minimum requirement, and a high cost of living allowance. The basic wage does not change frequently, but frequent increases are made in the allowance.

Since the daily and monthly rate payrolls constitute over 90 per cent of the total labor force of the industry, the discussion will be restricted to these two groups. Table 24 shows the wage structure of the Iraq Petroleum Company and its affiliates as of January 1953. In April 1954 there was a general boost in allowances bringing about an increase of 10 to 15 percent in total wages.

There are seven grades (one to seven) in the monthly rate payroll. Within each grade there are four basic wage increments. The allowance remains constant within each grade. Similarly, there are seven grades (zero to six) in the daily rate payroll, with identical arrangements with the exception of grades zero and six.

TABLE 24

WAGE STRUCTURE OF THE I.P.C., B.P.C., M.P.C.
IN IRAQ AS OF JANUARY, 1953. IRAQI DINARS.

| | | Monthly Payroll | | | | Daily Payroll | |
|---|---|---|---|---|---|---|---|
| Grade | Basic/M | HCLA/M | Total/M | Grade | Basic/D | HCLA/D | Total/D |
| 1 | 11. | 10. | 21. | 0 | .17 | .24 | .41 |
| | 12. | | 22. | | .18 | | .42 |
| | 13. | | 23. | | | | |
| | 14. | | 24. | | | | |
| | 15. | | 25. | | | | |
| 2 | 15.5 | 11. | 26.5 | 1 | .20 | .26 | .46 |
| | 16.5 | | 27.5 | | .22 | | .48 |
| | 17.5 | | 28.5 | | .24 | | .50 |
| | 18.5 | | 29.5 | | .26 | | .52 |
| | 19.5 | | 30.5 | | .28 | | .54 |
| 3 | 20.0 | 12. | 32. | 2 | .30 | .28 | .58 |
| | 21. | | 33. | | .32 | | .60 |
| | 22. | | 34. | | .34 | | .62 |
| | 23. | | 35. | | .36 | | .64 |
| | 24. | | 36. | | .38 | | .66 |

| | | Monthly Payroll | | | | Daily Payroll | |
|---|---|---|---|---|---|---|---|
| Grade | Basic/M | HCLA/M | Total/M | Grade | Basic/D | HCLA/D | Total/D |
| 4 | 25.50 | 12. | 37.50 | 3 | .40 | .30 | .70 |
| | 26.75 | | 38.75 | | .43 | | .73 |
| | 28.00 | | 40.00 | | .46 | | .76 |
| | 29.25 | | 41.25 | | .49 | | .79 |
| | 30.50 | | 42.50 | | .52 | | .82 |
| 5 | 32.00 | 12. | 44.00 | 4 | .55 | .35 | .90 |
| | 33.25 | | 45.25 | | .58 | | .93 |
| | 34.50 | | 46.50 | | .61 | | .96 |
| | 35.75 | | 47.50 | | .64 | | .99 |
| | 37.00 | | 49.00 | | .67 | | 1.02 |
| 6 | 39.00 | 12.5 | 51.50 | 5 | .70 | .40 | 1.10 |
| | 40.75 | | 53.25 | | .73 | | 1.13 |
| | 42.50 | | 55.00 | | .76 | | 1.16 |
| | 44.25 | | 56.75 | | .79 | | 1.19 |
| | 46.00 | | 58.50 | | .82 | | 1.22 |
| 7 | 49.00 | 12.5 | 61.50 | 6 | .87 | .40 | 1.27 |
| | 51.00 | | 63.50 | | | | |
| | 53.00 | | 65.50 | | | | |
| | 55.00 | | 67.50 | | | | |
| | 57.00 | | 69.50 | | | | |

Source: I.P.C., Kirkuk, *Personal Communication*, January 21, 1953. Basic/M·
means basic wage per month. HCLA/M. means high cost of living allowance
per month. The same applies to D., meaning Daily.

There is little doubt that the oil industry is the wage leader
in the country. Its wage policy apparently attempts to stay
just a little ahead of the going market rate. For instance, the
lowest wage paid by the I.P.C. and its affiliates in 1953 was
410 fils per day for a newly-hired unskilled worker. Actually
very few workers remain at this wage level for long. Prevailing
wages for such workers at Baghdad and Basrah in 1953 were
250 fils and 280 fils per day respectively (*see Table 25*).

The great majority of the labor force falls within grades
one to six in both the monthly and daily rate payrolls. These
range from semi-skilled workers with few months of training
to skilled mechanics, electricians, fitters, turners, wireless
operators, painters, carpenters, clerks, draftsmen, store-
clerks, accounts clerks, etc. The wage for this group (one to
six) begins with a low of nearly 500 fils (half a dinar) per day
for a new semi-skilled worker and proceeds to a high of
nearly two dinars a day for a grade six monthly worker. As
can be seen from Table 25, these rates are higher than prevailing rates in both 1953 and 1955.

TABLE 25

DAILY WAGES FOR CONTRACTORS' LABOR IN BAGHDAD
LIWA AND THE PORT OF BASRAH IN 1953 AND 1955
(in Iraqi Fils)

| | Contractors (Baghdad Liwa) | | Basrah Port | |
|---|---|---|---|---|
| | End 1953 | Jan. 1955 | End 1953 | Jan. 1955 |
| Carpenter | 900 | 900- 1,200 | 425- 555 | 465- 595 |
| Tractor Driver | 800 | 750 | 425- 525 | 465- 565 |
| Electrician | 700 | 1,200 | 425- 525 | 465- 565 |
| Turner | 1,000 | 1,300 | 600- 700 | 640- -740 |
| Mechanic | 700 | 700- 900 | 525- 660 | 565- 700 |
| Blacksmith | 700 | 800 | 425- 525 | 465- 565 |
| Crane Driver | 1,000 | 1,000 | 515- 595 | 545- 635 |
| Fireman | 600 | 600 | 355- 395 | 395- 435 |
| Greaser | 450 | 400- 600 | 335- 375 | 375- 415 |
| Laborer | 250 | 250- 350 | 280- 335 | 320- 375 |
| Storekeeper | 1,330 | 1,500 | 1,930- 2,130 | 1,970- 2,530 |
| Clerk | 1,330 | 1,500 | 615- 860 | 655- 900 |

Source: Lord Salter, *Development of Iraq*, A Report Submitted to the Iraq Development Board (London: Caxton Press, 1955, p. 153.)

An idea of the wage position of the oil industry in the industrial sector of the economy can be gained from comparing annual wage bills. In 1954 the annual wage bill of the four oil companies which then employed 15,249 (including refineries and distribution, otherwise 12,770) was 6,200,349 dinars. This amount exceeded by some 444,000 dinars the total wages paid by all other manufacturing industries in the country (total wage bill: 5,756,024 dinars) which then numbered 22,460 establishments and employed 90,291 workers.[11] It should be pointed out that approximately 37 per cent of the workers in these industries are small owners, partners, or unpaid family workers and do not therefore receive wages.

Wages in the final analysis are not the only criteria for

comparison. Workers in the oil industry receive many other tangible and intangible benefits which in most cases are not available outside the industry: fairly speedy advancement; assurance of a steady job; good working conditions; subsidized meals, housing, medical treatment and so forth.

Table 23 shows the disbursements of the oil companies in Iraq for both wages and services. It is assumed that the major part of the expenditures went to the payroll. On the whole they indicate a steady increase in wages per worker even though the number of workers also increased considerably. Expenditures rose from about 600,000 dinars in 1938 to nearly nine million in 1954. The increase in real wages, however, is not as great as might be surmised from the table. This is because the purchasing power of the dinar has declined to more than half its pre-war level.

*Hours and Conditions of Work*

Conditions and hours of work in the industry are governed by the Iraqi Labor Law No. 72 (1936) as amended by Law No. 36 (1942). A new labor law recommended by the International Labor Organization was approved by the Cabinet in June, 1956 for presentation to parliament, but was not, at the time of writing, passed.[12] The existing law covers daily workers only and, until recently, it applied in practice only to the oil industry and a few other enterprises, since there was hardly any other industry in Iraq.

In accordance with the law, the work day in the industry is eight hours and the work week forty-eight hours, for which the worker receives seven days' pay. Since 1945 the work day during the month of Ramadhan (the Muslim fast) has been only seven hours.

Friday, the Muslim Sabbath, is the weekly holiday. The law requires that workers receive leave with full pay at the rate of one day for each month employed and sick leave at the rate of four days for every three months. In case the sick leave has been utilized and the worker still requires treatment, he may use his ordinary leave.

Workers receive a week's notice before being discharged.

After four years of consecutive service, a worker receives compensation equal to two weeks' wages for each year served, in addition to wages for all leave due him.

Generally speaking, conditions of work in the industry are either equal to or better than the legal requirements. In any case, they are far superior to conditions prevailing in other industries in the country.

*Industrial Compensation and Pensions*

Industrial disability compensation is also governed by the labor law. According to it, compensation is paid in the following manner:

1. *Temporary Incapacity.* The worker receives free medical treatment, in addition to half his regular wages during the period in which he is unable to carry out his work, provided that such period shall not exceed one year. If it does, then the injury is regarded as permanent and compensation is provided accordingly.

2. *Partial Permanent Incapacity.* Compensation is assessed on the basis of a schedule of "organic incapacity" issued by the Ministry of Social Affairs.

3. *Total Permanent Incapacity or Death.* The worker or his relatives receive compensation equal to two years' wages.

The social welfare movement in the oil industry began only after 1951. Up to the present the I.P.C. and its affiliates have no retirement or disability pension plans. Theoretically, a person may spend his life in the service of the company, as some do, then retire to a life of destitution. One may receive injury and become completely disabled, but aside from a maximum compensation of two years' wages, he is left to shift for himself. The compensation scale of the labor law is a legal minimum. There is no law which prohibits the company from setting up an adequate scale. The I.P.C. and its affiliates have two schemes, but neither of them is designed to meet the human problem of old age or total disability:

1. *The Provident Fund.* The fund applies only to monthly workers since the daily workers are covered by the indemnity clauses of the labor law. Under this scheme 10 per cent of the monthly wages of the employe are deducted, and together

with accumulated interest on them, are called "A" account. The company contributes a similar 10 per cent plus a yearly bonus of 5 to 7.5 per cent of the total annual earnings of the worker. These contributions, together with accumulated interest on them, are called "B" account. Upon leaving the service of the company, the monthly worker receives the whole of "A" account in addition to:

50 per cent of "B" account after five years of service.
75 per cent of "B" account after ten years of service.
100 per cent of "B" account after fifteen years of service.

2. *The Employees Saving Scheme.* This plan is open to both the monthly and daily rate workers. It is designed to help the workers save part of their earnings. Membership and amount of saving are voluntary. Upon joining, the employe decides on the amount he desires to save, and it is then checked off by the paymaster and sent to the thrift office. The money is deposited in banks at rates of interest between 2.5 and 3 per cent.

The company's contribution lies in its encouragement of workers to join, and in providing the clerical and administrative staff, office space, and equipment free of cost. The scheme was initiated around 1950 in Kirkuk and subsequently introduced at Ain Zala and Basrah. It has been fairly successful, although some of the employes use it as a checking account.

The year 1956 may be regarded as a turning point in the history of labor in Iraq. It has already been stated that a new comprehensive labor law was approved by the Cabinet in June, 1956. According to press accounts, the proposed law extends the definition of workers to include white-collar employes, expands the indemnity clauses of the 1942 labor law and provides for more adequate compensation for industrial injury. It further provides for compulsory unionization in industries which employ over a certain number of workers.

During the same year the first Social Security Law in the history of the country was passed. On December 1, 1956 it was put into effect in five of Iraq's fourteen provinces. These five—Baghdad, Basrah, Mosul, Kirkuk, and Hilla—were chosen because of the heavy concentration of workers in them. The law gave initial coverage to some 65,000 workers in private enterprises, oil companies, and government establishments.

The main provisions of the law are as follows:

1. *Coverage.* It brings under coverage every employe who is working for an employer—whether for wages, or as an apprentice or as a probationer. The coverage is not restricted to industry but extends to every occupation.

2. *Contributions.* The employer is required to pay the Social Security Fund fifteen fils for every day of service of the employe excluding rest days, provided that such rest days are not more than one day a week. The state pays fifteen fils, and the worker ten fils. In other words, the employer pays 37.5 per cent, the state 37.5 per cent and the worker 25 per cent of the fund.

3. *Benefits.* The law provides for the following benefits which the worker covered can receive from the fund at one time or another: (1) old age benefit, (2) permanent invalidity benefit, (3) survivor's benefit, (4) marriage benefit, (5) maternity benefit, (6) funeral benefit, (7) unemployment benefit, and (8) sickness benefit.

4. *Administration.* Responsibility for the program is lodged in a Social Security Commission of three members appointed by the Council of Ministers. The Commission has a juristic personality and is authorized to buy property and otherwise invest the funds. The operation of the program is administered by a directorate in the Ministry of Social Affairs.

Before its passage, the law had been under discussion since 1951. Representatives from both industry and commerce were consulted concerning its various provisions. The knowledge that such a law would be passed may have been the reason why the oil companies took no action on their own in recent years to give their workers more adequate protection. It should be remembered that the policy of the industry is one of integration. Such a concept implies not being too far ahead, and not too far behind general trends and developments in the country.

*Labor Unions and Relations*

The labor law provides for the formation of labor unions.

In actual practice, there is a mass of cumulative evidence from impartial observers indicating that, on the whole, the government does not look with favor on the union movement. Moreover, union leaders seem to have no clear concept of union work, and it is believed the union membership (total in the country about 500) is infiltrated with state security agents.

According to a report of the United States Embassy in Baghdad, the government activity in the labor field is mainly confined to suppressing elements of potential threat to internal stability.[13] For instance, the union of cigarette workers which organized an effective strike in 1953 was disbanded by the government in 1954. In September, 1954, a new ordinance authorized the Council of Ministers, upon the recommendation of the Minister of Interior, to suspend or close down permanently any association, including labor unions, for actions endangering public security and order. The following month (October, 1954) the government issued regulations and set up machinery for conciliation and arbitration of labor disputes. One provision requires strikers to give a minimum of fourteen days' notice to the Ministry of Social Affairs before stopping work.

Whatever may be the attitude of the government, as of this writing no labor union exists in the oil industry. The only organizational channel through which the workers have some way of presenting their views or grievances to management is the Joint Consultation Committee System. This system was found effective in England during the war. It was introduced in one department in Kirkuk in 1950 and has since then been installed in all departments at Kirkuk, Ain Zala and Basrah.

a. *Objective.* The objective of the Joint Consultation Committee, according to the charter of the oldest committee at Kirkuk, is "to provide regular meetings between management and employes' elected representatives to discuss matters of mutual interest, to secure cooperation through explanation of measures proposed or taken on behalf of the interest of both parties."

b. *Functions.* The functions of the committee are completely advisory. They are limited to discussion of such subjects as promotion of physical welfare, improvement of working conditions and general work discipline. No subject covered by the labor law may be discussed.

c. *Composition.* Each department elects three sub-committees (each sub-committee has between six and eight members), one for each group of workers—the daily paid, the monthly paid, and the staff. Each sub-committee then elects two members to represent it on the Joint Consultation Committee of the whole department. In addition, management appoints two members to represent it. Thus the Committee is made up of eight members; two each, to represent management, staff, daily paid and monthly paid workers.

*Housing*

Up to 1950 the oil companies in Iraq to all practical purposes provided no housing for their employes. Very adequate housing was provided for the "staff," composed mostly of Europeans, and also housing for everyone on the pipeline stations in the desert. Other than that, there was hardly any housing scheme worthy of mention. Since 1950, however, housing has been provided for a larger and larger number of employes and workers.

At Kirkuk, a modern housing development was begun which by the end of 1952 had some 500 houses. The development has a shopping center, schools, a modern sewage system, and all the other necessary amenities.

The houses are of current design and are of two sizes. The larger size has three bedrooms and the smaller two. Both have a living room, a kitchen, a store-room, a bathroom, and a toilet. They are provided with electricity and running water, in addition to electric ceiling fans and radiators. Heat is supplied from a central plant.

Rent is very low. Priority is based on a point system. Each year of service is given two points, and each grade two points. But in any case, before becoming eligible, a worker must have served two years with the company. In effect, the point system leaves most of the daily workers out, until the needs of the monthly rate employees and those who have been long with the company are satisfied.

A slightly different scheme was begun in the Basrah area in 1952. At Ain Zala in the extreme north, no family housing is provided except for the staff. Bachelor accommodations are provided for technical and clerical labor. Unskilled workers usually come from nearby villages and go home at the end of the day.

In April, 1952 a home ownership scheme was initiated in Kirkuk and since then has been applied in Basrah. In one of its publications the company explained the reasons for the scheme as follows:[14]

> ...The company recognizes that any circumstances tending toward the segregation of its employees from the rest of the community—which is unavoidable in a Company Housing Estate—is contrary to the best interests of all concerned; and that the alternative of integration with local townships is more likely to promote the development and prosperity of the community as a whole, which must be the objective.
>
> It has become apparent that the construction of Company Camps or Estates has several drawbacks. Such estates, in which the inhabitants are precluded from many of the features of a normal community, fail to render the desired contribution to public welfare. Moreover, the employee occupying a house on a Company Estate, which he cannot make his own, is unable to attain the independence and security for his family that a house of his own provides.

The scheme operates in the following manner:

1. *Location.* The house must be located in Kirkuk, Basrah, and other townships, and not on company compounds. The selection of the location is left to the worker, but preference is given to locations which allow the worker to live within the circle of his group, such as his religious community, relatives, friends, and so forth.

2. *Procedure.*

a. The company prepares the designs, free of cost, makes the drawings, estimates the building costs, arranges for and supervises the construction of the house. It also defrays the costs of registration fees, building permits, legal charges, and all other incidental expenses. It also arranges for the insurance of the house against damage by fire and other destructive agencies.

b. The employee makes a specific down payment (officially 20 per cent but actually varying according to ability). The company then arranges to finance the balance needed by means of a long-term bank loan at 4.5 per cent interest per annum. The loan is paid back in small installments deducted from the employes' wages.

c. In the event of death, the company pays half the balance of the debt outstanding on the house, and the other half is paid through an insurance policy which the company takes out on the life of the employe. In this manner, the total debt on the house is liquidated, and the house is left free for the heirs.

The scheme has proved extremely popular with the workers and successful in Kirkuk. By the end of 1954, 202 houses had been built and were inhabited, while forty-two more were under construction and due to be completed in 1955. At Basrah the scheme was not launched until the end of 1953 when government approval was granted.

*Training*

Prior to 1951 the training facilities of the oil industry were very limited. Since the conclusion of the new agreement, however, many new training programs have been introduced, and the "educational" facilities have been considerably expanded. Several programs are now in operation, some of which affect the company directly and some indirectly.

a. *University Students.* The I.P.C. and its associated companies are obligated under the new agreement[15] to finance fifty Iraqi students annually for university study in the United Kingdom. The course of study must be technical. The students are nominated by the Ministry of Education and selected by a committee made up of government and company representatives. The students are under no obligation to the company in any way.

b. *Industrial Training Center.* Under this scheme, fifteen- to eighteen-year-old boys (with priority for children and relatives of company workers) who have completed at least their elementary education are selected by the company for a five-year course of apprenticeship training. During this period the students receive from the company about ten dinars a month each month the first year. The pay is then annually increased until by the last year it reaches twenty dinars a month. Part of the pay is withheld, either as savings for the student or payments to the parents. Kirkuk students live at home but they are charged for books and sports gear. The others are housed and fed by the company, for which seven dinars a month are deducted from their pay.

The training is divided into two parts: during the first two years all students go through a broad program of study with concentration on English, mathematics, physics, chemistry, engineering drawing, laboratory work, and workshop training in wood and metals. After the first two years the students are divided into three groups according to aptitude and ability. One group receives artisan training, the second, training in advanced engineering and science, and the third, training in commercial practice.

The Center opened at Kirkuk in late 1951. It has a modern classroom building, and an imposing array of training workshops. By the end of 1952 the Center had 100 students and it was expected that enrollment by 1956 would be around 300 students.

In addition, the Center carries out an adult education program in the evening. Workers between the ages of twenty-five and thirty-five are given instruction in English, commercial subjects, and office methods. It should be noted that day students under the regular program are not under obligation to work for the company when they complete their five-year course.

c. *Training in the United Kingdom.* Company artisans who show ability and promise are sent to the United Kingdom for one or two years of practical industrial training with part-time attendance at technical colleges. The scheme was initiated around 1951.

d. *Trainees' Schemes.* There is a complex variety of "learner" and "trainee" schemes at the Training Workshops in Kirkuk, to which the associated companies send the men they select. The training varies in length from a six-months basic course to a two-year program.

e. The company pays the tuition fees and other incidental expenses of approved correspondence courses with schools in the United Kingdom. Payment, however, is conditional upon the worker's successful completion of the course.

f. *On the Job Training.* Workers receive training while on the job under the direction of skilled artisans.

g. *"Sandwich" Training.* The companies accept a limited number of students from technical schools in the country for training at company workshops during their summer vacations.

h. *Evening Classes.* Evening classes at various installations of the companies and under a variety of arrangements are given in either English or Arabic or both. An increasing number of workers, especially from the lower grades, are taking advantage of this opportunity.

These various training programs are probably one of the more valuable and permanent contributions of the industry to the development of the country. There is an acute shortage of skilled labor in Iraq which is expected to become progressively more severe. The industry's efforts in this field are part of a countrywide drive to produce as many skilled workers as possible within the shortest period of time. This will be discussed later in another connection.

*Medical Facilities and Services*

In all, the oil companies have six hospitals with a total capacity in 1955 of 200 beds. The central hospital of the industry is located at Kirkuk. It serves the Kirkuk area and takes care of the major operations of the Mosul area and the pump stations. The hospital is fully equipped and competently staffed. It carries out an average of 1,200 operations a year. The total number of outpatient attendances at the hospital in 1952 were 72,005 of which 13,668 were non-employees.

Both Ain Zala and Basrah have smaller hospitals. In addition all areas have several clinics. Every pump station has its own medical arrangements including a doctor, a clinic, a detention ward, etc., to handle minor cases.

The services of the medical departments extend over a wide area:

a. Every employe prior to his engagement is examined and vaccinated against smallpox and inoculated against typhoid and paratyphoid.

b. All employes receive free medical treatment including hospitalization. This service in many cases extends to the employe's immediate family.

c. The company hospitals and clinics, especially in isolated areas, serve not only company personnel but also neighboring villages.

d. The medical departments are responsible for the general sanitation of the camps including supervision of water, food in the canteens, sanitation in houses on company estates, and other such functions.

e. They carry out, in cooperation with the local authorities, various campaigns to control disease in the areas in which they operate. The most extensive are the malaria campaigns which include larval control (spraying of water, etc.) and adult control (spraying of buildings).

*Welfare*

The welfare movement in the companies started around 1950. There are now welfare committees elected by workers in all areas. Their functions are purely advisory.

1. *Food.* In all areas the cost of food is subsidized. It is provided to monthly and daily rate personnel in most areas by contractors. The company usually supplies the contractor, free of cost, room space, equipment, part of the fuel, electricity and water, in addition to a straight monthly subsidy, or a per person subsidy or per plate subsidy, In return, it specifies the meal prices which the contractor may charge, specifies the kind of food he may serve and supervises the cleanliness of the mess hall. In addition there are tea and coffee rooms which are also subsidized.

2. *Recreation.* The extent of recreation facilities depends on

the location. In isolated areas, such as pump stations and Ain Zala, full recreation facilities are provided, including movies, a library, a recreation center, and, more recently, swimming pools.

In areas where there are nearby towns no moving pictures are provided for the daily and monthly payrolls. However, recreation centers and swimming pools are becoming widespread. There are several in the Kirkuk area and three were completed in 1954. In Basrah a recreation center was completed in 1955. In both Kirkuk and Basrah townships (not on the company compounds) two employe clubs were opened in 1950 and 1951 respectively. The clubs are heavily subsidized by the company.

3. *Schools.* In isolated areas where no schools are available, the company provides the space and equipment for a primary school; and the government, the teachers and their salaries, for the children of local employes.

### Conclusion

The oil industry is basically an extractive and not a manufacturing industry. It was financed and developed by British, American, French, and Dutch capital, but it is British in nationality and governed by British law.

Production of crude remained low until after the war. From there on it made a very steep rise reaching in 1955 over 33 million tons, or six times its 1950 level. The demands of the world and particularly the European market call for continued increase in the rate of production. It is doubtful that there will be any appreciable increase over the 1955 level until new pipelines or other transport facilities are available.

There are two plans under discussion for expanding the pipeline system. One calls for diverting the idle Kirkuk-Haifa lines to Tripoli in Lebanon; another, for a pipeline commencing in Kuwait and terminating on the Mediterranean either in Turkey or Syria or Lebanon. Such a pipeline would serve Kuwait, Iran, and Iraq. The implementation of either of these plans is governed to some degree by political considerations.

Between 1927 and 1950 the industry made valuable contributions to Iraq. Its influence, however, was not seriously felt. Production was low, the labor force was small, royalties comparatively meager, and local disbursements not too significant.

With the conclusion of the 1952 agreement, however, the oil industry became suddenly the central factor affecting the stability and development of the country. Negatively, there is little doubt that, if the industry were to close down suddenly, the government machinery would collapse and economic and social chaos would follow. Positively, it is the one important single force responsible directly or indirectly for economic progress and social reform and for pushing Iraq by forced march into the twentieth century.

The industry is the largest enterprise in the country. From its inception it set the pace for wages, industrial social welfare, and liberal treatment of labor. Since 1950 labor benefits such as housing, training, recreation, food, medical treatment, and so forth have been vastly expanded. Periodic increases are also made in wages, and the wage scale is higher than prevailing rates in the country. The industry's attitude towards the labor force is, however, paternalistic and there is reason to believe that the formation of labor unions is discouraged. In any case, no labor unions exist in the industry.

About 1950 the industry initiated a policy of integration with the country and its people. In one sense, such a concept implies not being distinctly recognizable as "different" or "foreign," not creating an élite labor force physically and spiritually segregated from the community and in general not being too far ahead nor too far behind developments in the country. In another, it implies identification with local interests and local life, increasing the number of Iraqis in responsible positions, better and more humane treatment of labor, participation in community affairs, rising along with local interests to meet emergencies, constructive sensitivity to public opinion and, in general, overt concern for the welfare of the country.

1. Owned equally by Standard of New Jersey and Socony Mobil.
2. Iraq, *Agreement Between the Government of Iraq and Khanaqin Oil Co., Ltd., and Rafidain Oil Co., Ltd., 25th December, 1951* (London: Cooper and Sons, Ltd., 1952.)
3. The formula has several variations, but is generally known as the "Fifty-Fifty" agreement.
4. I.P.C., M.P.C., B.P.C., *Agreement with the Government of Iraq Made on the 3rd Day of February, 1952, Together with Law No. 4 of 1952*, (Hertford, Herts, England: Stephen Austin and Sons, n.d. In English and Arabic.)
5. This was not actually part of the agreement. The promise was made by an exchange of letters between the Minister of Economics, dated September 28, 1951, and a reply from the General Manager of the three companies, G. S. Gibson, also dated September 28, 1951.
6. USIA, Baghdad, Press Dispatch, October 4, 1956.
7. USIA, Baghdad, Press Dispatch, December 13, 1956.
8. See, for instance, *Time Magazine*, May 27, 1957, pp. 29-30.
9. United Nations, Department of Economic and Social Affairs, *Economic Developments in the Middle East, 1945-1954* (New York: 1955, p. 102.) Hereafter referred to as *EDME, 45-54*.
10. I.P.C., Kirkuk, *personal communication*, January 23, 1953.
11. Industrial Census, 1954, *op. cit.*, pp. 9, 211, 213.
12. *Iraq Times*, June 12, 1956.
13. U. S. Embassy, Baghdad, *Annual Labor Report*, Iraq 1954 (Dispatch No. 562 of May 21, 1955). Quoted by *Iraq Handbook*, New Haven, H.R.A.F., 1955.
14. I.P.C., Kirkuk, *Home Ownership Scheme Handbook*, an unpublished typescript.
15. This obligation is actually not part of the 1952 agreement. It is more in the nature of a gentleman's understanding—probably based on article 29 of the 1925 concession agreement.

# CHAPTER 9

## INDUSTRIALIZATION, COMMUNICATIONS, AND ELECTRIFICATION

*The Existing Establishment*

The economic activity from which the majority of the people of Iraq derive their income is the raising of foodstuffs for the domestic and export markets. Modern industry, excluding oil, began to emerge only after World War II.

In 1954 it was estimated that there were 22,460 manufacturing establishments (excluding oil), employing some 90,000 workers. Total investment in machinery was estimated at about 15.6 million dinars. Over 96 per cent were small shops employing between one and nine workers each. They accounted, however, for only 50 per cent of the labor force. A large majority of them were family enterprises, and approximately 37 per cent of the workers were owners, partners, or family workers who received no money wages. There were ninety-five industries employing 100 workers and over (*see Tables 26, 27 and 28*).

As can be seen from Table 27, spinning and weaving, bakeries, cigarette-making, motor vehicle repair shops, metal products, shoemaking, tailoring, and carpentry were the most numerous, accounting in all for some 16,000 establishments. From the point of view of employment, spinning and weaving lead, followed by fruit-preserving and date-packing, tailoring, brick-making, metal products, bakeries, construction, motor vehicle repair, cigarette and tobacco and grain-milling. In terms of annual wage bills, spinning and weaving were also the most important, followed by construction, brick-making, railway workshops, bakeries, grain-milling, cigarettes and tobacco, electricity and water, motor vehicle repair, and cement. The wage bill of each of these industries was over 200,000 dinars.

TABLE 26

INDUSTRIAL SUMMARY OF IRAQ: 1954
(Excluding Oil)

| | | |
|---|---|---|
| Number of Establishments | | 22,460 |
| *Number of Workers:* | | |
| Men | 67,373 | |
| Boys | 10,611 | |
| Women | 10,270 | |
| Girls | 2,037 | 90,291 |
| Literate | 22,813 | |
| Illiterate | 67,478 | 90,291 |
| Total Value of Machinery, etc., in Dinars | | 15,658,000 |
| *Annual Expenditures in Dinars:* | | |
| Costs of raw materials | | 15,024,000 |
| Costs of oil and electricity | | 995,000 |
| Annual Wage Bill | | 5,756,000 |
| | | 21,775,000 |
| Total Annual Receipts (Gross) in Dinars | | 39,198,000 |

| Motive Power Used: | No. | Horsepower |
|---|---|---|
| Electric Motors | 6,157 | 37,403 |
| Oil Engines | 1,561 | 98,052 |
| Steam Engines | 26 | 59,256 |
| | 7,744 | 194,711 |
| Water Wheels | 216 | 1,110 |
| | 7,960 | 195,821 |

Source: Iraq, *Industrial Census of Iraq, 1954.* (Baghdad: 1956), pp. 9-19.

TABLE 27
MAIN INDUSTRIES OF IRAQ: 1954

| Industry | Number of Establish- ments | Number of Workers | | | Annual Wage Bill in Dinars |
|---|---|---|---|---|---|
| | | Men | Women | Total | |
| Spinning, Weaving, etc. | 2,248 | 7,871 | 1,187 | 9,058 | 695,881 |
| Construction | 39 | 4,644 | 35 | 4,679 | 546,848 |
| Brick-Making | 203 | 6,770 | 70 | 6,840 | 485,802 |
| Railway Workshops | 8 | 2,506 | | 2,506 | 434,690 |
| Bakeries | 1,563 | 3,754 | 1,445 | 5,199 | 311,566 |
| Grain-Milling | 954 | 3,648 | 135 | 3,783 | 273,373 |
| Cigarettes & Tobacco | 1,057 | 3,417 | 571 | 3,988 | 267,173 |
| Electricity Generating | 49 | 1,338 | 21 | 1,359 | 250,008 |
| Electricity & Water | 22 | 1,383 | 1 | 1,384 | 249,603 |
| Motor Vehicle Repair | 1,239 | 4,044 | 2 | 4,046 | 219,999 |
| Cement, Juss, Gypsum, etc. | 266 | 2,552 | 6 | 2,558 | 215,759 |
| Fruit-Preserving, Date- Packing, etc. | 98 | 3,166 | 5,051 | 8,217 | 175,883 |
| Metal Products | 2,346 | 5,370 | 5 | 5,375 | 169,770 |
| Shoemaking | 1,239 | 3,103 | 83 | 3,186 | 166,452 |
| Tailoring | 4,236 | 6,072 | 1,313 | 7,385 | 166,300 |
| Printing | 132 | 955 | 4 | 959 | 118,155 |
| Soap & Misc. Chemicals | 53 | 1,020 | 80 | 1,100 | 112,884 |
| Water Supply | 34 | 815 | | 815 | 79,900 |
| Shipbuilding & Repair | 5 | 442 | | 442 | 74,124 |
| Carpentry | 1,914 | 3,318 | 19 | 3,337 | 70,868 |
| Soft Drinks & Soda Water | 56 | 567 | | 567 | 68,758 |
| Canneries | 96 | 641 | 5 | 646 | 68,608 |
| Furniture-Making | 184 | 696 | 2 | 698 | 65,682 |
| Pottery- and Tile-Making | 140 | 718 | 12 | 730 | 63,922 |
| Sweets-Making | 176 | 732 | 77 | 809 | 51,602 |
| Spirits, Brewing, etc. | 7 | 303 | 1 | 304 | 50,864 |

Source: Industrial Census, 1954, *op. cit.*, pp. 10-13.

TABLE 28
INDUSTRIES OF IRAQ AND BAGHDAD CITY: 1954

| Size of Firm— No. of Workers | Iraq | | Baghdad City | |
|---|---|---|---|---|
| | No. of Firms | Total No. of Workers | No. of Firms | Total No. of Workers |
| 1- 4 | 19,896 | 35,406 | 3,874 | 7,420 |
| 5- 9 | 1,837 | 10,475 | 456 | 2,750 |
| 10- 19 | 433 | 5,718 | 119 | 1,556 |
| 20- 99 | 199 | 8,185 | 75 | 3,041 |
| 100-249 | 59 | 9,527 | 32 | 4,886 |
| 250-499 | 24 | 7,835 | 7 | 2,628 |
| 500-999 | 8 | 5,336 | 7 | 4,499 |
| 1,000-Over | 4 | 7,809 | 3 | 6,587 |
| TOTAL | 22,460 | 90,291 | 4,573 | 33,367 |

Source: Computed from Industrial Census, 1954, *op. cit.*

The three preceding tables show statistically the basic characteristics of the industrial establishment in Iraq. It is still in an embryonic stage, using for the large part human labor and simple machinery. It consists mostly of hundreds of small shops and family enterprises, a very large number of which cannot be classified as "modern industries" but are more in the nature of handicraft and cottage industries. For instance, most of the spinning and weaving, tailoring and shoemaking establishments fall into this category. It consists entirely of light industries, including some service industries such as vehicle repair shops. It produces entirely for the domestic market and, finally, it is very highly concentrated in the city of Baghdad. In the whole country there were 22,460 firms employing 90,291 workers. Baghdad City accounted for 4,573 firms or 20 per cent of the total and 33,367 workers or 36 per cent of the total. Included in these totals are ninety-five firms employing over 100 workers each, with a total labor force of 30,507 persons. Of these, Baghdad City had forty-nine firms or 51.5 per cent, and 18,600 workers or sixty-one per cent.

Another index of the concentration of industry in Baghdad City is its share of the annual wage bill and the value of industrial machinery, plant, and equipment. The annual wage bill for the 22,460 establishments mentioned was estimated in 1954 at 5,756,000 dinars of which the industries of Baghdad City paid 3,359,000 dinars or 58 per cent. The value of machinery and other installations in factories employing twenty persons and over in the whole country (excluding oil) was found to be about 12.1 million dinars. Of this, Baghdad's share was eight million or 66 per cent.

*Industrial Policy*

Although the economic structure of the country precludes the immediate creation of substantial large-scale industry, Iraq has either entirely neglected or inadequately exploited some very valuable industrial raw materials. Industrial expansion based on these resources can produce new wealth, raise the standard of living, and, perhaps most important of all, develop human skills. In particular, Iraq possesses an abundance of potential thermal and hydroelectric power, mineral deposits and chemicals, and agricultural lands. A fairly sizeable industrial complex can be built on the basis of these resources.

Since 1950 several reports have been submitted by specialists to the Iraqi Government concerning industrialization. Basically, they all subscribe to the same thesis: that industrialization should not be forced through tariff protection and government subsidies and that primary attention should be given to agriculture in preference to industry.

The International Bank Mission, after recommending certain specified industries, warned that "Particular care should be taken that government assistance does not foster inefficient industries at the expense of the country's standard of living."[1]

Professor Iversen in his report to the National Bank of Iraq came to the conclusion that:[2]

> Since fertile land is undoubtedly the most valuable asset of Iraq (even counting oil) it seems to be most appropriate to choose the first alternative [i.e., agriculture].
>
> This does not mean, of course, that industry should not be allowed to develop; on the contrary, it is to be expected that in the very long run Iraq will have to follow the path of other countries towards an increasingly industrialized stage of development. But in a world in which the problem of providing food for an evergrowing population is one of the most serious, it seems in the best interest of Iraq not to force this development, but to concentrate on raising the efficiency of agricultural production.

Iversen, in discussing the "diversification of exports," adds: "Iraq has large comparative advantages in agricultural production, whereas the possibilities of creating new industries able to compete on equal terms with producers abroad are more limited and more remote." He further states that, from this, it is not to be inferred that industrialization should be neglected, but that "to force this development, e.g., through strong protective measures . . . would probably in most cases be unwise . . . ."[3]

Lord Salter, in his report to the Development Board, sub-scribed to both the reasons and conclusions of Iversen and added a few of his own. He points out that "There is every prospect that, in spite of short-term variations, there will be a chronic and increasing tendency for the terms of trade to be adverse to those industrialist countries which do not include large primary-producing areas."

Salter further pointed out that the self-sufficiency argument does not hold in the case of Iraq since "Her rich oil supplies require foreign markets and provide the resources which enable her to import advantageously all the manufactured goods she needs as an addition to those which she can produce economically." A case for industrialization can be made for countries whose population is already too great for the limited land available. "Here," he argues, "under penalty of starva-tion or semi-starvation, industrial production is a necessity." In the case of Iraq, he states, this does not apply, and "will not do so for many years to come. On the contrary, the poten-tial increase in cultivable land largely exceeds the labor re-quired for it."[4]

In short, the basic argument of the Bank Mission, Iversen, and Salter is that forced industrialization should be avoided. The Arthur D. Little Report (1956), which proposed a com-prehensive plan for immediate industrial development, was generally in sympathy with the above view. In recommending specified industries the report applied the following criteria:

1. The proposed industry must be able to produce at a cost below the landed price of comparable imported goods or materials before import duty is levied. "If an industry can produce goods in Iraq at a price equal to or lower than the landed price without import duty, its establishment is truly economic. In the future it may be desirable to apply a less stringent test, but at the moment a number of industrial opportunities promise a profitability that does not need ad-ditional assistance. It is clearly desirable that they should be established first."

2. The technical processes of the proposed industries must have been in successful use elsewhere for a reasonable period of time.

3. Because of the present limitations of the domestic market, several industries were recommended which will produce mainly for the export market. "Improved levels of national income can be obtained only by fuller utilization of domestic economic resources. As Iraq's two great resources are agricultural and chemical, development cannot proceed on the basis of the internal domestic market alone."[5]

Some of the principal factors contributing to lack of industrial development in Iraq follow the familiar pattern in underdeveloped countries. Lack of technical knowledge and industrial labor; inadequate markets and marketing facilities; lack of stock market and banking institutions and the inability or unwillingness to invest in industrial enterprises. Savings in the past were either hoarded (in the form of gold, silver, or jewelry) or invested in land, urban property, or commerce where the capital was believed to be more secure and the returns much higher.

For the above reasons, industrial expansion in recent years is almost exclusively sponsored by the state. Expansion has taken three forms: (1) State enterprises mainly financed by the Development Board. The major part of industrial investment in Iraq goes to these industries. (2) Enterprises initiated and financed by both private capital and the government mainly through the government Industrial Bank. (3) Private enterprises which, however, do receive extensive aid in the form of loans, tax exemptions, and tariff protection. Each of these will be discussed separately.

*State Enterprises*

Major industrial projects in Iraq are usually undertaken by the Development Board. The allocations of this agency for industrial development have increased each year since its establishment. In the first Six-Year Plan (1951-56) allocations amounted to 31 million dinars. In the second program (1955-59) they rose to 43 million and in the third plan (1955-60) they rose further to 67 million. It should be noted that in the previous two plans the budgeted targets were never reached, mainly because technical studies were not complete.

Most of the Board's enterprises are still either under construction or in the planning stage. However, the first results began to appear in 1955 with the emergence of the state oil-refining industry.

## The State Refining Industry

The creation of a refining industry in Iraq has been the subject of government and public concern since the genesis of the oil industry. Up to 1951 the production of the Alawand refinery did not exceed 375,000 tons a year and considerable quantities of refined products were imported from Abadan in Iran.

After the Abadan refinery was closed down in 1951, production at Alawand was stepped up to 492,000 tons in 1952, and in order to close the gap between domestic supplies and requirements a new refinery was hastily constructed by the government at Muftiyah near Basrah. It was built largely from improvised materials and was put into operation in September, 1952.

In 1952 the government took the first steps to create a state refining industry capable of meeting the country's requirements. In that year it organized the Government Oil Refineries Administration (GORA) to be responsible for the administration of all government refineries. It also constructed the Muftiyah refinery and purchased from the Khanaqin Oil Company its marketing facilities in Iraq and the Alawand Refinery. Since then three more plants have been constructed by the government.

1. *The Dawrah Refinery.* This refinery, located near Baghdad, was completed in 1955 at a total cost of 10.5 million dinars. It was designed to have a capacity of 24,000 barrels of crude per day, but has proved capable of handling 27,000 b/d, and if necessary its capacity can be stepped up to 30,000 b/d. It produces gasoline, kerosene, gas oil, diesel oil, fuel oil, and Bunker "C" oil. The refinery commenced operations in June, 1955 with a staff of about 1,000 workers. Plans are already in progress to expand its capacity to 40,000 barrels per day.

Crude oil for the refinery is supplied by a new government twelve-inch 135-mile pipeline extending between the main

I.P.C. pipeline system at Baiji (K2) and Dawrah. The refinery was sited at Dawrah because of its proximity to Baghdad City, which consumes about 40 per cent of the country's total demand for refined products. The refinery is largely self-sufficient. It has adequate storage facilities for both refined and crude oil, a tin-can factory, filling stations, maintenance workshops, power plant, and electricity generating station.

*The Dawrah Lubricant and Asphalt Plant.* This plant is an extension of the Dawrah refinery. It is financed by the Development Board and was scheduled for completion in April, 1957 at a total cost of 3.6 million dinars. The plant is designed to produce annually 25,000 tons of various grades of lubricants in addition to 18,000 tons of road asphalt.[6]

*The Qayarah Asphalt Refinery.* This refinery located at Qayarah, south of Mosul, was financed by the Development Board and completed in early 1956 at an estimated total cost of 2.2 million dinars. It now employs some 250 workers and has an annual production capacity of 60,000 tons of asphalt and 29,000 tons of various gas oils. A drum manufacturing plant with a capacity of 600 drums daily was recently erected near the refinery. It is said to be able to produce asphalt at eight dinars a ton as against thirty dinars per ton which Iraq had to pay for imported asphalt.

*The Muftiyah Asphalt Refinery.* This is a small plant located at the refinery near Basrah. It was completed in 1955 and has a production capacity of 6,000 tons of asphalt a year.[7]

By the end of 1957 Iraq was to have attained a large measure of, if not full, self-sufficiency in refined products. Since 1955 it has not imported for local consumption any motor spirit, kerosene, gas oil, or fuel oil. Aviation oil continues to be imported, although plans are in progress for its domestic production. Iraq will also produce all its needs of asphalt and most lubricating oils.

Between 1952 and 1957 state investment in the refining industry reached some 16.3 million dinars, excluding the costs of the Muftiyah refinery and the purchase price of the Alawand refinery and the marketing facilities of the Khanaqin Oil Co. This investment is justified for many reasons. Production costs are lower than the costs of similar imported products. The state will not only be able to make a profit, but may be able to sell at lower prices. This is particularly true of lubricants and asphalt. Local consumption of refined products is expected to rise steadily. For instance, imports of lubricating oils rose in value from 0.6 million dinars in 1949 to 1.1 million in 1955. Between 1951 and 1955 local consumption of kerosene rose from 31.6 million gallons in 1951 to 61.6 million in 1956; fuel oil from 895 million to 135.7 million; motor spirit from 26.6 million to 53.7 million; gas oil from 9.1 million to 32.3 million gallons. When the industry is operating at full capacity it will probably be able to provide employment for some 5,000 workers. Finally, it will help increase the skilled labor force in the country.

### Mosul Textile Factory

The consumption of cotton fabrics has declined considerably in recent years in Iraq. For instance, in 1949 Iraq imported 51.5 million square meters of cotton yard goods. By 1956 imports declined to 27.9 million square meters. Part of the decline is due to local production, but part of it is also due to lack of demand and the shift in tastes. This is evidenced by the rise in the imports of rayon fabrics. Such imports rose from 4.2 million square meters in 1949 to sixty-six million in 1955.

Although the domestic market for cotton fabrics was not expanding, the Development Board properly concluded that the market was large enough to justify the establishment of a factory using local cotton for raw material. Consequently, construction of such a plant, located near Mosul in the north, began in 1954 and was completed in late 1956 at an estimated total cost of 4.9 million dinars. This figure included costs of housing for workers (894,000 dinars) and the cost of a training program (62,000 dinars). The housing is not yet complete.

The factory has a production capacity of twenty million square meters of cotton fabric a year. It is believed that its production, together with the production of other private factories, will meet the major part of Iraq's present needs for cheap cotton yard goods. The factory will commence operations with 400 workers on one shift, but gradually raising the number to 1,200 on three shifts.

## Cement Plants

A serious problem which confronts the Development Board—and indeed the whole country—is the acute shortage of building materials, notably cement, due to countrywide construction, both public and private. It is estimated that at the present time some 8,000 new and reconditioned houses are being built annually and that by 1960 the rate will reach 12,000 per year.[8]

In addition to private construction, various government agencies, including the Development Board, have housing programs for workers and lower income groups. It is held as a rough guess that by 1960 the government rehousing program will reach about 10,000 housing units a year, thus bringing the total to 22,000 units annually. Moreover, the dams, bridges, roads, factories, and other projects planned or under construction require relatively vast quantities of building materials. For instance, Lord Salter reported that a dam now under construction will require an average of 3,250 tons of cement a month for two years, with a peak demand of 5,000 tons a month.

Up to 1956 there were only four privately owned cement factories in Iraq, with a total combined production capacity of 3,300 tons a day. Urgent requirements of cement have to be imported (in 1955, 76,000 tons). According to Salter, this imposed an additional stress on an already overburdened railroad system and on the road systems of neighboring countries. Moreover, there is a cost differential of some five dinars a ton between locally produced and imported cement.

Mainly to help relieve the shortage and the transportation system, but also to add to local productive capacity, the Development Board began construction on two cement plants with a capacity of 350 tons a day each. Both were scheduled to be completed in late 1956. The cost of the plant near Mosul is estimated at 3.2 million dinars and the one at Sarchinar (Sulaimaniya) 2.5 million.[9]

### The Sugar Industry

Up to 1956 Iraq produced no sugar. Its consumption of this commodity has been steadily increasing in recent years. The volume of sugar imports rose from 52,000 tons in 1949 to 140,500 tons in 1956. The establishment of a local industry would indeed be attractive, if it were feasible, since there is an expanding domestic market.

The establishment of such an industry has been under study since 1951, when the International Bank Mission recommended that the project be held in abeyance until there was a reasonable certainty that the necessary raw materials would be available locally.

Since then the government has been experimenting with growing a variety of sugar raw materials in Iraq. Sugar beets were found to be suitable for cultivation in the north and the government encouraged the development of sugar beet culture there.

In 1956 the Development Board felt justified in proceeding with the project. On May 9, 1956, it awarded a contract for two million dinars to a German firm for the construction of a plant near Mosul to be completed in November, 1957. The estimated total costs of the plant, including workers' housing, is three million dinars. The plant will produce 10,000 tons of sugar a year from locally-grown beets and, until such time as beet production in Iraq is sufficient to keep it operating the whole year, it will also refine 25,000 tons of imported raw sugar annually.[10]

In 1956 a new law was in the process of being drafted to make the manufacture of sugar a state monopoly. Its stated purpose is the encouragement of local sugar beet agriculture, since, it is suggested, private sugar manufacturers may turn to imported raw materials, and in this way destroy the infant sugar beet culture.[11]

Plans for the possible expansion of the sugar industry are already in progress. The Development Board is considering establishing another factory at Sulaimaniya[12]. It was also suggested by consultants that a sugar plant might eventually be established in Basrah, since soil and climatic conditions in the Basrah region are suitable for the growing of certain types of sugar beet.[13] In addition, the Board approved plans in 1956 for the construction of a liquid sugar factory using dates as raw material.[14]

## The State Tobacco Monopoly

Since 1939 the government has had a monopoly on the purchase and sale of tobacco. The monopoly was established for three reasons: to improve the quality of tobacco, to assure farmers stable and reasonable prices, and to raise revenue.[15]

According to the Bank Mission, the first objective was a failure; the second was partially successful since the government did insure stable and reasonably high prices, but the difference between its purchase and sale prices and its stricter grading of tobacco resulted in illegal traffic. Moreover, merchants were able to inject themselves between the tobacco farmer and the government because of their ability to advance money, to transport the produce to distant centres and to obtain higher grading for the tobacco.[16] The third has been highly successful.

No information is available as to whether any measures have been taken to correct the misuses brought out by the Mission. The assumption is that some effort has been made. In any case, in 1956 the state assumed full control over the tobacco industry. At the request of the Council of Ministers, the Parliament passed a bill on February 25, 1956 which made both the production and manufacture of tobacco a complete state monopoly. Existing tobacco factories will be bought out, but the owners will be allowed to participate in the stock capital of a government holding company which will be created under the control and supervision of the Tobacco Monopoly Administration[17]

In early 1957 the Monopoly began the construction of a new cigarette factory at Sulaimaniya. It is expected to be ready at the end of 1957, and will produce initially four million cigarettes a day with an eventual production target of six million.[18]

*Industrial Planning*

From the previous discussion it can be seen that between 1952 and 1956 investment in state industries exclusive of the refining industry came to some fifteen million dinars. In each case the industry depends on local raw materials, caters to the domestic market only, and was selected after years of study and planning. The state industrial program fell behind its scheduled targets, but in the long run it seems much more advisable to fall behind schedules than to be hurried by various pressures into establishing, without adequate study, industries which might later prove inefficient and uneconomical—provided, of course, that "adequate study" is not taken as a blanket excuse for laxity and ineffectiveness.

Many new industries are either being planned or are ready to be launched by the Development Board or some other government agency. The Little Report, mentioned previously, proposed a phased program for implementation in a period of some six years (*see Table 29*). The program contemplates creating a chemical industry with a variety of by-products, establishing date industries, a steel-rolling mill and a steel furnace, and expansion and improvement of the agricultural products, metal products, and building materials industries.

TABLE 29

SUGGESTED PHASING OF INDUSTRIALIZATION PROGRAM
(The *Little Report:*1956)

| PHASE I | PHASE II | PHASE III | PHASE IV |
|---|---|---|---|
| Rayon Textile Mill | Rayon Textile Mill | Rayon Plant | Steel Furnace |
| Sulfur Extraction Plant | Steel-rolling Mill | Plastic Materials Plants: | Plastic Materials Plant: |
| Paper Plant | Fertilizer Plant | Ethylene | Polyvinyl Chloride |
| Date Industries: | | Polyethylene | Caustic Soda Plant |
| Syrup Plant | | | Date Industries: |
| Animal Feed Plant | | | Syrup Plant |
| | | | Animal Feed Plant |

| *PHASE I* | *PHASE II* | *PHASE III* | *PHASE IV* |
|---|---|---|---|
| *Extension &* | *Extension &* | *Extension &* | *Extension &* |
| *Improvement of:* | *Improvement of:* | *Improvement of:* | *Improvement of:* |
| Agricultural Products Industry | (Same as First Phase) | (Same as Previous Phase) | (Same as Previous Phase) |
| Metal Products Industry | | | |
| Building Materials Industry | | | |

Approximate Total Investment in Million Dinars:

| 7.5 | 14 | 13.5 | 8 |
|---|---|---|---|

Source: The *Little Report,* p. 6.

The Six-Year Plan (1955-60) of the Development Board seems to follow fairly closely the program suggested above.

In addition to electrification (to be discussed below) the Board's program contemplates the following breakdown:

|  | Estimated Expenditures: |
|---|---|
| *Industry* | *1956-60* |
|  | In Millions of Dinars |

1. *Extension and Improvement of:*
   Agricultural Products Industry
   Metal Products Industry
   Building Materials Industry                    $\Big\}$      11. 5

2. *New Industries:*
   Sulfur Extraction Plant
   Paper Mill
   Date Syrup Plant
   Date Animal Feed Plant
   Rayon Textile Mill
   Steel-Rolling Mill
   Steel Furnace                    12. 3

3. *New Plants (Under Study):*
   Fertilizer Plant
   Plastic Materials Plant
   Caustic Soda Plant
   Mining Projects
   Natural Gas Pipeline                    10. 7

4. Development of Other Industries,
      including Atomic Energy.                    4.67

                    Total:                    39.17

The above program is to be understood as a general and tentative plan and not as an inflexible schedule. Some projects may be deferred or rejected, while others may be pushed ahead or new ones introduced. The estimated expenditures include allocations to the Industrial Bank and to the Ministry of Economics to help private capital participate in, or undertake in full, certain industries, particularly agricultural products, metal products, and building materials industries as indicated above. These industries are ill-suited to be state enterprises. At the same time, although many establishments may be needed, the individual production unit would be comparatively small in size and would not require large capital outlay, so that private capital with state aid—if and when necessary—can finance them.

In the case of the building materials industry the climate is very favorable for both improvement in quality and vast expansion. There is an almost unlimited market owing to the housing boom. Because demand far exceeds supply, the profits are handsome. Units can be dispersed throughout the country and are not dependent on each other.

The situation is the exact opposite in the case of Iraq's mineral resources such as natural gas, sulfur, and salt. According to the Little Report and others before it, their most effective utilization "can be accomplished through an integrated chemical industry." The market for chemicals in Iraq is now extremely limited. At the same time, to be profitable, chemical plants have to be fairly large, since production costs in the chemical industry bear a direct relationship to plant size. Hence the establishment of a chemical industry in Iraq would be justified only if it produced primarily for export markets. In this way, it would also supply the internal market with chemicals at low prices, thus giving impetus to their use and a gradual expansion of the local market.

Basically, then, the problem resolves itself to one of finding adequate foreign markets and meeting competition. According to the Little Report, "the local cost of production that [Iraq's] plentiful chemical resources make possible, will help to overcome the difficulties of competition from industrial countries and the obstacle of tariff barriers; her geographical position places her in a favorable position to supply the expanding Near and Far Eastern markets." The Report then proceeds to suggest the possible lines along which a chemical industry might be developed in Iraq. It states:

> The nature of the chemical industry is such that joint products or by-products often result from the productive process. The economics are generally such that, unless markets can be found for these extra products, it is not profitable to produce the main product. As a result, the chemical industry consists of a series of complex, interdependent plants; despite the large sales of products to other industries, the chemical industry has now become its own best customer. Products of one plant are used by another in manufacturing a product required by an external industry; the second plant in turn produces joint or by-products that are used by a third plant; and so on. The possible line of development of a chemical industry in Iraq illustrates this interdependence.

> Investigation has disclosed that the establishment in Iraq of plants to produce rayon and paper and to recover sulfur from natural gas is economically justified. A rayon plant and a paper mill of the recommended size would between them require 5,600 tons annually of caustic soda. This, coupled with the demand of existing industries, would by 1960 result in a probable total demand of 8,000 tons of caustic soda, which would justify its production in Iraq. The only method of producing this chemical that would be economical on this scale, the electrolytic method, would result in the production of about 0.9 ton of chlorine for each ton of caustic soda produced. Unless markets can be found for this it would be cheaper to import the caustic soda. The proposed plastic-material industry offers a potential market for chlorine, as it is required as a raw material for polyvinyl chloride. Natural gas can be used to produce ethylene, a raw material for both polyvinyl chloride and polyethylene, which are widely used plastics with growing world markets.

> The sulfur in the Kirkuk natural gas could supply, in addition to export markets, the rayon plant with the sulfur and sulfuric acid it would need. At the same time it would make it possible to produce fertilizer in Iraq, as sulfur would be required in substantial quantities to produce ammonium sulfate. Ammonium sulfate, or the other nitrogenous fertilizers, ammonium nitrate

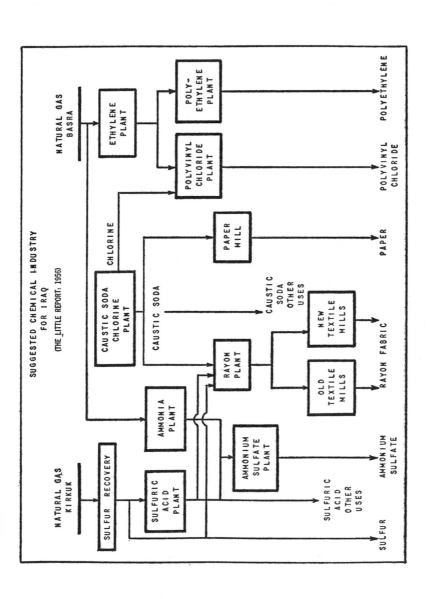

SUGGESTED CHEMICAL INDUSTRY FOR IRAQ (THE LITTLE REPORT: 1956)

and urea, would require ammonia, which could also be manufactured from natural gas.

Between these two extremes—a chemical industry (which is fairly large, interdependent, and for which domestic and foreign markets have to be created or found), and a building materials industry (consisting of medium or small independent production units, with domestic market demand far ahead of supply)—lie the agricultural and animal products industries. In this case, both domestic and foreign markets exist with considerable potential for growth. An industry also exists but requires some expansion and vast improvement.

The leather products industry is a good example. Iraq produces its own leather in addition to some imports. Local tanneries are protected by high import tariffs. Yet local leather is generally of poor quality, has a limited range of colors, and is expensive compared with foreign products. At the same time, the annual *per capita* consumption of shoes is 0.2 pair.[19] It is quite obvious that, with the rising standard of living, a substantial increase in the consumption of shoes is most likely. If the consumption rises to no more than one pair a year per person, this would entail a fivefold increase. Measures for improvement would have to begin at the source and proceed all along the line, such as improvement in livestock nutrition, protection from diseases, etc., forcing tanneries to improve their processes, possibly through removing tariffs on imports of leather, and so on.

Another illustration is the dairy products industry. The consumption of dairy products is extremely low in Iraq, but with the rise in the levels of income, a substantial increase is to be expected. Hence, there is a potentially expanding market for products of modern dairy industries.

Similarly, there is a potential domestic market for vegetable oils and fats. The *per capita* consumption of these products in Iraq is 4.3 kilograms annually, as against a world average of ten kilograms and a United States average of 30 kilograms.[20] There are two modern factories at Baghdad more than capable of meeting the present local market demands, even if all imports were to be disallowed. However, as the level of income rises, consumption of oils, fats, soap, and similar products will almost certainly increase and lead to expansion of the industry. As the industry develops in size and techniques, it will produce new commodities (such as detergents, glycerine, potassium carbonate, etc.). Since additional supplies of oil-bearing seeds will be needed, agriculture will also be stimulated.

So far the discussion has been restricted to possible industrial expansion which would depend exclusively on local raw materials. According to the Little Report present and potential local market demands and price differentials would make the establishment and expansion of some industries depending on imported materials economically justified. This would include the establishment of a small steel industry consisting initially, of a steel-rolling mill to be followed by a steel furnace and a small foundry. It would also include expansion of the metal products industries.

It is quite obvious that mass production of metal products will not be possible in Iraq for many years to come. Small plants form, nevertheless, an important base for industrial expansion and are vital to economic growth. They supply many products which otherwise would have to be imported from distant suppliers, and provide support and services to other segments of the economy. The Little Report suggests expansion in three possible fields:

1. Products to supply the building and construction industry, such as the manufacture of steel doors and windows. The demand for these products will more than double in five years, owing to housing development.

2. Household Products. Although it is impossible to assess accurately future demands of the local market for household goods and articles, *prima facie* evidence indicates that significant increases are to be expected in the immediate future. This assumption is supported by two arguments. First, rise in levels of income is usually accompanied by a corresponding expansion in the horizon of wants—a universal human tendency. A sample survey of lower middle and lower income groups (i.e., a majority of the population) conducted in 1954

in the city of Baghdad, where the standard of living is generally higher than the rest of the country, showed that people
spent only a little over 1.5 per cent of their incomes on
household furniture and utensils.[21] In other words, they bought
only absolute minimum necessities. Since the houses are almost bare, it is therefore reasonable to assume that people,
with the rise in their real income, would want to spend more
on furnishing their homes, an important prestige factor.

The estimated rate of some 22,000 housing units to be constructed annually by 1960 will, in effect, lead to a substantial
increase in the demand for household goods, since new
houses need furnishings. The demand will not be only for more,
but also better furniture. The houses being built or planned are
much better in design and quality than those the public,
especially in the lower income groups, has been used to.
There would be little inclination to furnish a hut nicely, but
there would be much incentive to do so in a nice house, signi-
fying a change in social status.

In any case, the potential local market demand would
probably justify establishment or expansion in the near future
of modern light industries manufacturing such articles as
kitchen utensils (in oversupply at the time of the report),
metal furniture, kerosene stoves, and heaters (widely used in
Iraq), air coolers (now being manufactured there), small
low-cost refrigerators with imported motors, and similar
articles.

3. Service Industries. There is an urgent need for service
industries to supply other industries, such as those of agricultural machinery and motor transport, with spare parts
and components and to provide servicing and maintenance
facilities. The lack of spare parts and service facilities usually
results in long delays, considerable expense to owners, and
waste to the country. The Little Report suggests the establishment of central machine shops and foundries in Baghdad,
Basrah, Mosul, and Kirkuk (the four main cities), and a
central garage in Baghdad. The machine shops could organize mobile repair units to service agricultural equipment in
the various provinces. In Turkey this procedure has proved
fairly successful.

The discussion on industrial planning above serves to illustrate two main points. First, the wide range of opportunities for industrialization to meet the demands of the present and future local market. Second, the type of policy questions the Development Board will be seized with for the next five years. For example: which industries should receive priority? Which industries should be undertaken by the Board and which by private capital? Which private industries should receive assistance from the Board? What are the best ways of providing assistance? What organizational structures should be established to administer state industries and to supervise private industry? What are the best ways of insuring efficiency, high standards, and high quality? What are the best ways to increase the skilled labor force at such a short notice? The list could go on.

*State Participation in Private Enterprise*

The chief instrumentality of state assistance to private industry is the Industrial Bank. The concept of direct state aid to industry was put into practice in 1936, when the State Agricultural-Industrial Bank was organized. The assistance which the bank afforded industry was insignificant. The total value of its industrial loans—its only contribution—from 1936 to 1945 came to some 64,000 dinars.[22] In 1946 it was replaced by the Industrial Bank and the Agricultural Bank.

In 1946/47 the government created the Industrial Bank with a capital of half a million dinars. In 1952, its nominal capital was raised to three million. According to its charter, its functions are: (1) to grant loans for the establishment of new industries or the expansion or improvement of existing industries, (2) to participate in stock industrial enterprises, (3) to start new industries on its own initiative if necessary, and (4) to offer various services connected with the import of machinery and materials and the export of products.[23]

In many ways the Bank has been very successful. It has contributed materially to the development of private industry through capital participation, and has shown substantial profits. Table 30 shows twelve companies in which the Bank

TABLE 30

INDUSTRIES IN WHICH THE INDUSTRIAL BANK
IS A PARTICIPANT: 1954

| Company | Year Formed | Nominal Capital I.D. | I. Bank Nominal Share | Per cent |
|---|---|---|---|---|
| 1. Iraq Cement Co. | 1951 | 1,000,000 | 269,810 | 27 |
| 2. Vegetable Oil Co. | 1940 | 600,000 | 120,000 | 20 |
| 3. Iraq Spinning & Weaving Co. | 1947 | 1,200,000 | 425,100 | 35.4 |
| 4. Iraq Milling Co. | 1945 | 250,000 | 6,000 | 2.4 |
| 5. National Tanning Co. | 1947 | 175,000 | 68,811 | 39 |
| 6. Iraq Jute Co. | 1951 | 400,000 | 75,000 | 18.75 |
| 7. Date Industries Co. | n.a. | 100,000 | 20,000 | 20 |
| 8. Baghdad Bakeries Co.[a] | n.a. | 100,000 | 25,000 | 25 |
| 9. Iraq Textile Co.[b] | 1953 | 250,000 | 125,000 | 50 |
| 10. Iraq Lime Co. | 1954 | 100,000 | 20,000 | 20 |
| 11. Building Materials Co.[c] | 1954 | 500,000 | 100,000 | 20 |
| 12. National Insurance Company[d] | 1951 | 1,000,000 | 150,000 | 15 |
| TOTAL | | 5,675,000 | 1,504,731 | |

Source: Industrial Bank, *Annual Report for 1953/54*, pp. 9-14.

[a] The Baghdad Municipality participates to the same amount.

[b] The other 50 per cent is owned by the Army Memorial Fund. It was reported that this factory will expand its operations to meet all army needs of blankets, socks, clothing, and other material. The capital, it is reported, has been raised to 1.25 million dinars. For this purpose the Memorial Fund borrowed 150,000 dinars from the Development Board, *Iraq Times*, January 30, 1956.

[c] The Mortgage Bank, a government agency, participates to the same amount.

[d] This is actually a government company. The government owns forty per cent of the stock capital, and the Industrial Bank, the Mortgage Bank, the Rafidain Bank, and the Agricultural Bank, all state banks, own 15 per cent each.

was a participant in 1954. These happen to be among the major companies in the country. They all use modern power-driven machinery. They are all fairly successful and have shown reasonable profits.

The total stock capital of these companies is 5,670,000 dinars, of which the Industrial Bank's stock participation is 1,504,731 dinars. If the stocks of other government agencies are added, then the total government participation comes to 2,479,731 dinars or 43.7 per cent.

It should be remembered that the purpose for which the

Bank was created is to assist in the industrial development of
the country and not to involve government in business. Consequently, once a company is established as a going concern
and its success is assured, the bank tries to dispose of its stock
to the public. This has two objectives: (1) to release the
Bank's funds for investment in new industries, and (2) to help
create a very badly needed capital market and to educate
the public in the use of stocks.

TABLE 31

LOANS OF THE INDUSTRIAL BANK

| Year | No. of Loans | Total Value of Loans in Dinars |
|------|-------------|-------------------------------|
| 1948/49 | 35 | 50,298 |
| 1949/50 | 81 | 132,110 |
| 1950/51 | 87 | 281,225 |
| 1951/52 | 151 | 655,380 |
| 1952/53 | n.a. | n.a. |
| 1953/54 | 172 | 734,140 |
| 1954/55 | 242 | 1,367,602 |

Source: Industrial Bank, *2nd and 3rd Annual Reports* for the years 1948-49,
1949-50; National Bank of Iraq, *Annual Report for 1952; Statistical Abstract* for
1955, p. 181.

On the other hand, the Bank has been criticized on two
counts. It seems to set a high value on profits and has a tendency to measure its success in that context. Although the
Bank should make some profit in order to create public confidence in its operations, it was not created to make money
but to assist and develop industry. Therefore, it should participate not only in ventures that show considerable profits
but also in industries which benefit the country as a whole,
even though their profit margin may be low.
   The Bank has a tendency to participate only in fairly large
enterprises. It should in addition help in the establishment
and improvement of handicraft industries and small repair

shops. This would contribute to social stability since it helps to create a class of independent artisans in the cities.

The second main function of the Bank is to assist in the improvement and expansion of industry through loans. The Bank has become increasingly active in this field as a glance at Table 31 will show. In 1948/49—the second year of its operation—it made thirty-five loans totaling in value 50,-298 dinars. Six years later, in 1954/55, the number of its loans rose to 242 with a total value of 1,367,602 dinars. They vary in amount from 150 to 150,000 dinars and more, and are extended to small and large establishments, although the latter seem to receive the lion's share.

It is apparent that the Bank is playing an increasingly vital role in the industrialization of Iraq. It will be recalled that among the major allocations of the Development Board for the 1955-60 industrial program were included unspecified amounts for the Industrial Bank and the Ministry of Economics. Apparently, insofar as private industry is concerned, the Bank is to become the executive arm of the Board.

Lord Salter recommended that where industrialization was concerned the Board should separate policy function from administrative functions and should delegate administrative functions to a separate body. This was endorsed by the Little Report. The report specifically recommended that the Industrial Bank be reorganized and transferred to the Ministry of Development, with additional loan and capital funds above those now at its disposal. It further recommended that the Board facilitate the establishment of an Industrial Development Finance Corporation owned by private and state banks. Such a corporation should have a line of credit from the Board. Its function would be to provide capital and loan funds to private industry. Once it is formed it should take over the functions of the Industrial Bank with regard to private industry. The Development Board would, however, remain the policy-making body determining the scope and direction of industrialization. The report cites the Industrial Bank of Turkey as a successful example of an industrial bank in the Middle East.

*Private Industry*

Basically, the rise of modern private industry dates back to the war years. From 1936 to 1943 total capital investment in industry came to a little over one million dinars.[24] During the war, shortages of manufactured goods and expectations of high profits resulted in some industrial expansion. From 1943 to 1948 private industrial investment totaled 3.1 million dinars.[25] Some of the factories that were established were inefficient and could survive only as long as there was no competition from foreign goods. Consequently, in the years immediately following the war, these industries experienced considerable distress.[26]

In any case, by the end of 1952, in addition to other industries, there were ten large-scale industries totaling in number twenty-two establishments.[27] Their total capital was nearly five million dinars (4,835,755), and the value of their annual output was 4.4 million dinars (4,424,339). They employed 4,553 workers with an annual wage bill of close to 600,000 dinars (599,366).[28]

Since 1952 there has been substantial development. In 1954, according to the census, there were ninety-five firms employing 100 workers and over each, with a total labor force of 18,600 workers.[29] Four of these employed 1,000 workers and over each, with a total of 7,800 workers (*see Table 28*). These figures exclude the oil industry.

It can be stated—probably without much exaggeration—that since 1950 private industry has come into being almost exclusively as a result of state effort. The activities of the Industrial Bank have already been discussed at some length. But in addition to direct financial aid, new industries receive extensive privileges. In 1950 a new law (No. 43 of 1950), called the Encouragement of Industry Law, replaced an old one passed in 1929. The new law awards new industries the following benefits: (1) exemption from income and surtaxes for four years, (2) exemption from import duty on machinery, material, equipment, and spare parts, (3) exemption from property tax for ten years, and (4) use of government land not in excess of 25,000 square meters, free of rent for ten years.

Also, industry is afforded varying degrees of protection. For instance, heavy import duties are imposed on leather, while the importation of cotton yarn and beer is entirely prohibited. Other goods are subject to a quota system.

The main obstacles which have so far stood in the way of the development of private industry are being gradually removed. The foremost is probably lack of capital, with a concomitant hesitancy or reluctance to invest in industry. Through state financial aid and various other inducements the volume of private capital invested in industry is increasing year by year. As knowledge of the "mysteries" of industry increases and the benefits from it become clear, it is reasonable to expect that the rate of investment will increase and that private capital will become more venturesome in spirit. The second main obstacle is lack of technical knowledge and shortage of skilled labor. This, again, is being rectified by the state. The third main obstacle is market limitation. As has been demonstrated, the market in Iraq for many commodities is no longer static. It is either expanding or expandable.

On the whole, however, state investment in industry for some years to come will far exceed private investment. If the present trend continues, the state may eventually own most— if not all—the most important industrial enterprises in the country. This raises the question of the desirability of state ownership of industry versus private ownership.

It is argued that state investment in industry is only a temporary measure, necessitated by the lack of private capital and the immediate need and/or desire for a measure of industrialization to utilize valuable natural and human resources now completely idle or only partially exploited.

The wisdom and the need for the present state action are beyond question. There is little doubt that, if there is to be any significant industrialization, major investment will have to be by the state since it alone has the necessary capital. However, there is a real possibility that what began as a temporary measure, until a capital market could be developed, may become permanent. Three main arguments support this conclusion:

1. Experience in other countries has shown that once an

organization is created, it becomes extremely difficult to dislodge it, for it generally entrenches itself and develops vested interests. Particularly in government, temporary measures and organizations have a way of becoming permanent.

2. Ownership of industry by the state may become more and more attractive as a revenue-raising instrument. As the volume of profits from state industries increases, there will probably be considerable reluctance to give up this lucrative source of revenue. On the contrary, this may provide further temptation to increase state industrial holdings.

3. Although there is no conclusive evidence based on actual study, there is reason to believe that, generally speaking, the vocal segments of the Iraqi public and particularly the intelligentsia, would prefer state ownership of the important industries to private ownership. This statement would probably hold true in all countries of the Middle East. Conceptually, state ownership has the advantage of appealing to the public in terms of "public property" to be used for the general good rather than to enrich the few. Conversely, private ownership of industry brings with it mental association with "capitalism," a term which in the Middle East carries unpleasant and sometimes even sinister connotations.

The ultimate outcome will probably depend on state policy. At present the tendency, whether by choice or necessity, seems to be toward more state ownership. It remains to be seen whether this trend will continue.

*Electrification*

The consumption of electricity in Iraq is still almost entirely restricted to the four main cities of Baghdad, Kirkuk, Basrah, and Mosul. Among them, they account for about 90 per cent of the consumption of electricity in the country. The other ten per cent is distributed among the other smaller towns. No electricity is consumed in rural areas.

Between 1947 and 1955 consumption increased over eight times (*see Table 32*). However, as can be seen from the table, the greatest part of the increase took place in the two cities of Baghdad and Kirkuk. Over 90 per cent of the electricity in Kirkuk is consumed by the oil company.

Table 32 is interesting in many respects, for in a certain sense
it can be regarded as an index of the change taking place in
the country. First, it shows that electricity is gradually replacing kerosene for lighting in the cities. It shows as well
the growth of modern industry in Iraq, and its concentration

TABLE 32

CONSUMPTION OF ELECTRICITY IN IRAQ,
BAGHDAD CITY AND KIRKUK PROVINCE
(In Thousand Kilowatt Hours)

| Year | Lighting | Manufacturing | Other[a] | Total |
|------|----------|---------------|----------|-------|
| | | IRAQ | | |
| 1947 | 32,974 | 24,038 | 1,559 | 58,571 |
| 1950 | 58,706 | 54,850 | 3,336 | 116,892 |
| 1952 | 77,084 | 119,653 | 10,504 | 207,241 |
| 1953 | 98,540 | 159,083 | 14,001 | 271,624 |
| 1954 | 116,184 | 260,954 | 12,896 | 390,034 |
| 1955 | 139,990 | 331,883 | 17,301 | 489,174 |
| 1956 | 159,980 | 323,940 | 22,457 | 506,377 |
| | | BAGHDAD CITY | | |
| 1947 | 15,967 | 8,948 | 177 | 25,092 |
| 1950 | 24,613 | 13,022 | 333 | 37,968 |
| 1952 | 28,708 | 25,239 | 354 | 54,301 |
| 1953 | 31,755 | 36,929 | 396 | 69,080 |
| 1954 | 39,708 | 44,769 | 465 | 84,942 |
| 1955 | 47,792 | 67,182 | 463 | 115,437 |
| 1956 | 55,878 | 82,608 | 354 | 138,840 |
| | | KIRKUK PROVINCE | | |
| 1947 | 2,338 | 13,887 | | 16,225 |
| 1950 | 12,150 | 39,463 | | 51,613 |
| 1952 | 15,402 | 91,003 | 5,675 | 112,080 |
| 1953 | 19,251 | 117,290 | 7,847 | 144,388 |
| 1954 | 31,562 | 209,554 | 5,827 | 246.943 |
| 1955 | 34,510 | 231,386 | 5,852 | 271,748 |
| 1956 | 38,986 | 199,234 | 9,231 | 247,451 |

Source: Iraq Government, *Statistical Abstracts* for 1950, pp. 63-64; for 1952,
pp. 133-134; 1955, pp. 191, 192; 1956, pp. 214-215.

a "Other" includes electricity used for cinemas, laundries, heating, refrigeration, cooling, etc.
b To all practical purposes "Kirkuk Province" here means Kirkuk City.
The main consumer is the oil company (I.P.C.). The company produces its
own electric power and supplies part of the needs of the city of Kirkuk. In
other words most of the consumption is by the oil company located at the city of
Kirkuk.

in the city of Baghdad (other than oil). Finally, it shows an increasing use of electricity for other purposes than lighting. This indicates that electrical appliances are in much greater use in the country.

Iraq possesses plentiful supplies of low-cost thermal and potential hydroelectric energy resources. Nevertheless, until 1956 these resources were not utilized, although electric supply is inadequate and comparatively expensive.

The question of increasing the supply of electricity has been under discussion and study for several years. Lately it has become more urgent, since the demand for domestic use has been increasing steadily and the development of industry depends to a large measure on the availability of low-cost electric power. An electrification program was included in the first Six-Year Plan, but no concrete steps were taken until 1956.

The program contemplates the gradual electrification of the whole country. Present plans are based on the use of natural gas and oil as sources of energy. This is because under present conditions of low demand (i.e., in relation to potential production capacity) and low-cost thermal fuels, the comparatively high cost of constructing hydroelectric plants would be unjustified. Thirdly, intensive cost studies have shown that electric power can be sold to industry and other consumers at two fils (0.28 cents) per unit.

The program also calls for the construction of a power plant at Dibbis near Kirkuk to serve northern Iraq, with an initial generating capacity of 60,000 kilowatts, another at Baghdad to serve central Iraq with a capacity of 60,000 kilowatts[30] and a third at Basrah to serve southern Iraq, with a capacity of 45,000 kilowatts.[31] The Development Board allocated 12,669,000 dinars for electrification in its 1955-60 plan.

In July 1956 the Board awarded contracts to two German firms to supply and install turbogenerators, boilers, and other equipment for the Dibbis and Baghdad power plants. The Dibbis station will use Kirkuk natural gas and the Baghdad station crude oil, but the Baghdad plant will revert to natural gas at a later date. According to the contract one generator (15,000 k.w.) in each station should be installed and handed over to the Board not later than twenty-one months after the signing of the contract. The due date will then be in the spring of 1958. The latest information available indicates that the Board was ready in October 1956 to award contracts for the Basrah station to be completed in 1959.[32]

*Communications*

### Administration, Nature, and Problems
### of the Transport System.

Control over the transportation system in Iraq is vested in several government agencies. The railways are state-owned and are operated by the Railway Administration, an autonomous agency which has its own budget independent of the ordinary government budget. The Railway Administration is also responsible for operating the Iraqi Airways.

Control over and maintenance of the road system is vested in the Public Works Department under the Minister of Communications and Public Works. Roads within municipal boundaries are the responsibility of municipal authorities. The construction of major roads and bridges is carried out by the Development Board. The Port of Basrah is operated by the Basrah Port Directorate which, like the Railway Administration, is an autonomous body with its own separate budget.

Geography and demography have bequeathed two distinct features to Iraq's transportation system. First, the major part of the traffic in Iraq moves along a north-south axis from Mosul to Basrah. This is the backbone of the transportation system. Southwards must move the great quantities of grain and other produce for the domestic and export markets; northwards go all goods entering Basrah, the country's only port and its southern extremity. Second, the system is concentrated mainly in the populated and cultivated eastern part of the country. It converges on two main points: Baghdad, the capital and trade center, and Basrah.

A good transportation system is essential to economic growth. Expansion in agricultural production, for instance, is meaningless unless there are adequate facilities to carry the produce to market centers. Industrial development is also dependent in a similar manner.

At present the main north-south traffic axis is served (1) along the entire length by a single track railway of two different gauges, (2) part of the way, by road, and (3) to a limited and diminishing extent, by river transport. The possibilities of developing internal river navigation are very limited. This is due to natural difficulties and to the fact that the river system is to be used primarily for irrigation. Consequently, the policy concerning expansion is reduced to one main issue: Should the emphasis be on developing the railway or on roads or on both? As for the railroad system, there are two alternatives: (1) conversion to one gauge or (2) a new line while maintaining two gauges.

## The Railroad System

By far the most important means of internal transportation in the country is the railroad system. It consists, excluding sidings, of 1,030 miles (1,648 kms.), of which 330 miles (529 kms.) are standard gauge and 700 miles (1,119 kms.) are meter gauge.[33]

These make up three main lines: two meter-gauge lines, and one standard gauge. Of the two meter-gauge lines, one connects Baghdad with Basrah, passing southwards through the most densely populated part of the country and with a branch line to Karbala. The second connects Baghdad with the northwestern provinces east of the Tigris, passing through Kirkuk and terminating in Erbil. The track from Kirkuk to Erbil was completed only in 1949. The third main line, the

TABLE 33

THE RAILROAD SYSTEM
GOODS AND PASSENGERS CARRIED

| Year | Goods (tons) | Passengers |
|------|------|------|
| 1945/46 | 2,304,038 | 5,292,441 |
| 1950/51 | 2,052,456 | 3,809,412 |
| 1953/54 | 2,519,266 | 3,014,401 |
| 1954/55 | 2,663,610 | 3,405,422 |

Source: *Statistical Abstracts* for 1950, p. 246; 1955, p. 228; 1956, p. 177.

standard gauge, connects Baghdad with Mosul and continues to Syria and up to Turkey and from there to Europe. It is the only railroad link which Iraq has with its neighbors. The railway system consists entirely of single track lines.

Up to 1950 the system was more than adequate for the country's needs and was estimated to be able to carry about 15 per cent more than its 1950 average. Expansion was nevertheless deemed necessary because a sharp increase in the movement of goods resulting from the development program was anticipated. Moreover, a large part of the rolling stock and engines was very old and needed immediate replacement.

In 1951 the International Bank Mission made the following recommendations:

1. Extension of the railroad system to meet expected rise in the movement of goods and passengers.

2. Gradual conversion from steam to diesel traction. It was argued that diesel traction is much more efficient, especially since diesel fuel is available locally at favorable prices.

3. Conversion from narrow gauge to standard gauge throughout the system. It was suggested that large segments of the narrow-gauge lines were old and would need replacement in any case. In this way, too, the system would be unified and facilitate the movement of goods and passengers. As things stood, goods transported from Basrah to Mosul, for instance, would have to go up to Baghdad on the narrow-gauge line and there be moved to the standard-gauge line and then transported to Mosul. In the words of the Mission, "the operation is costly, inefficient, and time-consuming."[34]

The Iraqi Railways administration, supported by Lord Salter, did not agree with the last recommendation of the Mission. It is in favor of building a new standard-gauge line from Baghdad to Basrah and, at the same time, retaining the old meter-gauge line. In this way the country would have two complete systems: standard gauge from the Syrian border-Mosul-Baghdad-Basrah and meter gauge from Erbil-Kirkuk-Baghdad-Basrah. Transhipment of goods at Baghdad would thus become unnecessary.

The Administration and Lord Salter argue that converting

the Baghdad-Basrah meter-gauge line at present would play havoc in the movement of goods necessary for the development program. It is further argued that the increase in the movement of goods during and after the development program would in any case necessitate a new line. It would therefore be best, according to Salter, to build a new standard-gauge line serving new areas and, when this is completed, to replace the meter-gauge line with a new standard one at the appropriate time.[35]

The new line, also according to Salter, should follow a slightly different route (i.c. Baghdad-Kut-Nasiriyah-Basrah) from the old one. This has two advantages. It is shorter by thirty-seven kilometers and can serve new areas which have no railroad connections. Apparently this recommendation has been accepted by the Railways Administration.

In its 1955-60 program, the Development Board allocated 24,940,000 dinars for expansion and improvement of the railways. Among other things, the program includes construction of the Baghdad-Basrah line, a meter-gauge line from Baghdad to Dawrah (a very short distance), purchase of locomotives and rolling stock, expansion of work shops, new stations and housing for workers.

According to reports, construction on the Baghdad-Kut-Nasiriyah-Basrah standard-gauge line began in 1956 and is due to be completed late in 1959.[36] It will be 576 kilometers long (360 miles) and will cost around 15 million dinars.[37]

## The Road System

The road system is the least developed means of communication in the country. In 1950/51, it consisted of about 8,000 (5,000 miles) kilometers of roads, 2,500 of which were metalled and surfaced, 500 metalled only, and some 5,000 kilometers of earth roads. It is still concentrated in the vicinity of Baghdad, in the north, and primarily connects the capital with the north and the east. All roads in the southern plains were earth roads, most of which became impassable in the winter due to rain and river floods. In 1956, with the completion of various flood control structures, the flood danger was removed, and ceased to be a factor inhibiting development.

The road system in 1950-51 was limited, and road conditions were (and still are) very bad. Road traffic was very light and the number of vehicles in the country even now continues to be comparatively small (*see Table 34*).

TABLE 34

REGISTERED VEHICLES IN IRAQ

|  | 1945 | 1950 | 1955 | 1956 |
|---|---|---|---|---|
| Passenger cars | 3,771 | 11,438 | 20,603 | 23,815 |
| Buses | n.a. | 3,007[a] | 3,311 | 3,451 |
| Trucks | 2,017 | 5,907 | 9,043 | 10,543 |
| Motorcycles | 127 | 1,626 | 2,091 | 2,420 |

Source: *Statistical Abstracts*, 1950, p. 249; 1955, p. 213; 1956, p. 135.

[a] Source: *IBRD*, p. 330.

The broad objectives of the road-building program were laid down in 1950 by an Interdepartmental Committee of Government Officials, assisted by a foreign expert. The Committee devised a ten-year program with the following order of priorities: (1) trunk roads connecting Baghdad with Basrah and Kirkuk, (2) roads in areas which do not and are not likely to have railroad connections, (3) roads between centers which are served or are likely to be served by rail, and (4) strengthening the existing paved roads.

There has been no basic change in policy since the Development Board took over. Roads, in the words of Lord Salter, are to serve as "ribs in the transport anatomy with the railroad system as the backbone." Emphasis is on trunk roads connecting main centers and on feeder roads connecting rural areas with main centers to facilitate the movement of agricultural products. Whenever possible, roads will not follow the railroad routes, in order to avoid duplication and prevent wasteful competition.

The basic difference between the Board's program and that of the Committee is one of timing and speed. The former is much more extensive and geared to be completed in a

shorter time. This is due to three factors: (1) much larger
amounts of money are available, (2) a sharp rise in road
traffic is expected, resulting from expansion in agricultural
and industrial production, and (3) the flood menace, which
used to inundate roads in the south and obstruct road construction, has since 1956 been removed, so that work in
southern areas can proceed at a much faster rate.

In its 1955-60 program the Development Board allotted
a global sum of 63.6 million dinars for road construction and
22.9 million for bridges (*see Table 35*). Some of the main road
projects which are either under construction or programmed
for are as follows:

|  |  | Estimated cost in Dinars |
|---|---|---|
| 1. | Basrah-Amara-Kut-Baghdad | 10,125,000 |
| 2. | Ba'quba Junction-Kirkuk | 3,550,000 |
| 3. | Baghdad-Shargat-Mosul | 6,100,000 |
| 4. | Roads leading to dam sites | 9,480,000 |
| 5. | Kirkuk-Kuisankak | 2,000,000 |
| 6. | Baghdad-Hilla | 1,420,000 |
| 7. | Hilla-Diwaniya-Najaf | 3,850,000 |
| 8. | Karbala-Najaf | 1,500,000 |
| 9. | Diwaniya-Samawah-Nasiriyah | 5,000,000 |
| 10. | Basrah-Fao | 1,250,000 |
| 11. | Dujailah-Nasiriyah | 2,250,000 |
| 12. | Raniyah-Dokan | 1,350,000 |
| 13. | Baghdad-Khanaqin | 1,100,000 |
| 14. | Ramadi-Rutba | 900,000 |
| 15. | Musayyib-Karbala | 750,000 |
| 16. | Sulaimaniya-Qara Dagh | 795,000 |

Until 1956 the road construction program proceeded at a
very slow pace in relation to schedules. This was due to the
need for adequate time to locate and plan roads, to acute
shortages in skilled labor and materials, and to floods. Although the work is now proceeding at a satisfactory pace, it
is doubtful that the targets set for 1960 will be reached. Table
35 shows the work that was accomplished between 1952 and
January 1, 1956.

TABLE 35

ROAD AND BRIDGE CONSTRUCTION IN IRAQ
(1952—January 1, 1956)

*Road Design:*                                                          *Kilometers*

    a. *Location Surveys:*
        Completed                                              765
        75% completed                                         108
        Under 75% completed                                   116

    b. *Construction Plans:*

        Completed                                              685
        50% completed                                         227
        Under 50% completed                                    85

*Road Construction:*

    a. *Completed:*

        By P. W. D.*                              101
        By Contract                                42            143
                                                  ———

    b. *Under Construction:*

        By P. W. D.                               60
        By Contract                               329           389
                                                  ———

    c. *Contracted but not started*                                     85

*Bridge Construction:*                                                   *Number*

    a. *Completed:*

        By P. W. D.                               3
        By Contract                               15            18

    b. *Under Construction:*

        By P. W. D.                               7
        By Contract                               18            25
                                                  ———

Source: U. S. A., I. C. A., Baghdad, *Iraq Progresses*, Baghdad, August, 1956, n.p.

* Public Works Department.

## Navigation

In recent years river navigation has ceased to be a significant factor in the country's transportation system. This is because river conditions have deteriorated steadily by heavy silting, shifts of the channels, and a rising of the river bed. Emphasis is now on using the river system for irrigation rather than navigation. Consequently, the plans of the Development Board do not include improvement of river transportation.

Basrah, Iraq's only port for general cargo, was first developed as a modern port by the British during World War I. Since then it has experienced considerable expansion and improvement. It now handles very efficiently an ever-increasing volume of passenger and cargo traffic (*see Table 36*). Its varied activities extend along the Shatt al-Arab from the main wharves at Magil (Basrah) to Fao, the oil terminal.

TABLE 36

MOVEMENT OF OCEAN-GOING VESSELS
AT THE PORT OF BASRAH

| | *1945* | *1950* | *1953* | *1955* | *1956* |
|---|---|---|---|---|---|
| *Vessels:* | | | | | |
| Arrived | 128 | 372 | 430 | 434 | 453 |
| Departed | 128 | 363 | 424 | 434 | 457 |
| *Cargo Tonnage:* | | | | | |
| Imported | 147,769 | 238,725 | 478,145 | 727,446 | 659,086 |
| Exported | 316,958 | 687,497 | 719,417 | 561,194 | 475,613 |
| *Passengers:* | | | | | |
| Arrived | 2,344 | 16,415 | 14,466 | 20,753 | 15,670 |
| Departed | 428 | 16,075 | 12,830 | 16,224 | 11,808 |

Source: *Statistical Abstract*, for 1950, p. 257, and 1955, p. 118; 1956, p. 128.

At various times the Iraqi government has considered the construction of a new port at Umm Qasr, on an inlet of the Persian Gulf south of Basrah. The project has a certain appeal in case of war and in view of the present congestion at Basrah. Both the Bank Mission and Lord Salter recommended that the project be abandoned, at least for the present. There were many technical reasons for their position. They also felt that the port of Basrah can handle a much larger volume of traffic if its facilities are expanded. Apparently the Iraqi Government is not fully convinced. In its 1955-60 program the Development Board allocated a round sum of four million dinars for the expansion of Basrah and the construction of a port at Umm Qasr.

The Iraqi Government has been considering the formation of an Iraqi shipping company. Although the port of Basrah is fairly well served by shipping lines, Iraq has experienced some difficulty in recent years in exporting her products, in particular the date crop. There have been many occasions when date cargoes were ready for shipment but there were no ships to carry them.

The Bank Mission recommended against the proposed project. Nevertheless, in 1952 the government passed a law establishing the Iraq Shipping Company, Limited, mainly with government capital. No action has so far been taken to implement the law. It is reported that the government is giving thought at present to engaging an expert to study and report on the whole question.

## Air Transport

Iraq has two good class "B" international airports favorably located at Basrah and Baghdad, in addition to several small airports in various parts of the country.

The state-owned Iraqi Airways operates a charter service, mainly for pilgrims, and a regular service between Baghdad-Basrah-Kuwait-Bahrain, Baghdad-Damascus-Cairo and Baghdad-Teheran. In addition, planes of almost all the international airlines make regular stops either at Basrah, or Baghdad, although Basrah is the better served since it lies along the main traffic routes to Southeast Asia and the Far East.

Since 1950 air traffic has been increasing steadily (see *Table 37*). In April, 1956, Iraqi Airways opened a weekly service between Baghdad and London via Istanbul and Vienna.[38] Two more international airlines began making regular stops at Baghdad in 1956 (Swiss Airlines and Lufthansa), and a third, Pan American Airlines, in 1957.[39]

TABLE 37

AIR TRAFFIC IN IRAQ

|  | 1947 | 1950 | 1953 | 1955 | 1956 |
|---|---|---|---|---|---|
| *No. of Planes:* | | | | | |
| Arrived | 5,394 | 5,443 | 5,995 | 6,716 | 7,813 |
| Departed | 5,394 | 5,443 | 5,995 | 6,716 | 7,813 |
| *Passengers:* | | | | | |
| Arrived | 12,376 | 21,453 | 31,412 | 45,818 | 57,744 |
| Departed | 12,882 | 44,448 | 30,962 | 42,976 | 57,204 |
| In Transit | 31,672 | 44,456 | 43,921 | 47,646 | 40,500 |

Source: *Statistical Abstract*, 1950, pp. 263-270; 1955, p. 123; and 1956, p. 133.

It has become fairly apparent that the facilities of the Baghdad Airport are no longer adequate to meet the increase in air traffic. In its 1955-60 program, the Development Board allocated 8.85 million dinars for the expansion of the existing Baghdad airport, the construction of a new modern airport (at Baghdad) and other airports throughout the country. Apparently, when the allocation was made no final policy decision had been taken whether to enlarge the present airport or to build a new one. This is indicated by the recommendation of the Council of Ministers to the Development Board in October, 1956 that it take immediate steps either to build a new modern international airport or to enlarge and improve the existing Baghdad airport to meet the proposed standards.[40]

*Summary and Conclusions*

The present industrialization program in Iraq represents the first major step which the country has taken toward industrialization. No doubt it is also the first phase. The program has certain distinct features:

1. For all practical purposes it is sponsored, planned, financed, and executed by the state. Even private industrial enterprises receive, in one way or the other, state financial aid in addition to other benefits.

2. It is organic in the sense that it is primarily designed to put into use idle national resources which have been either completely neglected or only partially exploited.

3. With the exception of the chemical industry and certain agricultural products, it is primarily designed to meet the present and future demands of the domestic market. Even in the case of the chemical industry, one of its indirect objectives is to create and expand domestic demand.

4. The program consists entirely of light industries.

5. With some exceptions (in private industry, already established), it maintains stringent criteria for selecting industries. Generally speaking, only industries which can produce at costs below landed prices of comparable foreign products before import duties are imposed have been chosen.

On the whole, little criticism can be made of the broad features of the program. It is extensive but not pretentious, and generally tends to make the most economical use of the country's resources. It has avoided grandiose schemes which may be emotionally satisfying but bring the country little or no economic benefit. Two major criticisms have been made of it, however:

1. It tends to give too much attention to fairly large establishments and too little attention to small industries, which are also important. This tendency seems to have been checked as a result of the recommendations of the Little Report. The change is reflected in the 1955-60 program.

2. The Little Report maintains that the most economical method of industrialization is through private capital. Although the need for present state investment is recognized, due to the limitations of private capital, the state, according to the Report, should make much more intensive efforts (through the Industrial Bank and/or an Industrial Development Corporation) to have private capital undertake as large a part of the industrialization program as possible.

In its early stages the program proceeded at a rather slow pace, but in 1955 it began to pick up momentum and has since increased its pace considerably. One of its main problems is the shortage of skilled and technical manpower.

Both the electrification and transportation programs are complementary to the industrialization program. The first provides low-cost power necessary for industry and the second is necessary for the movement of industrial and agricultural products.

Concrete steps for electrification were taken only in 1956. The program should be fully completed by 1960. It represents, however, one phase. Further expansion will be necessary later.

In terms of allocations, the transportation program is the second most important part of the Development Board 1955-60 plan. This underlies the recognition that agricultural and industrial expansion is of little value unless there are adequate transportation facilities to carry the goods and the products.

The major part of expenditures goes to the building of roads and bridges, with emphasis on trunk roads connecting main centers and feeder roads connecting main centers with rural areas. Next in size of expenditures is the railroad system, the backbone of the transportation system. The major part of the allocation goes to the construction of a standard-gauge line from Basrah to Baghdad. Thus, when completed, the country will have two complete systems, one standard gauge and the other meter gauge. Third in importance is the port of Basrah. It is being expanded to meet the expected increase in the export and import trade. Finally, plans are under consideration either to improve and enlarge the Baghdad airport or to build a new international airport capable of landing large airliners.

When and if the present program is completed, Iraq will indeed have traveled a long way on the road of progress. The program will create additional wealth, bring in more foreign exchange, create and improve human skills, expand the domestic market, increase population mobility, and generate new wealth-producing factors.

1. *IBRD*, p. 40.
2. Carl Iversen, *A Report on Monetary Policy in Iraq*, (Copenhagen: Ejnar Munks-gaard Publishers, 1954), p. 147.
3. *Ibid.*, p. 177.
4. See Salter, *op. cit.*, pp. 15-19, *passim.*
5. Arthur D. Little, Inc., *A Plan for Industrial Development in Iraq.* Summary Report. (Cambridge, Mass.: May 1956), pp. 3-4. Hereafter referred to as Little Report.

6. *Iraq Times*, June 4, 1956; *USIA*, Baghhad, Press Dispatch, July 27, 1956.
7. *EDME, 45-54*, p. 117.
8. The Little Report, p. 32.
9. Salter, *op. cit.*, pp. 159-60, 215-16.
10. *Iraq Times*, May 10, 1956.
11. *Ibid.*, May 1, 1956.
12. *USIA*, Baghdad, press dispatch, October 3, 1956.
13. The Little Report, p. 45.
14. *Iraq Times*, May 28, 1956.
15. *IBRD*. p. 26.
16. *Ibid.*, pp. 26-27.
17. *Iraq Times*, February 17, 27, 1956.
18. *USIA*, Baghdad, press dispatch, October 24, 1956.
19. The Little Report, p. 47.
20. The Little Report, p. 48.
21. See Chapter I, section on disposition of family income.
22. Muzaffar H. Jamil. *The Trade Policy of Iraq.* (Cairo: 1949), pp. 300, 583. (In Arabic.)
23. Industrial Bank, *Compilation of Laws, regulations, etc.* (Baghdad: Government Press, 1951.)
24. Industrial Bank, *Annual Reports for 1947/48* and *1948/49*, p. 49.
25. Industrial Bank, *Annual Report for 1947/48.*
26. Industrial Bank, *Annual Report for 1948/49*, p. 10.
27. These were: cotton spinning and weaving (1); cement (1); wool spinning & weaving (2); modern tanning (5); beer (1); alcohol (3); vegetable oil (1); modern soap making (1); silk weaving (6); jute spinning and weaving (1).
28. Iraq Government, Directorate General of Industry, *Annual Report for 1951/52*, pp. 24-26. (In Arabic.)
29. These figures include government industries, but exclude the government refineries. They also include the railway workshops and public utilities such as electricity and water supply.
30. This figure is not certain. Original planning was for 40,000 kilowatts. Further study showed that future needs of central Iraq were conservatively estimated. Consequently the plan increased the generating power of the station.
31. Original planning was for 20,000 kilowatts only.
32. *USIA*, Baghdad, press dispatch, October 3, 1956.
33. The actual total length of the system in 1954/55 was 1,060.6 miles (1,697 kms.) excluding sidings.
34. For analysis of railways, see *IBRD*, pp. 44-46, 314-26.
35. Salter, *op. cit.*, pp. 65-68.
36. *Iraq Times*, February 9, 1956.
37. Salter, *op. cit.*, pp. 211-12. Actual appropriations by the Board were 13,920,000 dinars which includes the cost of sidings, engines, and rolling stock.
38. By Viscount airliner.
39. Pan American used to make stops only at Basrah. TWA also makes stops only at Basrah.
40. *USIA*, Baghdad, press dispatch, October 4, 1956.

PART IV  *The Department of Human Resources*

**CHAPTER 10**

## THE CHALLENGE OF EDUCATION

No more serious challenge confronts Iraq today than that of education, both as a means of building a new social structure and as an instrument of technological progress. The problem is one of vast dimensions, In 1947 when the first census was taken, only eight per cent of the population (excluding nomads) could read and write. Of the total male population about 14 per cent were literate, while the corresponding figure for females was three per cent.

The problem is not only vast, but its solution has assumed critical urgency in view of Iraq's development program. There has to be some balance, a proportional relationship, between material and intellectual progress. In order to run efficiently, the new physical plant abuilding in agriculture, industry, etc., has to be manned and maintained by a fairly skilled and literate labor force. However, the time gap between physical production and personnel training is wide. It takes two to four years to build a factory or a dam, but it takes a larger number of years to build up a skilled and intelligent labor force. The terms "skilled" and "intelligent" are used here in a broad sense. They include not only the ability to read and to manipulate machines, but also the acquisition and/or adaptation of philosophies, attitudes, behavior, and other intangible components necessary for a society which aspires to a higher standard of living.

The tables that follow in this chapter serve to illustrate two central points: (1) the almost pathetic inadequacy of the educational establishment and (2) the desperate efforts that are being made (since 1950) to improve it and enlarge it.

In Iraq, education is a state function. Authority, however, is divided among various government departments. The Ministry of Education has full administrative and financial responsibility for intermediate, secondary, vocational, and technical schools, teachers' training schools, six colleges, and most of the students studying abroad at government expense. Until 1951 it also had similar authority over elementary schools, but in that year, with a view to decentralization, the government transferred responsibility for them to the Provincial Administrative Councils.[1] The Ministry, however, retained supervisory powers and set the curriculum.

Seven other colleges come under the jurisdiction of various other ministries, depending on the subject of specialization. Finally, the Development Board is responsible for the construction of schools and other educational institutions. In

TABLE 38

ACTUAL EXPENDITURES OF THE MINISTRY OF
EDUCATION, AND THEIR PERCENTILE RELATIONSHIP
TO TOTAL GOVERNMENT EXPENDITURES

| Year | Thousand Dinars | Percent |
|------|-----------------|---------|
| 1920/21 | 130[a] | 2.3 |
| 1925/26 | 171 | 4.2 |
| 1930/31 | 294 | 7.3 |
| 1935/36 | 431 | 9.6 |
| 1940/41 | 848 | 11.8 |
| 1945/46 | 1,612 | 9.0 |
| 1950/51 | 3,599[b] | 14.0 |
| 1953/54 | 6,787 | 13.5 |
| 1956/57 | 10,560 | 16.3 |
| 1957/58 | 12,887[c] | 18.3 |

Source: For 1920/21 to 1953/54, Ministry of Education, *Annual Report for 1953/54*; for 1956/57 and 1957/58, Education in Iraq, *op. cit.*, p. 2.

[a] All figures include costs of elementary education.
[b] All figures exclude high cost of living allowances.
[c] Estimated.

addition, the Board supports either directly or indirectly educational enterprises that come within the purview of the development concept as such.

Table 38 shows actual expenditures of the Ministry of Education in selected years and their percentile relationship to total government expenditures. These include the costs of elementary education but exclude high cost of living allowances and the expenditures of colleges and other institutions not attached to the Ministry. They also exclude expenditures of the Development Board.

In the 1920's expenditures began to rise slowly, and they registered appreciable increases during the 1930's. During the war years there was a considerable decline both in real terms and in percentage of the total budgetary figure. The increase in expenditures in 1945-46, for instance, was actually offset by the decline in the purchasing power of the dinar and a corresponding rise in the cost of materials and services.

After the war, expenditures on education began to recover. In 1950/51, they reached a high of 14 per cent. Since then they have risen sharply year after year. In fact, the table does not show the full extent of the rise since, in the past, part of the expenditures used to go to school construction. The apparent percentage decline in 1953/54 is not real, for in that year the Development Board assumed full responsibility for the costs of school construction.

The role of the Development Board in the field of education has increased considerably since it was organized in 1950. In the first program (1951-56) its projected activities were restricted to the building of schools, sending students abroad to study technical subjects—mainly to meet part of its own needs for skilled personnel—and to developing and improving research facilities.

The conception of its role became broader in each succeeding program. In the 1955-60 plan there were included the establishment of technical schools, schools to develop agricultural education, a public library, swimming pools, and sports fields. In other words, in addition to increasing and improving the physical plant, the Board also became concerned with the development of human resources and skills.

TABLE 39

ALLOCATIONS OF THE DEVELOPMENT BOARD
FOR EDUCATION:  1955-60

|  |  | *Dinars* |
|---|---|---|
| 1. | Student Missions | 1,650,000 |
| 2. | Research and Laboratories | 1,550,000 |
| 3. | Scientific Institutes and Primary Schools | 8,000,000 |
| 4. | Other Scientific Institutes | 750,000 |
| 5. | Technical Schools | 1,250,000 |
| 6. | Schools and short courses to develop agricultural education | 750,000 |
| 7. | Iraqi University | 2,000,000 |
| 8. | Public Library | 350,000 |
| 9. | Students' House | 250,000 |
| 10. | Swimming pools and sports fields | 2,000,000 |
|  | TOTAL | 18,500,000 |

*Elementary Education*

Iraq is committed to the ideal of universal literacy. The task is so formidable that only little progress has been made. The achievements between 1920 and 1950 are impressive in absolute terms, but are only "a drop in the bucket" in terms of ultimate goals.

In 1920/21 there were eighty-eight primary schools with some 8,000 students. Thirty years later, in 1950/51, their number had increased to 1,101. In other words, they increased at the rate of some thirty-three schools a year.

From 1950/51 on there was a radical departure from previous patterns. This was due to the establishment of the Development Board, which had become financially responsible for the construction of schools, and to considerable increases in the budget of the Ministry of Education. The Board began building "schools by the hundreds" so that between 1950/51 and 1956/57, a period of six years, 760 new elementary schools were added, amounting to 70 per cent of the number of all elementary schools opened during the previous thirty years. Perhaps as significant is the fact that even the annual rate of increase is not static. In 1951/52, 108 new schools were added.  In 1953/54, the number rose to 128 schools. Between 1954/55 and 1956/57, it increased further to 141 new schools per year. It would not be sur-

prising if, by 1960, the number reached 200, or even 250, schools a year.

A much more intensive increase took place in the number of children attending government elementary schools. The figure rose from 180,000 (*see Table 40*) in 1950/51 to 378,000 in 1956/57, an increase of 198,000—amounting to 110 per cent. Between 1945/46 and 1950/51 the increase averaged a little over 10,000 a year. By 1956/57 it reached 42,000 a year. If the present trend continues, it should reach somewhere around 60,000 a year by 1960.

Despite the increased efforts of the state, the problem continues to be one of vast dimensions. The elementary school age group in Iraq is conservatively estimated to constitute more than one million children. Of these, in 1956/57, some 35 per cent were receiving fundamental training. This percentage in fact does not reflect the true situation because of the extremely high turnover. A large majority of the children attend one, two, or three years, then drop out to join the ranks of the functional illiterates. Thus a considerable part of the effort to increase literacy is wasted. This partially accounts for the fact of almost universal illiteracy despite evident increases in expenditures, schools, and enrollment.

The primary cause of the high drop-out rate is believed to be economic. On the one hand, to a poor family a boy is an economic asset which must be put to productive use. On the other, although schooling is completely free, even the minimum necessities of the primary student impose an economic burden on the parents which many of them, in their marginal existence, cannot afford. The "economic thesis" has been recently substantiated by UNICEF programs in Iraq. Simple free lunch meals in pilot projects resulted in increasing enrollment and in maintaining attendance. In 1955 UNICEF initiated a large-scale program to feed school children, starting with 60,000 in 1955 and reaching 100,000 in 1957. Ninety per cent of the costs of the program are borne by the Iraqi Government.

In addition to the general problem of an adequate number of schools to meet requirements, there is also the problem of maldistribution of existing facilities between urban and rural areas and between the sexes. In 1953/54 the government elementary schools (excluding coeducational, night schools, and railway schools) were divided as follows:

|        | City Schools |          | Rural Schools |          |
|        | Schools | Students | Schools | Students |
|--------|---------|----------|---------|----------|
| Boys   | 450     | 119,085  | 574     | 55,070   |
| Girls  | 237     | 50,176   | 19      | 1,296    |
|        | 687     | 169,261  | 593     | 56,366   |

From a glance at the above data two important facts emerge: (1) that the towns have about 60 per cent of the primary schools in the country, although more than 70 per cent of the population lives in rural areas. In addition, the number of children attending school in urban areas is over three times those of rural areas; (2) that education of girls in the cities seems to have made considerable progress. The number of girls attending primary schools in the towns, which comes to a little over 40 per cent of the number of boys, indicates that prejudice against "girls' education" has been substantially broken down, and that basically it has ceased to be a serious problem. By contrast, girls' education in rural areas hardly exists. In eight of the most densely populated provinces no facilities whatsoever existed in 1953/54. The nineteen schools that did exist were unevenly distributed among the other six provinces. What is more significant is the fact that in all rural areas only 1,296 girls were attending school in addition to those who went to coeducational schools. Girls' education is still not socially acceptable there. The main hurdle, therefore, is not the lack of schools but lies rather in the attitude of the peasant.

A comparatively new and interesting development in elementary education is the kindergarten-junior school movement. It is a refreshing and a hopeful sign of the progress

---

a Elementary schools include night schools and kindergartens (co-ed.) where only women teach. The number of private schools in the country is relatively small. In 1954/55 they were divided as follows: Elementary schools, 84, with 19,912 students and 645 teachers. Secondary schools, 56, with 12,397 students and 865 teachers. A large number of the schools were for boys.

(Table 40 footnote)

TABLE 40

GOVERNMENT ELEMENTARY AND SECONDARY SCHOOLS[a]

| | 1945/46 | 1950/51 | 1951/52 | 1952/53 | 1953/54 | 1954/55 | 1955/56 | 1956/57 |
|---|---|---|---|---|---|---|---|---|
| | | | | Elementary Schools | | | | |
| *Schools* | | | | | | | | |
| Boys | 723 | 819 | 901 | 984 | 1,094 | 1,154 | 1,062 | n.a. |
| Girls | 169 | 190 | 204 | 228 | 256 | 270 | 261 | n.a. |
| Co-Ed. | 52 | 92 | 104 | 117 | 101 | 155 | 425 | n.a. |
| Total | 944 | 1,101 | 1,209 | 1,329 | 1,451 | 1,579 | 1,748 | 1,861 |
| *Teachers* | | | | | | | | |
| Men | 3,361 | 4,376 | 5,051 | 5,544 | 6,070 | 6,679 | 7,274 | n.a. |
| Women | 1,418 | 1,991 | 2,237 | 2,491 | 2,749 | 2,948 | 3,196 | n.a. |
| Total | 4,779 | 6,367 | 7,288 | 8,035 | 8,819 | 9,627 | 10,470 | 11,607 |
| *Students* | | | | | | | | |
| Boys | 90,419 | 138,530 | 153,653 | 173,341 | 195,803 | 224,253 | 252,732 | n.a. |
| Girls | 28,068 | 42,249 | 45,600 | 52,487 | 62,530 | 70,744 | 79,949 | n.a. |
| Total | 118,487 | 180,779 | 199,253 | 225,828 | 258,333 | 294,997 | 332,681 | 378,384 |
| | | | Intermediate and Secondary Schools | | | | | |
| *Schools* | | | | | | | | |
| Boys | 36 | 64 | 73 | 86 | 92 | 109 | 107 | n.a. |
| Girls | 23 | 31 | 31 | 39 | 42 | 50 | 45 | n.a. |
| Total | 59 | 95 | 104 | 125 | 134 | 159 | 152 | 210 |
| *Teachers* | | | | | | | | |
| Men | 451 | 698 | 814 | 1,027 | 1,185 | 1,350 | 1,439 | n.a. |
| Women | 141 | 301 | 356 | 430 | 535 | 662 | 699 | n.a. |
| Total | 592 | 999 | 1,170 | 1,457 | 1,720 | 2,012 | 2,138 | 3,072 |
| *Students* | | | | | | | | |
| Boys | 9,480 | 17,594 | 18,553 | 23,015 | 26,666 | 32,036 | 34,040 | n.a. |
| Girls | 2,693 | 5,112 | 5,525 | 6,926 | 8,144 | 9,448 | 10,558 | n.a. |
| Total | 12,173 | 22,706 | 24,078 | 29,941 | 34,810 | 41,484 | 44,598 | 60,389 |
| | | | | TOTALS | | | | |
| Schools | 1,003 | 1,196 | 1,313 | 1,454 | 1,585 | 1,738 | 1,900 | 2,071 |
| Teachers | 5,371 | 7,366 | 8,458 | 9,492 | 10,539 | 11,639 | 12,608 | 14,679 |
| Students | 130,660 | 203,485 | 223,331 | 255,769 | 293,143 | 336,481 | 377,279 | 438,773 |

Sources: For 1945/46 through 1953/54, Iraq, Ministry of Education, *Annual Report for 1953/54*; for 1954/55, Iraq, *Statistical Abstract, 1955*, pp. 109-111; for 1955/56, *Statistical Abstract*, 1956, pp. 74-76; for 1956/57, Iraqi Embassy, Office of the Cultural Attaché, *Education in Iraq* (Washington, D. C.: n.d.), pp. 7 and 12.

of education in Iraq. In these schools only women teachers are employed, progressive techniques are practiced, and—unlike most other schools in the country—they are coeducational.

In 1933-34, the Ministry of Education opened a few kindergartens on an experimental basis, but they proved so popular that by 1944-45 (they were by then called junior schools and first and second grades were added to them) there were fifty-six schools attended by 8,512 children, of whom 4,322 were boys and 4,190 were girls.[2] By 1953/54 the number had risen to 101 schools with 19,652 students, of whom 11,058 were girls and 8,594 were boys.[3]

Coeducational schools are still mainly city institutions. Few of them, however, are tolerated in the villages where no facilities for girls are available. The movement holds great promise, since it can be used to break down the prejudice against education for girls, particularly in rural areas.

The content of elementary education is undergoing change. Traditionally it has been highly academic, with great emphasis on book-learning and often on subjects which have little relation to the life of the student. Textbooks are often literal translations of their Western sources, with illustrative material absolutely meaningless to the Iraqi child.

The system is gradually being overhauled. In the first place, a differentiation is now being made between urban and rural schools. In the latter a little more emphasis is placed on agricultural subjects and on practical application outside the schoolroom. Secondly, the curriculum throughout the whole system is shifting a little toward subjects that meet the particular needs of the Iraqi child, with a little less emphasis on book-learning and more on "learning by doing." Finally, better and more meaningful textbooks are being introduced.

The system has also been characterized by a high degree of centralization. In 1951 a welcome change took place when control over elementary education was transferred from the central government to local provincial councils. It is too early to assess the results but, ideally, it is a move in the right direction. In the final analysis, local people know their needs better than a central bureaucracy. It is also more democratic and, by giving local authorities responsibility (with assistance), expansion of school facilities will probably proceed at a faster rate. Some have expressed fear that the move may increase divisive tendencies. This fear seems unjustified, since the central authorities still retain supervisory powers and still prescribe the curriculum and the rules and regulations.

In addition to a few minor ones, elementary education in Iraq confronts two special problems: (1) the problem of the Yezidi minority, and (2) the problem of Bedouin education.

The Yezidis are a closely-knit, semi-political religious minority comprising some 32,000 persons. Some of their religious beliefs and taboos prohibit the education of children, and the pronunciation of certain sounds and words. Even if schooling were allowed, the second prohibition makes instruction nearly impossible.

The problem of Bedouin education has been the subject of serious thought for many years. Since tribes migrate from one area to another, the usual school organization does not apply. A few mobile schools have been organized and move with the nomads; and some of the tribes, such as the Shammar in the north, are anxious to have their children receive instruction. By and large, no serious effort has been made to solve the problem. Probably, as the nomads become sedentarized— and they are gradually becoming so—the educational system will be expanded to include their children. In the meantime, Bedouin children continue with little or no schooling.

*Secondary Education*

In order to qualify for secondary school, the student must have completed a six-year elementary course and passed a general examination set up by the Ministry of Education. The secondary school system itself is divided into two stages: an intermediate stage consisting of three years of study; and a preparatory stage consisting of two years. The preparatory stage has three divisions: science, literature, and commerce. After completion of the intermediate stage, the student must pass another general examination before proceeding to the preparatory stage. Similarly a third examination must be passed at the end of the two-year preparatory course before receiving the secondary school certificate.

Both inadequate economic resources and conscious government policy have tended to reduce substantially the number of students who may continue their education from the elementary to the secondary stage. Each examination hurdle eliminates between 40 and 50 per cent of the candidates. Those who fail cannot proceed further. For instance, in 1955, out of 21,045 students who took the general examination after the six-year elementary course, only 12,531 or 60 per cent passed. Out of 7,256 participants in the intermediate examination, only 3,715 or 51 per cent passed. Out of 3,406 students who took the secondary school examination, 1,644 or 48 per cent passed. In all the three examinations, out of 31,707 participants, 17,890 or 56 per cent passed.

Despite these limiting factors, the number of schools and students rose sharply, particularly in recent years (*see Table 40*). In 1920 there was only one school in the whole country, located at Baghdad. By 1951 the number had risen to ninety-five, including thirty-one schools for girls. As in the case of elementary schools, 1951 was a year of departure from previous patterns. In a period of six years between 1951 and 1957, 115 new schools were added, bringing the total to 210.

Until 1956 secondary education in Iraq followed the European tradition. Heavy emphasis was placed on classical and literary subjects with a marked tendency toward preparing students for the universities and the professions. The repeated examinations tend to have a stultifying effect on the students. In particular, the general examination after the six-year elementary course categorizes students too sharply and usually affects the candidate for the rest of his life. Similarily the "science" examination, held at the end of the two-year preparatory period, is so difficult as compared with the "arts" examination that few students elect to take a science major, thus creating another impediment to technical education, so very badly needed at this stage in the development of Iraq.[4]

The whole conception of what intermediate and secondary

education should achieve is at present undergoing critical
appraisal. In 1955-56 a committee was set up by the Ministry
of Education to examine and consider the various stages of
education as well as textbooks and the curriculum. It made
the following recommendations:

> The Committee considers primary schools as an independent
> unit which supplies the intermediate schools of theoretical or
> practical study. For this reason we approve the scheme of
> differentiating the branches of study. The intermediate schools
> should include theoretical study for the graduate of the pri-
> mary schools who wishes it (after he has passed the examinations
> in the three subjects put by the Ministry of Education). This
> kind of study would reveal the ability of the student and direct
> him to the way of most use to his surroundings and to himself.
> If he proves his capability he may continue his studies in the
> scientific or literary departments of the secondary school. If, on
> the other hand, he discovers that he is not capable of this kind
> of study or that he desires another field, he is allowed to shift
> to technical study...
> As for professional learning as differentiated from theoretical,
> it should include agriculture, commerce, industry, and home
> economics. Students who hold a primary school certificate (*from
> the examinations set by the school, not the one set by the Ministry of
> Education*) may enter these schools. The purpose of the technical
> schools is to prepare skilled and semi-skilled technicians and
> workers who can undertake the various crafts and semi-technical
> work. Intermediate schools of home economics would prepare
> girls who will make successful housewives and mothers in the
> future.
> The Committee in setting the above recommendations has
> tried to draw a line between the two kinds of studies—theoretical
> and practical—and to prepare more students for solid and
> useful fields, particularly along practical lines, where a student
> may find his chief interest is in being a skilled workman or
> continuing, if he wishes, to higher practical study.
> Those who prove capable may go on to higher education.
> The Committee, however, is very anxious to see this kind of
> education put to practical use to the graduates in order that
> they may make a living out of it.[5]

The recommendations of the Committee have been accepted. Schools above the elementary level are to be reclassified

into separate and optional programs: science, literature, industry, agriculture, commerce, and home economics.

Since 1952 secondary education has been completely free. In addition, boarding school facilities are to be established for students from small villages not likely to have secondary schools of their own.

Progress—to the extent that money can achieve it—has been impressive in recent years. Iraq has still to solve the curriculum problem and the related problem of availability of qualified teachers to meet the requirements of the new curriculum proposed.

*Technical and Vocational Training*

Because of the development program and the growth of industry, services, and mechanized agriculture in recent years, the question of technical education has now assumed a special significance. The level of technical knowledge in the country is very low, even by Middle Eastern standards, and both the number of technicians and of training facilities are entirely inadequate to meet the present needs of the country.

Various theories have been offered from time to time to explain the present dilemma. "The Arab mind," it is said, "has a flair for literature but none for natural science"; young men prefer "white collar" jobs; working with one's hands is not considered dignified,[6] and so on. Some of these generalizations are no doubt true, but they fail to provide an adequate explanation, for—time and again—actual experience has seemed to disprove them. The numerous oil companies with specific objectives have found the Arab receptive and capable, once given the incentive and opportunity, of acquiring quickly a relatively high level of technical skill.[7] The oil companies have been able to train large bodies of men in a bewildering variety of skills and trades. It seems to this writer that the explanation is a simple one. On the one hand, until recent years there has been no particular demand in Iraq for artisans. The wages of skilled workers were generally lower than those of office workers. Therefore, no strong enough incentive existed for acquiring technical skills. On the other hand, "white collar" jobs, in addition to being better paid, carried with them social prestige, so that it was only natural for young men to seek them in preference to skilled work.

In any case, the technical training movement has gathered considerable momentum in recent years. This was inevitable since the success of the development plans rests to a large degree on the availability of an adequate labor force.

In 1955 there were three technical schools (at Baghdad, Kirkuk, and Basrah), and a fourth was opened the same year at Sulaimaniya. In 1955/56 they had a total of some 808 students and were able to graduate 92 students. So far, following the recommendations of the Committee mentioned previously, the Ministry of Education opened, in addition to the above, three commercial secondary schools, three agricultural secondary schools, and two technical secondary schools. The Development Board has allocated large sums of money for the establishment of technical and agricultural schools and other "scientific" institutes. The next few years will probably see considerable expansion in technical training facilities although, for some years, the expansion will not keep up with the demand.

Some progress has also been made in vocational education. Courses in agriculture (since 1950) have been set up in rural primary schools; in gardening for boys in the cities; in home arts for girls. In addition, there is a school for nursing and midwifery attached to the College of Medicine, which in 1954/55 had 134 women students; a Home Arts School for girls (799 students in 1955/56), and an Institute of Fine Arts (361 students in 1955/56).

*Teachers' Training*

In spite of the increased and heavy demands on the supply of teachers, training facilities have generally kept abreast of the needs of the country, so that only occasional shortages occur. Between 1950 and 1957 the number of elementary school teachers increased by 82 per cent; that of secondary school teachers by more than 207 percent (*see Table 40*).

In 1953/54 there were three schools for the training of elementary school teachers: two for boys and one for girls.

These admit graduates of intermediate schools for a four-year course of study. Their total enrollment was then 863 students: 623 boys and 240 girls. In addition, as an emergency measure, the Ministry had (in 1953/54) eight training sessions of one-year duration for graduates of secondary schools. Their total enrollment was 881 students: 636 boys and 245 girls.

During the same year (1953/54) there were two colleges for the training of secondary school teachers: the coeducational Higher Teachers Training College and the women's Queen Aliya College. Both are located at Baghdad and admit only secondary school graduates for a four-year course. Their combined enrollment in 1953/54 was 1,191 students.

Since 1954 considerable changes and expansion in training facilities have taken place. The Institute of Fine Arts (mentioned previously) has been changed into a teacher training center in that field. Queen Aliya College has been transformed into a secondary teacher training college in the field of Home Economics only and a Physical Education College was added (in 1954/55) to train secondary school teachers in that field. In 1956/57 the total number of elementary school training centers and short educational sessions increased to thirty-seven: twenty for men, twelve for women, and five mixed. Their 1956/57 enrollment was 3,612 students.

Present planning of the Ministry of Education includes, among other projects, the following: (1) the training of 2,000 teachers every three years over the next ten years, and (2) the establishment of elementary teacher training centers in all the provinces. This plan has a dual objective: (1) to provide teachers to meet the continued expansion in the number of schools and students, and (2) to be able to apply compulsory education throughout Iraq. In 1940, with the passage of the General Education Law, primary education became compulsory. Obviously, however, the provision could then only hope to lay the legal foundation for future action, as school facilities in many areas were not available. So far the law has not been implemented, although the country has reached a point where further delay would not be justified.

*Higher Education*

In 1921 there was one institution of higher learning in the whole country—the Baghdad Law College. In 1956/57, the system of higher education consisted of thirteen colleges with a total enrollment of over 5,000 students (*see Table 41*). Four of these colleges have been established only since 1950: The College of Agriculture (1950), the College of Dentistry (1952), the College of Physical Education (1954), and the Veterinary College (1956).

Financial responsibility and jurisdiction over the thirteen colleges arc divided among various government departments. The Ministry of Education has jurisdiction over seven colleges; the Ministry of Health over three, the Ministry of Agriculture over two; and the Directorate of Waqf over one. All the colleges with the exception of Queen Aliya College (for women), and the College of Religious Jurisprudence (for men) are coeducational.

The College of Medicine admits only "science" majors from secondary schools for a six-year course of study, including one year of internship. After the successful completion of the six-year course it grants the degree of *Licencié* in Medicine. The same regulations apply to the College of Pharmacy and Chemistry, except that it offers only a five-year course which includes one year of internship for pharmacists and a four-year course for a B.S. degree in chemistry. All the other colleges admit only graduates of secondary schools for a four-year course. All of them grant the degree of *Licencié* to students who pass the prescribed examinations in the final year of study.

In addition to the above colleges, there is a school of nursing and midwifery and a school for health officials. Both are attached to the College of Medicine. A police college under the jurisdiction of the Ministry of Interior completes the list.

Some of the colleges, such as the College of Arts and Sciences, have attained a fairly high academic standing. However, they all suffer from the fact that they are not

TABLE 41

COLLEGES IN IRAQ
1956/57

|  | Student Enrollment |
|---|---|
| *Under Ministry of Education:* | |
| 1. Law College | 705 |
| 2. Higher Teacher Training College | 923 |
| 3. Queen Aliya College (for Women) | 394 |
| 4. College of Arts & Sciences | 697 |
| 5. College of Engineering | 397 |
| 6. College of Commerce & Economics | 644 |
| 7. College of Physical Education | 33* |
| *Under Ministry of Health:* | |
| 8. Royal College of Medicine | 656 |
| 9. College of Pharmacy & Chemistry | 181 |
| 10. College of Dentistry | 107 |
| *Under Ministry of Agriculture:* | |
| 11. College of Agriculture | 203 |
| 12. Veterinary College | 20 |
| *Under Directorate General of Waqf:* | |
| 13. College of Religious Jurisprudence | 193 |
| TOTAL | 5,153 |

Source: Education in Iraq, *op. cit.*, p. 40.

* Data for 1954/55 from *Statistical Abstract for 1955*, p. 106.

covered by a university structure which would give them the advantages of a central organization, pooling of resources, and planned budgeting. A University Bill was under debate for more than three years. It was finally passed late in 1956 (Law No. 60: 1956). Under the law most of the above colleges will be incorporated into a university to be called the University of Baghdad. The Development Board in its 1955-60 program allocated two million dinars for the construction of the buildings. Expropriation of the land site (at Jadriyah) has already been completed.

As in elementary and secondary education, no tuition fees are charged in the college system. In addition, gifted and deserving needy students receive room, board, laundry, and other facilities free of charge. In return such students must serve the government for a certain number of years after their graduation.

*Foreign Study*

In addition to the system of higher education in Iraq itself, the Ministry of Education and other government departments send students to foreign universities to specialize in various fields, and give partial financial assistance to others studying on their own.

Between 1921/22 and 1949/50 the Ministry sent abroad, at its own expense, a total of 1,295 students. Since 1950 the number has increased very sharply.[8] From that year (1950) to date, the Ministry of Education and the Development Board together have been spending an average of 1.5 million dinars ($4.2 million) a year on scholarships for foreign study.

In 1952/53 there were 840 students in foreign universities supported either in full or in part by the Ministry of Education and 175 supported in full by the Development Board, in addition to 1,331 others studying at their own expense. In 1954, it was estimated that over 3,000 Iraqis were studying at foreign universities, most of them in the United States, Britain, and Lebanon, and considerable numbers in France and Egypt. In 1956 over 1,100 students were in the United States alone, about a third of whom were bursary students.

The very large majority of bursary students undertake natural science courses, with heavy concentration on the various branches of engineering, agriculture, chemistry and physics. Social sciences follow, with concentration on economics, finance, statistics and social planning. A very small number undertake courses in the humanities. In recent years, about 120 of the bursary students complete their studies and return home each year. It would probably be safe to assume that, of those who are studying on their own, at least twice this number return, so that a total of between 300 to 400 students complete their studies and return home each year.

Foreign study has not been an unmixed blessing, although it must be stated that, on balance, it has proved not only a very valuable but also a necessary experience. On the positive side, it has provided Iraq with a large body of experts which otherwise it would have been unable to obtain in such a short time. Since Iraq has no facilities for such training, it is hard to see how the needs of the Development Board, the other government departments, agriculture, industry, etc., can otherwise be met. Certainly, in the long run, Iraq cannot depend on the services of foreign experts.

Secondly, it offers the intelligent among the new generation a far greater margin of social and economic mobility, and in the process it creates a new élite based not only on family heritage but on intelligence and on achievement.

Thirdly, it helps in the breakdown of narrow provincialism. The students bring back a wide variety of personal experience and a broader realization of the world which cannot but have an impact on Iraqi society.

On the negative side, it is claimed that some students choose inferior universities and do not receive enough reward for their time and money; that many often choose subjects of little value to themselves and to their country;[9] that social conditions in the foreign countries they go to are so radically different from their own background that considerable damage is done to their personalities; and that some become so acculturated to the West that when they return they are unable to readjust themselves to the traditional environment of their country.

Some of the above statements are probably true, although perhaps somewhat exaggerated. On the whole, however, the benefits far outweigh the harm. Some of the misuses can be corrected. Universities and disciplines can be more carefully selected. In any case, until such time as Iraq has adequate facilities there is no alternative to advanced foreign study. Perhaps the most potent argument that can be made against it is that it is comparatively very expensive. Iraq, therefore, should begin to establish such facilities. This would have the advantage of being less expensive and leaving the student in his own environment.

*Illiteracy Centers*

The campaign against illiteracy began in the late twenties. However, statistical data indicate that no consistent policy was followed until 1950, so that the number of centers and students used to fluctuate radically from year to year. In 1927/28 there were thirty-one centers, all for men, with 2,074 students. In the thirties the movement gained considerable momentum, reaching in 1938/39 a high of 205 centers for men, with 16,415 students, and seven centers for women, with 218 students. During the war it declined sharply reaching in 1948/49 a low of eighteen centers, all for men, with a total of 1,498 students. From then on, however, the number of centers and students began to climb steadily, with no setbacks, until in 1954/55 there were 309 centers for men, with 26,178 students, and thirty-seven centers for women, with 3,693 students. In 1955/56 the number rose to 506 centers with a total enrollment of 34,695 men and women.

Students attend two consecutive courses of four months duration each, six nights a week, two classes each night. In the first course, they study reading, writing, and arithmetic. In the second, reading, writing, arithmetic, hygiene and civics are studied.

In addition to the above centers, illiteracy classes are conducted in jails, in the army and in the police. Also many government departments, such as the Railways and the Port Directorate, private companies, such as the oil companies, and private philanthropic and volunteer organizations conduct similar classes.

## *Conclusions*

Officially, the system of education in Iraq is described as "democratic, progressive, and nationalist." It is democratic in the sense that available facilities are open to all without discrimination for reasons of race, color, or creed. It is progressive in the sense that it is basically secular and has followed Western methodologies of education. It is nationalist in a dual sense. It attempts to inculcate in the Iraqi child love and devotion to Iraq as a country and a political entity, and similar sentimental loyalty to the "Arab Nation" of which Iraq is only a part.

The country still faces a formidable task. Over two-thirds of the children (at least) of primary school age receive no instruction. The administrative structure is cumbersome, the curriculum needs a radical reform, and considerable expansion in technical education is required. Perhaps the most hopeful thought lies in the fact that the government is conscious of these problems, and that it is bending every effort to meet the challenge and forge ahead in creating an enlightened society.

1. A law passed in 1945 provided for the creation of an administrative council in each of the fourteen provinces. It is to be composed of representatives of the province and presided over by the provincial governor representing the central government. The purpose of the council is to assume some of the responsibilities of the central government with regard to local affairs. Among these is education. The Council receives grants-in-aid from the central government for specific purposes. In a certain sense, these councils—very limited in their powers as they are—represent an interesting experiment in real democracy. Although the law was passed in 1945, the first council was not organized until 1954—some ten years later—in the province of Baghdad.

2. For details of the history of the movement see R. D. Matthews and M. Akrawi, *Education in the Arab Countries of the Near East*. (Washington, D. C.: American Council on Education, 1949), p. 146.

3. Ministry of Education, Annual Report for 1953/54, *op. cit.*, p. 23.

4. In 1953/54, 52.5 per cent of those who took the science examination passed, as compared with 61.4 per cent for the "arts" examination, and 57 per cent for the "commerce" examination.

5. Office of the Cultural Attaché, Embassy of Iraq. *Education in Iraq*. (Washington, D. C.: 1957, pp. 10-11.)

6. This writer has seen Arab students in the United States (who had never done any manual work in their lives in their home countries) work as manual laborers, waiters, and in factories. This goes to show that attitudes are not inflexible and that under given incentives and circumstances they change quickly.

7. For instance, British labor supervisors at the I. P. C. in Kirkuk told this writer that members of the Jabbur tribe have an amazing knack for handling machinery.

8. The number of students who were sent by the Ministry or the Board (fully supported) are as follows: 1950/51, 133 students; 1951/52, 234 students; 1952/53, 125 students; 1953/54, none (because of disturbances); 1954/55, 114 students; 1955/56, 120 students. Of these, the Development Board sent a total of 317 students, of whom 102 have already returned.

9. In the case of bursary students, I have been unable to find evidence to support this allegation. In the first place, the subject of specialization is selected by the Ministry of Education on the basis of the demands of government departments. Secondly, I went through the subjects of specialization of all

bursary students sent between 1950/51 and 1953/54. The subjects are mostly in the natural sciences, followed in a far smaller number by the social sciences. This is in line with what Iraq needs today. The allegation may, however, be true of students studying on their own.

# CHAPTER 11

## PUBLIC HEALTH

The concept that the state is responsible for the health of its citizens is accepted in Iraq without challenge. This is a natural development, since Iraq began its national life almost completely devoid of medical facilities, and the full burden of responsibility fell upon the state. Therefore, almost the entire medical profession itself as well as the physical plant existing today are the creation of and in the service of the state.

Responsibility for public health is vested in the Ministry of Health, which was created only in 1952. Prior to that, responsibility lay in a directorate attached to the Ministry of Social Affairs. In line with the general development of the country, expenditures of this department have increased steadily. Between 1947/48 and 1954/56, they rose from 450,-000 dinars to 4.3 million dinars, a ninefold increase in seven years (*see Table 42*). Expenditures in 1955/56 represented 7.8 percent of the total ordinary expenditures of the government.

Since 1950 almost all the expenditures of the Ministry have been for operational activities. Since that time the Development Board has assumed the major responsibility for financing the construction of hospitals, clinics, and other health establishments. As in the case of education, the Board's conception of the role it should play became broader in each successive plan and the magnitude of planned expenditures increased. Between 1952 and 1956, it built fifteen hospitals, forty-nine clinics, and a considerable number of houses for medical staff.

TABLE 42

BUDGET OF THE MINISTRY OF HEALTH
AND THE MEDICAL COLLEGE
(Selected Years)

| | Budget in Dinars | Per cent of Total Government Budget |
|---|---|---|
| 1947/48 | 448,332 | 7.8 |
| 1949/50 | 1,339,239 | 6.5 |
| 1950/51 | 1,829,198 | 6.2 |
| 1951/52 | 2,341,863 | 7.6 |
| 1952/53 | n.a. | n.a. |
| 1953/54 | 2,973,849 | 5.9 |
| 1954/55 | 3,794,658 | 7.0 |
| 1955/56 | 4,327,158 | 7.8 |

Source: *Statistical Abstracts* for 1950, p. 287; 1952, p. 258; 1955, p. 318; and 1956, p. 238.

In addition to its direct contributions, the Development Board plays an indirect role in improving health conditions: through loans to municipalities and other agencies for drinking water and sewage disposal schemes; through the drainage or filling in of swamps; construction of low-cost housing; extension and improvement of drinking water supplies; establishment of community centers and construction of sanitary slaughter houses and other establishments which have a direct bearing on raising the health standards in the country. The direct allocations of the Board for health in its 1955-60 plan are 18.2 million dinars. Direct and indirect expenditures during the same period are estimated, however, to reach the neighborhood of one hundred million dollars.

Since 1952 several international agencies have also been active in improving health conditions in Iraq. These include the United States Point Four Program, UNICEF, UNESCO, and WHO. These organizations either conduct independent programs of their own, collaborate in government programs, or train Iraqis to undertake specific tasks.

TABLE 43

DEVELOPMENT BOARD ALLOCATIONS FOR HEALTH:  1956-60

|  | Beds | Estimated Cost in Dinars |
|---|---|---|
| Baghdad Medical Center× | 1,000 | 4,000,000 |
| Karkh Hospital (Baghdad)* | 550 | 2,000,000 |
| Kazimain Hospital (Baghdad suburb)* | 300 | 700,000 |
| Basrah Hospital* | 400 | 900,000 |
| Amara Hospital* | 200 | 500,000 |
| Other Hospitals and Clinics* |  | 5,750,000 |
| Eradication of Malaria Campaign* |  | 2,000,000 |
|  |  | 15,850,000 |
| Improvement of Drinking Water* |  | 1,500,000 |
| Filling of Swamps* |  | 300,000 |
| Milk Pasteurization Plant (at Abu Ghraib)† |  | 550,000 |
| Grand Total |  | 18,200,000 |

× Planning completed.
* Construction in progress.
† Completed.

## Attitudes Toward Medicine

To all practical purposes, no native practice of medicine—as distinguished from modern practice—exists any longer in Iraq, except perhaps in isolated villages where no other facilities are available. On the contrary, people demand medical facilities and in recent years a village which has a clinic acquires prestige.

There are two exceptions to the above general rule: midwives are still preferred to obstetricians. This may be due to the traditional segregation of the sexes in Middle Eastern society and because it is felt that such an intimate life process as giving birth should be witnessed only by persons of the same sex. Midwives are regarded with considerable respect and affection, and homes are generally open to them at all times. In many respects, especially in the villages, they occupy a position similar to that of the priest. The government has recognized their importance and influence, and in recent years it has begun to establish training centers for them.

In contrast to midwifery, nursing, especially among the Muslims, is not regarded as quite a respectable profession.

This is particularly true for a girl of good family. This attitude prevails throughout the Middle East, but increases in intensity as one moves towards the Persian Gulf and farther east. A very serious problem of recruitment thus exists.

The second exception to the general lack of native medicine, although far less significant, is the bone-setter. In some isolated communities local bone-setters may still be found, who are generally surprisingly efficient and knowledgeable in their vocation.

An attitude which creates considerable difficulty is that which has developed throughout the Middle East, including Iraq, concerning tuberculosis. It is regarded as a "shameful" disease. Consequently every effort is usually made to conceal the fact from the neighbors, and there is great reluctance to report cases to hospitals. In many instances, only when the disease reaches a latent stage are the patient and his family willing to take this step.

In contrast to the attitude toward tuberculosis, no stigma seems to attach to *bejel*, a mild form of syphilis fairly common among the Bedouins of Iraq.

In recent years a new difficulty has begun to appear in the attitude of villagers toward mobile clinics. It seems that mobile clinics which make it possible to serve a number of villages (where a clinic for each would not be justified) are not regarded by the villagers with the same degree of confidence as permanent clinical installations. It may be that this is a transitory attitude which will disappear with more experience.

*Medical Facilities*

As in the case of education, in absolute terms the progress achieved has been remarkable. In 1918 there were one or two hospitals in the entire country. In 1950 there were eighty-two hospitals (seventy-one government, eleven private), 4,901 beds (4,483 government, 418 private), and 448 dispensaries. Assuming a population of five million in 1950, there was about one hospital bed for each 1,000 population.

Between 1950 and 1955 the number of hospitals rose to 115 (ninety-eight government, seventeen private), and beds to 7,745 (7,269 government, 476 private)—an increase of 40 per cent and 58 per cent respectively. The ratio of beds to population rose to one per 650 persons.

No exact data are available as to the number of clinics that have been constructed since 1950. A figure of sixty would probably not be far off the mark, so that it can be estimated that in 1955 there was a total of some 550 clinics.

Although statistically less impressive, similar increases took place in the medical staff. In 1951 there were 762 registered doctors (sixty-one of them foreigners), of whom 582 were government officials. There were 274 pharmacists, 557 nurses, 938 male dressers, and 682 midwives. The figures for 1955 were 1,014 doctors (ninety-four foreigners), 305 pharmacists, 781 nurses, 1,309 male dressers, and 767 midwives. These data do not include dentists, dental practitioners, vaccinators, health officers, laboratory analysts, etc.

Iraq is still confronted with serious problems in regard to both facilities and staff. Most of the hospitals are located in urban centers such as Baghdad, Basrah, Mosul, and Kirkuk. Some rural areas have no facilities whatsoever.

The most serious problem, however, is not the construction of hospitals and clinics (for this can proceed fairly rapidly) but the acute shortage of trained personnel. One new hospital in the south, it is reported, remained unopened for two years after completion because no personnel could be found to man it.

Doctors are usually extremely reluctant to work outside Baghdad. Of the 1,014 doctors in all of Iraq in 1955, 560 were located in the province of Baghdad alone. In essence, this means the city of Baghdad and its suburbs. Young doctors, after living in a foreign country or in Baghdad, find life in rural areas drab and uninteresting. There is usually no adequate housing, life is monotonous, and there is nothing to do besides one's job.

The shortage is not only in doctors but also in medical aides. The Jewish girls who used to be the main source of supply for nurses have gone with the general exodus of Jews in 1950. Male "dressers" are recruited in order to fill part of the need.

Some efforts are now being made to meet the problem of personnel. Doctors trained at state expense are required to serve a certain number of years outside the big cities (this has always been the case). As an inducement to serve in the provinces, adequate housing in rural areas is now being constructed for the medical staff. Training programs for doctors, nurses, and male dressers have been stepped up, but they still fall far short of meeting the requirements.

*Preventive Medicine*

Progress in preventive medicine has not been as evident as in curative medicine. In fact, the preventive medicine campaign can be said to have begun in earnest only since 1950. Between 1920 and 1950 epidemics which used to decimate the area, such as cholera, the plague, smallpox, and louse-borne typhus were either completely eradicated or brought under substantive control. However, the principal endemic diseases—such as malaria, trachoma, bilharzia, hookworm, and other intestinal diseases—remained widespread. The incidence of some of them, as will be pointed out later, actually increased.

The reasons why progress in this field has not been as marked are the complexity of the problem and the very heavy expenditures involved. Amelioration requires a large trained staff scattered throughout the country. It also requires considerable expenditures on sewage disposal, latrines in villages, pure drinking water, drainage works, and so forth. Awareness on the part of government officials and the public is needed; planning and coordination among the various government departments are required. An example cited by Salter gives a graphic illustration of this point. He writes:

> An old abandoned canal system was partly re-opened in 1941. By the summer of 1943 some 7,000 people were beginning to farm about 130,000 mesharas of newly irrigated land. Malaria from which the district had, before the new irrigation, been entirely free, at once appeared in a virulent form. Almost the entire population was stricken. Many of the villages were deserted. A review of the situation then showed that impervious

strata underlay much of the irrigated tracts, which therefore rapidly became water-logged. Drainage of these areas was then begun and the main drains for the whole area were completed by 1946. At the same time rice cultivation was strictly forbidden.[1]

Above all, attack on this complex of problems requires the cooperation and education of the public. In the final analysis, no government measure will be fully effective until the public understands that many of the diseases that afflict it originate in unsanitary habits and practices.

The preventive medicine movement has gained considerable strength since 1950. Work is being carried out on all fronts by the various ministries, local and municipal councils, and the Development Board. Expenditures in this field, compared to the pre-1950 level, are very high indeed. Campaigns (which will be discussed later) are now in progress to eradicate the main diseases at the source. Irrigation canals and ditches are being built with a view to health hazards. Sewage-disposal plants in the towns, latrines in the villages, and water purification systems are increasing. In addition, community welfare centers, greater distribution of pasteurized milk, a rise in the educational level and in real income, are in themselves preventive measures.

## The Chief Diseases

The degenerative diseases do not constitute a serious problem in Iraq. This may be due to the fact that the life span of the Iraqi is too short for him to develop them. The major and "problem" diseases of the country are those of socio-economic origin. They are all diseases originating in ignorance, poverty, overcrowding, uncleanliness, lack of sanitation facilities, water pollution, and malnutrition. Table 44 gives the number of main infectious disease cases treated in the hospitals and clinics of the country during 1946 and 1951-1956. Below, each of the major "problem" diseases will be discussed separately.

1. *Malaria.* In Iraq, malaria is the result of man-made conditions. Ironically enough, its incidence increased with the development of the water resources of the country until it became an endemic disease and the chief killer. Iraqi

doctors estimate that this disease alone kills some 50,000 persons a year.[2] Irrigation canals and stagnant pools are now the main breeding grounds of the malaria mosquito carrier.

Malaria threatens about three-fourths of Iraq's population. The worst areas are the north and northeast, and the foothills and uplands of the northern Zagros mountains. It is also serious in the low-lying coastal areas of Shatt al-Arab, Hammar Lake, and the alluvial plains of central and south

TABLE 44

MAJOR INFECTIOUS DISEASES TREATED

| | 1946 | 1950 | 1951 | 1952 | 1953 | 1954 | 1955 | 1956 |
|---|---|---|---|---|---|---|---|---|
| Trachoma | 558,323 | 484,323 | 677,599 | 618,403 | 489,527 | 481,272 | 406,514 | 431,245 |
| Malaria | 742,921 | 537,286 | 456,299 | 409,075 | 451,133 | 360,623 | 320,926 | 217,834 |
| Bilharzia | 21,029 | 23,372 | 35,287 | 32,672 | 29,249 | 37,784 | 42,495 | 54,669 |
| Hookworm | 13,992 | 9,518 | 16,188 | 23,686 | 19,167 | 14,170 | 24,035 | 24,866 |
| Dysentery* | 34,046 | 36,602 | 46,569 | 46,184 | 22,407 | 25,082 | 63,716 | 41,202 |
| Tuberculosis* | 8,660 | 9,905 | 9,925 | 11,066 | 6,171 | 6,754 | 6,969 | 10,405 |
| Venereal Diseases† | 47,547 | 36,600 | 22,892 | 18,376 | 4,925 | 11,398 | 3,537 | 4,002 |

Source: *Statistical Abstracts* for 1950, pp. 35, 54-57; 1952, pp. 87-92; 1955, pp. 314-316; and 1956, pp. 220-223.
*All forms.
†Includes syphilis, gonorrhea, and soft chancre.

Iraq.[3] Statistical data gathered over the years indicate that malarial incidence is much greater during flood years.

Little was done to combat the disease until after the war, due to the prohibitive costs of wide-scale larvicide and drainage projects, "the world's main recourse until the advent of DDT." Due to preventive measures taken since 1947, malaria has completely disappeared in the cities of Baghdad, Basrah, Mosul, and Kirkuk.

In 1950 the Endemic Diseases Institute (created in 1946) began concerting efforts to attack the malaria problem. Soon thereafter, the World Health Organization began cooperating by sending experts to train local specialists and to help develop a "national malaria strategy."

In 1952 UNICEF entered the scene. In addition to government effort, UNICEF began sending trucks, jeeps, sprayers, DDT, and field research supplies. Its efforts concentrated on the Tanjero Valley in northern Iraq. In 1954, U. N. and government operations were consolidated, giving protection to some 1.7 million persons.[4]

In late 1955, with continued U. N. and United States aid, 2,000 malaria workers launched an eight-year campaign which will protect two million persons during the epidemic season and achieve total protection for all the threatened population (three million) by 1963.

The UNICEF release cited previously states, "UNICEF aid will cease in 1956 when the Iraq government, which all along matched UNICEF's investment, plans to take over full responsibility. For the task, Iraq is enlarging the Endemic Diseases Institute at Baghdad; establishing five regional malaria centers . . . " The Development Board allocated two million dinars to the Endemic Diseases Institute to be spent between 1956 and 1960 on the eradication of malaria.*

The results of the work that has been accomplished since 1950 are reflected in the number of malaria cases treated at health institutions (*see Table 44*). In 1950 there were over 537,000 cases. In 1956, only 218,000, a decline of sixty per cent. The decline took place year after year (except in 1953), and has been too steady to be simply a statistical accident.

* In 1957 a Malaria Board was established.

The social and economic significance of the decline in the incidence of malaria is far-reaching. For one thing, malaria has been one of the major causes of the high rate of infant mortality—estimated to reach up to 500 per 1,000 babies born in malarial areas, with an average of 300-350 per 1,000 for the country as a whole. Once the malaria menace is removed, a considerable drop in the infant mortality rate should follow. This was, of course, the justification for UNICEF's joining the campaign against malaria in Iraq.

In addition to some 50,000 deaths it is said to cause each year, malaria also causes much disability and saps energy and vitality. It thus affects adversely the general level of productivity in the country, and limits the prospects of economic betterment for the individual.

2. *Trachoma.* With the decline in the incidence of malaria, trachoma has now moved to statistical first place among the problem diseases of the country. It is an eye disease, social in origin, and arises from unhygienic practices and general uncleanliness. It is carried from one person to the other by the common housefly.

Although the disease yields to curative treatment in its early stages, unlike malaria (for which comparatively inexpensive means of attack at the source has been found through insecticides), its eradication can only be accomplished through a general rise in the level of sanitation which would reduce fly-breeding areas and eventually eliminate the carrier. People come to health institutions to be treated in an ever larger number, while the source of the disease itself remains untouched year after year.

No data are available as to the incidence of the disease in the country as a whole. Illustrative examples only can be cited. Out of 140,451 students examined in 1950/51, 23 per cent were found to be afflicted with trachoma. In 1952/53, the rate was also 23 per cent out of 199,359 students. In the following year (1953/54), the percentage rose to 24.6 of 154,397 students examined.[5] A UNESCO worker recently estimated that trachoma incidence in the Dujailah settlement is as high as 80 per cent. A guess that some 60 per cent of the population in the entire country is afflicted with it would probably not be too far wrong.

There is reason to believe that incidence may be on the decline in Iraq. For instance, trachoma cases treated have been decreasing since 1951 (*see Table 44*). It must be admitted that this is not necessarily a reliable index, since many of those afflicted either have no access to, or do not take the time to visit, clinical facilities. Perhaps the best index is the province of Baghdad which has superior facilities, accessible to everyone, and where the population is more aware of the problem than in other areas. It would therefore be reasonable to assume that the majority of those afflicted would visit health institutions for treatment. This is statistically indicated, since about one-third of the cases treated in the entire country are located in this province.[6] The number of cases treated in Baghdad (province) dropped steadily year after year from 331,479 in 1951 to 102,789 in 1955, a decline of about 69 per cent. The pattern of decline followed that of the country as a whole.

3. *Bilharzia.* Bilharzia (schistosomiasis) is a parasitic ailment caused by a fluke which has a life cycle of human, vector snail, human. The fluke is picked up through the skin of the foot, develops in the human liver, reproduces, passes out through the urine into water, goes through a stage of development in the snail, and lives in stagnant and polluted waters until it finds a human host.

The disease is debilitating. The main components of its effects are lassitude, low vitality, and blood in the urine. It is therefore of profound economic significance. It lowers both the individual's capacity for work and his ability to resist and overcome other diseases.

As in Egypt—where the disease was first identified—it predominates in the flow-irrigated areas of the Iraqi countryside. A survey carried out by the Endemic Diseases Institute (around 1950) showed that the disease does not occur south of the town of Basrah; that it reaches its peak of incidence in the Lake Region, but from there northward, it declines steadily up to the Kurdish mountains, where it does not occur at all. The same survey showed that its highest incidence (i.e., per cent of all cases treated in hospitals that year) is in the provinces of Amara (67 per cent), Kut (48), Muntafiq (47), Dulaim (36), and Baghdad (35). Its incidence in both the provinces of Karbala and Diyala is 28 per cent and in the province of Basrah, 23 per cent.

The disease does not lend itself to easy clinical treatment, although this is possible. A wide variety of preventive measures which might reduce incidence substantially or eliminate it completely is known. The wearing of shoes reduces the possibility of contact between the victim and the snail almost to zero. The snail does not thrive in water flowing at the rate of three miles per hour, so that major and minor canals can be designed accordingly. Infected waters can be treated by dragging bags containing copper sulfate through them. The prevention of canal and water pollution through stricter laws, education, and provision of latrines in the villages (to prevent fouling of the canals) would also help considerably. Pure water supplies are also necessary.

Government departments and the public in general have become much more bilharzia-conscious in recent years. Irrigation canals and ditches are now being constructed with a view to eliminating bilharzia and other disease hazards. Drainage works now being built should help considerably by preventing waterlogging. The Endemic Diseases Institute has been expanded and is now doing valuable work in combatting the disease at the source. It has also been suggested that the government (perhaps the Development Board) should provide all school children with shoes free of cost, and even subsidize their general sale, particularly in infected rural areas.

The number of bilharzia cases treated at health institutions has risen considerably in recent years, over two and a half times between 1946 and 1956 (see Table 44). These figures in all probability reflect, not an increase in incidence, but rather a greater awareness on the part of the public and health authorities. Consequently, more cases are identified and treated. There will probably be a substantial increase in the number of cases treated over the next few years, followed later by a decline which would indicate an actual decline in incidence.

4. *Hookworm*. Hookworm (ankylostomiasis) is another parasitic disease. Among its effects are anemia and very low vitality. Like bilharzia, the parasite is picked up through the skin of the foot (and through infected drinking water) and lives in the intestinal tract. The disease thrives in areas where there are inadequate sewage disposal and open drains.

The disease seems to predominate in the south, although some Iraqi writers believe that some two-thirds of the entire population are afflicted with it.[7] In 1954, over 50 per cent of the pregnant women examined in one month at the Samawah Health Center were found to have one or more types of intestinal parasites.[8]

As is clearly evident, effective eradication of the disease is dependent, like that of bilharzia, on a rise in the level of sanitation, installation of sewage disposal facilities, stricter enforcement of sanitary laws, and economic betterment. In the meantime, of course, it can be treated clinically.

The number of cases treated during the last six years give no conclusive indication whether the disease is increasing or decreasing in the country (*see Table 44*). Cases which came to clinical attention rose from over 9,000 in 1950 to over 23,000 in 1953. Then they dropped to something over 14,000 in 1954, but rose to an all time high of over 24,866 cases in 1956. It is probable that there has been some decline since then, for improvement has occurred in sanitation and economic conditions. In any case, a decline is clearly indicated in the province of Baghdad. The number of cases treated there fell steadily year after year, from 13,794 in 1952 to 3,023 in 1955.

5. *Tuberculosis*. The number of tuberculosis cases brought to medical attention indicates that the disease does not represent a serious danger. There is reason to believe, however, that its incidence is much higher, owing to the social implications mentioned before.

In 1952 a national campaign, with the help of WHO and UNICEF, was launched to combat the disease, by attempting to discover its actual extent, by B.C.G. vaccination, and by public education. It is reported that by the early part of 1955 some 550,000 persons were X-rayed, and 220,000 were given B.C.G. vaccinations.

6. *Venereal Diseases.* The principal causes of venereal diseases in Iraq are prostitution, legal and illegal, and *bejel*, a mild form of syphilis common among the Bedouins and apparently passed on by parents to their children.

In recent years venereal diseases seem to have been brought under reasonable control. This may have been due to the widespread use of antibiotics and a much closer supervision of prostitution. In 1950, over 47,500 cases were brought for medical attention. Six years later in 1956, their number dropped to 4,000.

In 1950 the Directorate of Health estimated that some half a million persons were afflicted with *bejel*, mainly among the tribes in the provinces of Amara, Dulaim, Mosul, and Kirkuk.[9] No data are available on the progress achieved with this disease since 1950, although it is known that the Endemic Diseases Institute assisted by the World Health Organization is investing considerable time and effort in combatting it. The fact that the Bedouins attach no stigma to this disease should be of considerable help in eradicating it, once its exact nature is determined.

*Conclusions*

Considerable amounts of money have been invested and remarkable progress has been achieved since 1950 in the improvement and expansion of the medical facilities of the country. Despite this progress, Iraq, as in the case with education, is still a long way from solving its health problems. Health facilities, particularly clinics and health centers, are still extremely inadequate; severe shortages in medical personnel exist; and the death rate is still very high. There is, however, the desire to improve health conditions, and the funds to do it.

Generally speaking, no aspect of the development program has met with more enthusiastic response from the public than the measures taken to raise the health standards in the country.

1. Salter, *op. cit.*, p. 86.
2. A Committee of Officials, *Kingdom of Iraq*. (Baltimore: The Lord Baltimore Press, 1946), p. 91.
3. Iraqi Embassy, Washington, D. C., *Bulletin*, August, 1955, quoting a UNICEF press release of July, 1955.
4. *Ibid.*, p. 8.
5. Iraq, Ministry of Education, *Annual Reports* for 1950-51 and 1953-54.
6. Of course, it is possible that this is so because the incidence of the disease in Baghdad is higher than the rest of the country. Such reasoning, however, would be rather far-fetched and illogical since the level of sanitation is higher in Baghdad than anywhere else. In the absence of definite data, it would be more reasonable to accept the first assumption.
7. Khayyat, *op. cit.*, p. 33.
8. Adams, *op. cit.*, p. 160.
9. Iraq. Directorate General of Health, *Annual Bulletin of Health and Vital Statistics for 1950*. (Baghdad: Government Press, 1950), p. 20.

# CHAPTER 12

## COMMUNITY DEVELOPMENT AND WELFARE

After World War I the cities and towns of Iraq grew haphazardly with little planning or coordination. The old sections, medieval in many of their features, are characterized by narrow, winding streets and alleys, unsavory odors, open drains, and generally unhygienic living conditions. Not infrequently, livestock are kept within municipal limits of some of the main cities. To this day, not even Baghdad can boast an adequate sewage disposal system.

In contrast, the new sections look impressive with broad tree-lined, dual-carriage boulevards and modern apartment buildings and villas for the rich. According to the International Bank Mission, even the new sections were not properly planned. It stated in part:[1]

> Streets and traffic circles have been laid out according to pre-scribed geometrical patterns without paying much attention to their functions or to the need for creating integrated residential areas with appropriate housing for different income groups and provision for schools, shops and hospitals or clinics . . . Growth has been, in fact, piecemeal and spasmodic rather than coordinated and regular, and emphasis has been placed more on the ornamental than on the useful. Some traffic circles, for example, are unnecessary; others are even safety hazards . . . . Sometimes streets have been ruthlessly cut or widened through built-up

areas with little regard for the consequences; the remnants of buildings which have been sliced through at odd angles can still be seen.

A rising volume of immigration from rural areas has taken place, especially since World War II. Immigrants tend to recreate conditions in their former habitat. Many of them simply squat on vacant lots, or live in sarifa camps (mat huts) on the outskirts under conditions of extreme squalor. The immigration not only aggravates further the congestion and the severe housing shortage, but increases the danger of epidemics, disfigures the cities and towns, and impedes efforts for municipal improvement, in addition to creating other social problems.

Almost all the rural population lives in villages rather than in isolated homesteads. From necessity, villages are usually located near a source of water supply—a well or a stream in the north, a canal in the irrigation zone. In the north the common building material is stone; mud or mud brick in the south and center. Villages in the north have greater permanence. This is mainly because of a much longer tradition of settled agriculture there than in the south and center. Another factor is probably the salination of the soil and the silting of canals in the latter two regions. When this occurs, peasants have no choice but to move to new locations.

The village normally consists of a number of huts in very close proximity to each other. Usually the hut is composed of a thick-walled room with one door which opens on an enclosed yard where the cooking is done and the animals are kept. They are so designed as to keep out cold, heat, and sand at the least expense; hence the thick walls and very small or no windows at all. Furnishings consist of the absolute minimum necessities.

Ordinarily the village has no communal facilities or services. There are no schools or clinics; there is no system of collecting garbage; seldom, if ever, does a hut have a latrine of its own; very often, the water supply is either polluted or soon becomes so. Trees, which would provide a protective screen against sand, relief from the burning sun and firewood, are seldom seen.

TABLE 45

IRAQ HOUSING CENSUS: 1956
(Excluding Villages Under 15 Houses)

| Type of Housing | No. of Houses | Per cent |
|---|---|---|
| Brick | 111,871 | 15.1 |
| Stone | 46,127 | 6.2 |
| Mud | 304,296 | 41.1 |
| Sarifa (reed) | 194,629 | 26.2 |
| Tent | 15,282 | 2.1 |
| Other | 68,901 | 9.3 |
| Total | 741,106 | 100.0 |
| **Source of Water Supply** | | |
| Piped Water | 154,395 | 20.8 |
| River or Streams | 370,785 | 50.2 |
| Wells | 59,476 | 8.2 |
| Other Sources | 154,262 | 20.8 |
| Total | 738,918 | 100.0 |
| **House Facilities:** | | |
| Houses with Piped Water | 154,395 | 20.8 |
| Houses with Electricity | 125,672 | 16.9 |
| Houses with Toilets | 247,638 | 33.4 |
| Houses with Baths | 75,840 | 10.2 |

*Occupancy:*

| | |
|---|---|
| Persons per family | 5.65 |
| Families per house | 1.07 |
| Rooms per house | 2.07 |
| Persons per room | 2.37 |

Source: Iraq Government, *Statistical Abstract for 1956*, pp. 120-24.

In 1956, a housing census, the first of its kind in the country, was completed. The results, summarized in Table 45, paint a grim picture. Excluding villages with less than fifteen houses, it was found that about 79 per cent of all houses in the country were mud or reed huts (*sarifa*), tents or inferior habitation. Seventy-one per cent had no safe water supplies, and over 66 per cent had no toilets. Only 10 per cent had baths and 17 per cent electricity. The national average occupancy was found to be 2.37 persons to a room.

It is against this background that a conscious community development movement began in earnest only recently. Its general objectives are to make life more pleasant and bearable. Among other things, its program includes better and more coordinated planning of the physical layout of cities, towns, and villages; the provision of schools, clinics, health and community centers; better and more housing; gardens and playgrounds; clean water; better sewage disposal in the cities and latrines in the villages, etc. Some aspects of the community development movement are discussed below.

*Housing*

The present housing program is carried out by three main government agencies: the Development Board, the State Mortgage Bank, and the Ministry of Social Affairs. In addition, of course, should be mentioned private, municipal, and industrial housing.

1.  *The Development Board.* Initially, the Board's housing program was very limited in scope and conception. It was designed primarily to help government employes and workers of the Board. Between 1951 and 1956, however, thinking developed considerably on this subject. This is reflected in the fact that—against a small sum allotted for housing in the first Five-Year Plan—the new program calls for the expenditure of more than twenty-four million dinars between 1956 and 1960. In 1956 serious consideration was being given to the formation of a Ministry of Housing, Villages, and Municipalities to be financed by the Board.

The Board's ultimate objective is the construction of some 245,000 housing units; 125,000 in rural areas, and 120,000 in cities and towns. Of the latter, 47,000 are to be located in Baghdad and 13,000 in Basrah.

For all practical purposes, the Board's immediate program was launched only in 1955. A Greek consultant recommended by the International Bank acts now as the housing advisor to the Board. He has recommended a two-fold program: (a) a general program for the construction of 25,000 houses in five years and (b) a short-term program whereby several housing developments, each not to exceed 1,000 houses, would be constructed: four in Baghdad, two in Basrah, two in Mosul, one in Kirkuk, and one in Sarchinar (cement factory). The houses are to be built in complete groups. Each development will have its requirements of public services, i.e., roads, water supply, sewage system, electricity, and public buildings such as schools, mosques, clinics, social and recreational centers, markets, playgrounds, and parks.

The short-term program is now in operation. Some 2,000 houses are now under construction in Mosul, 600 in Kirkuk, 160 in Dibbis, 400 in Sarchinar, 5,000 in Baghdad, and about 1,800 at Basrah—a total of some 10,000 houses. Commissioning of new houses by the Board will probably reach some 10,000 a year by 1960.

The houses under construction seem to be designed primarily to meet part of the needs of government employes, workers of the Board's industrial plants, and sarifa dwellers at Baghdad and Basrah. Some of the houses are to be sold on a long-term installment basis, while others are to be rented at low rates.

2. *The Ministry of Social Affairs.* This department is primarily concerned with the construction of low-cost housing for government employes and workers. So far, it has constructed some 2,000 houses for that purpose. In addition, it is now building a new township, Topchi, near Baghdad. The township will include electricity, piped water, sewage disposal, a shopping center, streets, a mosque, a hospital, a school, a post office, a police station, and a park.

As planned, the Topchi development consists of 1,950 houses, some already completed, some near completion, and some under construction in late 1956. Twelve hundred and fifty of the houses will be allotted to government officials, employees and workers, and 700 to some of the 1954 flood victims.

The main housing projects of the Ministry are financed through grants from the Development Board.

3. *The Mortgage Bank* This state bank was founded in 1948 with a nominal capital of half a million dinars, and began actually operating in 1949. In 1952 its capital was raised to two million dinars but the amount was not fully

paid up by the government until 1954. In 1954/55, the bank had at its disposal a total of 3.2 million dinars in capital, deposits and loans.

The purpose for which the bank was created is to facilitate the construction of housing. It is authorized by law to perform two main functions: (1) to build houses on its own account and sell them at cost or at nominal profit on an installment basis and (2) to make loans to individuals and organizations to help them (a) construct new buildings or houses, (b) repair or purchase buildings and houses, and (c) pay off existing house mortgages which are usually at high rates of interest.

So far the bank has built 168 houses in Kirkuk, Baghdad, and Sulaimaniya, as well as eighty-two houses for teachers in Baghdad. In addition, eighty houses were under construction in Mosul in 1956.

Under construction, also by the Bank, are two Baghdad suburbs. Faisal City is primarily for army and police officers and will consist of 4,450 houses. The second suburb, al-Mamun Town—named after a famous caliph of Iraq—includes all the modern amenities such as electricity, piped water, and sewage disposal, as well as schools, a shopping center, a clinic, a park, and a police station.

This suburb is due to be completed in 1957 and will consist of 500 houses, each fifty being in a different style. Each house will include four rooms, a hall, a bath, and a kitchen. Evidently the suburb is designed for the middle-class income group.

Loans by the bank are limited to a minimum of 100 dinars and a maximum of 2,000 at five per cent interest and repayable over a maximum period of twelve years. Between 1949/50 and 1954/55 the bank made the following loans:[2]

|  | No. of Loans | Total Value in Dinars | Per Cent of Total |
|---|---|---|---|
| Conversion of Existing Mortgages | 3,008 | 1,727,343 | 32.4 |
| New Houses | 1,651 | 1,650,540 | 31.0 |
| Repairs and Purchase | 4,126 | 1,939.423 | 36.6 |
|  | 8,785 | 5,317,306 | 100.0 |

In size, 56.5 per cent of the loans were for less than 500 dinars, 20.6 per cent from 500 to less than 1,000 dinars, and 22.9 per cent for 1,000 dinars and over. This last category, however, accounted for 55.4 per cent (2,944,754 dinars) of the total value of the loans made. In length, 56.3 per cent of the loans were from one to four years; 28.8 per cent from four to eight years; and 14.9 per cent from eight to twelve years accounting for 38.5 per cent (1,871,654 dinars) of the total value of the loans made.

During the above period the activities of the bank were concentrated in the city of Baghdad, which accounted for 77.3 per cent of all the loans made. This was due to two main reasons. First, about 70 per cent of the private capital of the country invested in mortgages is located in Baghdad. Since these private mortgages were at high interest rates, there was a run on the facilities of the bank to liquidate them. Secondly, the only branch the bank had was in Baghdad. In other places, the facilities of the Agricultural Bank were used. In 1953, the Mortgage Bank opened a branch in Basrah, and in 1954/55 branches in four other towns were opened, bringing the total to six.

4. *Industrial Housing* Under Law No. 29 (1947), industrial plants employing 100 workers and over must provide housing for their workers. So far the law has not been enforced, and it will probably remain on the books as a foundation for the future. However, the oil companies, the Railway Administration, and the Basrah Port Directorate do provide housing and are expanding their programs. In all the new state enterprises housing for workers is provided for and is included in the cost estimates for their implementation.

*Evaluation*

The housing program, as it has operated to date, has two distinct features. First, with few exceptions, the houses by cost and type of construction seem to be designed for middle- and upper-class income groups, mostly government employes and officials. The poorer segments of society who need housing more than all others do not seem to be provided for. Then, too, the houses are mostly located in the cities and primarily

in Baghdad. Rural areas received hardly any benefits of the
program up until 1957. It must be said, however, that the
plan has only been launched. The 1955-60 program is expected to spread the benefits over a much larger geographical
area, including rural sections, and over a larger segment of
the population.

As in the case of almost every development activity, the
program confronts two main difficulties: scarcity of skilled
labor and shortages of materials. The first problem is being
met, at least in part, in three ways: (a) by employing foreign
workers, (b) by requiring all contractors to give unskilled
Iraqi workers on-the-job training, and (c) by establishing
training schools. For instance, one such school has now been
established, and has about 1,200 trainees. Most of the teachers
are foreign specialists.

The second problem is being met through (a) the encouragement of new building materials industries, and (b)
the use of new materials. For example, a new factory, probably the largest of its kind in the Middle East, was recently
built to mass-produce construction materials such as tiles,
bricks, etc.

*Pure Water Supply*

In 1951, out of a total of 131 municipalities of all four
classes in the country, about forty of them, including most
towns with a population of over 6,000, had modern piped
water supply systems.[3] In 1955, water purification systems
were in operation or under construction in ninety towns and
cities.[4]

The increase is reflected in the figures on consumption of
pure water in the towns. In 1951, more than 44 million
cubic meters were consumed. By 1955, the consumption
reached to more than 77 million, an increase of 75 per cent
(*see Table 46*). This indicates two trends—an increase in
per capita consumption, and extension of the system to new
towns.

The water systems are managed by municipal Boards
under the direction of the Department of Municipalities in
the Ministry of Interior. The Development Board administers

TABLE 46

CONSUMPTION OF PURE WATER IN THE TOWN OF IRAQ

| Year | 1,000 Cubic Meters |
|------|--------------------|
| 1947 | 37,081 |
| 1950 | 46,445 |
| 1951 | 44,456 |
| 1952 | 51,107 |
| 1953 | 55,354 |
| 1954 | 63,773 |
| 1955 | 77,326 |
| 1956 | 81,275 |

Source: *Statistical Abstracts* for 1950, p. 65; 1952, p. 193; 1955, p. 195; 1956, p. 201.

no pure water scheme as such. Rather it allocates funds for such purposes to the Ministry of Social Affairs, to the Department of Mines (to drill wells), and to the Department of Municipalities. It also makes direct loans to individual municipalities for such purposes. In its 1955-60 program, the Board had allocations of 1.5 million dinars for improvement of drinking water, and three million dinars for drilling artesian wells, presumably both for drinking purposes and irrigation.

The main difficulty which, prior to 1951, stood in the way of a faster rate of expansion of municipal water systems was lack of funds. This factor has since disappeared and progress in this field, with the financial support of the Development Board, has been satisfactory. The rate of expansion is increasing rapidly, so that it is probable that, by 1965, either all or most municipalities in Iraq will have modern water works.

The problem of pure water for human consumption is of a somewhat different nature in rural areas. In some cases, particularly in the north, all that is required is the construction of a well in the village itself, and if one is already available, providing it with such facilities as pipes and tanks, if necessary, to insure that the water, which is usually pure at the source, does not become infected.

In villages which depend on irrigation canals or streams the problem is more complex. Here the water is in most cases impure, and usually has to be carried long distances to the village. Consequently, canal water has to be pumped to the village, purified and disinfected, then stored in tanks for use.

Expenditures on clean water for villages have averaged in recent years about 200,000 dinars a year. They include costs of drilling wells, storage tanks, pumps, pipes to carry water, and training for villagers to maintain and keep wells clean.[5] The program will probably undergo considerable expansion in the near future.

By the end of 1956 the Development Board had completed the construction of 100 wells, in addition to fifty wells which were either under construction or being tested. The 1955-60 program provides for the construction of 200 more wells at an estimated total cost of three million dinars. Many of these wells are designed for nomads or semi-nomads. Apart from providing clean water for man and animal, they have also been found to be a very effective instrument for settling the tribes. It is estimated that ten to fifty families of the nomadic tribes have now settled permanently around each well.

*Improvements of Rural Life*

Several aspects of improvements in rural life—such as education, health, water, housing, etc., have been discussed above. The new settlements being created under government supervision provide perhaps the most hopeful beginning. Community and health centers have now been established in several villages and are now on the increase. The health centers serve not only as clinics but also as demonstration units where women are taught child care and the elements of sanitation and the courses of disease. A training program for rural social welfare workers has now been instituted.

The attack on the rural problem, however, has been piecemeal. In late 1956 an integrated ten-year rural community development program, drafted by UNESCO and requiring special legislation, was being prepared for presentation to Parliament during its December, 1956 session. The scheme was to be launched in 1957.

The plan calls for the formation of a Rural Community Development Council composed of the Prime Minister as chairman, the Ministers of Interior, Social Affairs, Health,

Education, and Agriculture as members, and a secretary-general with cabinet rank to administer the program.

The council will have a separate and autonomous Central Board with full executive, financial, and administrative powers. It is to be attached to the Council of Ministers, but directly responsible to Parliament.

The secretary-general of the Council will be the board chairman. He will be assisted by an advisory committee of top-level specialists from the Ministries of Education, Health, Agriculture, Social Affairs, Interior, Finance, Economics, and Development, as well as heads of any other relevant government department.

The object of the program is to improve the standard of living of Iraq's rural population, reduce the migration of farmers to larger cities and towns, step up farm production and provide solutions for such basic problems as ignorance, disease, and unemployment.

The program calls for a total expenditure of six million dinars over a ten-year period. Expenditures during the first year are to be 1.5 million dinars, and, thereafter, half a million each year for the duration.[6]

Several features of the plan are of special interest. First, unlike any previous attempt, it is integrated and coordinated, with all the appropriate departments participating. The rural problem is also placed on the highest executive level, i.e., the ministerial level. Too, the "autonomous board" idea, under the control of specialists isolated from politics, seems to have taken root.

From the meager information available and the relatively small amounts involved, it seems that the scheme is not intended to replace other projects but rather to supplement them. It is probable, however, that after some experience and confidence have been gained, the plan will undergo considerable expansion.

*Sanitation*

The extent of improvement in this field cannot be statistically determined. *Prima facie* evidence indicates, however, that progress has been more or less in line with the general development of the country. This is probably especially true in urban areas. There is definite evidence that sanitation laws are now much more rigidly enforced than before. For example, in Basrah a hygiene corps has been formed to inspect food shops, restaurants, bakeries, barber shops, and other establishments catering to people's consumption needs.

Perhaps the most spectacular development in this field is the installation of a sewage disposal system for the city of Baghdad, where the population is estimated to have neared the million mark. The system is estimated to cost some eight million dinars and will take several years to be completed. Specifications for bids by contractors were ready in the latter part of 1956. The project will be financed by the Municipality of Baghdad, mainly through loans and guarantees from the Development Board. Similar systems are now under consideration for Mosul, Basrah, and other towns.

The municipal boundaries of Baghdad were expanded in 1956 to include some 260 square kilometers as against the previous seventy-five. The area annexed is part of an expansion plan drawn by a British town-planner. Before 1956, no such expansion was possible because of the flood danger. This has now been removed.

*Conclusion:*

The community development and welfare movement is very new in Iraq. Very little was done in the past to improve conditions of life. This was particularly true in the case of rural areas which still lack, in most cases, even the elementary necessities of civilized existence. It is probably fair to say that the various government agencies began to pay serious attention to most of these needs only in the last three or four years. This is illustrated by the expenditures of the Development Board. The 1950-55 plan allocated only token amounts for such purposes. In contrast, the amounts allocated in the 1955-60 plan are by no means insignificant.

The Development Board, the various national governmental agencies and local administrations, now have elaborate plans to improve housing, safe water, and electricity supplies, sanitation, etc. Little, at least in terms of total needs, has so far been achieved, although these plans are gradually being put into effect.

1. *IBRD*, pp. 442-443.
2. Iraq, The Mortgage Bank. *A Statistical Report on the Operations of the Mortgage Bank from Its Establishment to 31.3. 1955.* (Baghdad, 1956.)
3. *IBRD*, pp. 442, 458.
4. Adams, *op. cit.*, p. 160.
5. *Iraq Times*, January 25, 1956.
6. *USIA*, Baghdad, Press Dispatch, October 3, 1956.

# PART V *Conclusions*

## CHAPTER 13

### CONCLUSIONS

Among the principal causes of political and social instability in the Middle East are the abject poverty of the majority of its peoples and their desire for a better life. The area contains sources of potential wealth which, if properly developed, can support a much higher standard of living.

All specialists agree that the best approach to development in the area would be through a coordinated regional program. For reasons which lie outside the scope of this book, such an approach has not been possible so far. Development, therefore, has taken place on a country basis, and, in most countries, it has been rather sporadic, lacking in coordination and clearly defined objectives, and ineffectual in terms of changing the basic pattern of the socio-economic structure. Some countries have the capital for investment, but no resources; others have the resources but no capital; some have both, but lack an imaginative and wise leadership.

Iraq is considered to be among the less advanced countries in the region. It is, however, blessed with the main components necessary for development: capital for investment, extensive resources in land, water, oil, undetermined quantities of minerals, and a low population density in relation to these resources.

The program initiated in 1950 is designed to employ these favorable factors in the development of the country. The program is by no means perfect. Justifiable criticisms may be made—and have been made— of the individual components of some of its schemes, of policies, of administration, and of the slowness with which the work is sometimes executed. Yet, as a whole, it remains a bold and imaginative program representing a refreshing and radical departure from the inefficient methods of previous years.

For the first time in the modern history of Iraq and, indeed, of all the Arab countries, development, through the creation of an organizational structure (the Development Board), is relatively insulated from politics and is left basically in the hands of competent specialists; large amounts of capital are being continuously invested; comprehensive and coordinated plans covering all sectors of the economy and aiming at fairly well-defined objectives have been drawn and are being implemented; and a large number of specialists, technicians, and engineering firms have been employed, not only to help in the execution of the program, but also to train Iraqis to help themselves.

Some of the more immediate benefits of the program are already visible. Unemployment has, for all practical purposes, disappeared, and the real wage income has risen. In 1956 the country, for the first time in its long history, achieved reasonable protection against the menace of floods, and, in the summer of the same year, produced bumper crops— almost double those of 1955. The number of children going to school in 1956/57 was more than double that of 1950. Malaria, which used to kill some 50,000 persons a year, is being brought under a substantial measure of control. The program should affect, either directly or indirectly, the very foundations of the economic, social, and political institutions of the country. It should be remembered that Iraq's intensive planned development began only in 1950. The various plans of the Board and other government agencies and departments represent only initial steps in a grand design which may take twenty to thirty years to reach fulfillment. It is also assumed here that intensive development as a state policy will not be interrupted except by circumstances over which the government has no control, such as war.

What then is the significance of the program? Basically, it is a means of speeding up the process of economic and social change taking place, not only in Iraq, but throughout the Middle East and most underdeveloped countries. The essential difference between Iraq and some of her neighbors is that she is forging ahead at a much faster pace and that the country, because of its resources, holds the promise of a more prosperous future for its people than some of her less fortunate neighbors.

There are limits to what heavy government spending and "crash programs" can do in bringing about change. Sometimes they create economic stresses, social dislocation, and cultural chaos. It may be desirable at times to slow down elements of a program so that its main components can develop proportionately. This is particularly true in the field of human relations. Habits, customs, and traditions do not change or disappear overnight and new ones cannot be imposed without explanation if they are to be effective. The most healthy change is that which springs from the "grass roots" with guidance and assistance from above. There is also the ever-present danger that designs for change may be borrowed from other societies without due regard to whether they are adaptable to the Iraqi environment or congenial to its people. This is probably the main criticism against the program in Iraq. It is for the people, but not from them. There is a considerable lack of communication between the bureaucracy which administers the program and the common people whom it is designed to benefit. The bureaucrat is contemptuous of the *fallah* and his customs, and believes him to be an unintelligent dolt who has little to contribute to progress, if anything; and the *fallah* has a deep-seated suspicion of the bureaucrat and his designs, gained from centuries of unpleasant contact with government which was usually restricted to military conscription and the collection of taxes. As one writer on Middle Eastern economic matters has observed, "Government is alien."

The possible impact of the program can be divided into three main categories:

*The Economic Impact*

1. The most obvious effect of the program is on the national income. There is little question that, not too far in the future, it may rise to several times its 1950 level, and it is not unlikely that the average *per capita* income may become the highest in the Middle East, including Turkey and Israel. Further, the distribution of the national income among various segments of the population will be more even, with *fallaheen*, the urban workers, and the middle classes receiving a more equitable share, and the wealthy class receiving a smaller proportion than it receives at present.

2. Iraq, like all countries of the Middle East, has been moving from a subsistence to a money economy. The program, by raising the horizon of wants, will tend to accelerate this process. Emphasis will increasingly tend to shift from production for personal consumption to production for the domestic and export markets. The closed or semi-closed village economy system will gradually break down, to be replaced by a system of economic interdependence with money as the primary medium of exchange and the main symbol of wealth.

3. Agricultural production should experience a tremendous rise and Iraq may become the granary and garden of the Middle East as it was in centuries past.

In addition to the monetary return, the increase in agricultural production will be of manifold significance. Iraq will become basically self-sufficient, and the population will be assured of abundant food supplies at cheaper prices at all times. Iraq will become a major exporter of agricultural products. In times of peace, Middle Eastern countries will be able to import from Iraq grains and other food commodities—presumably at cheaper prices than they can be obtained from distant lands such as Australia and Canada, thus increasing intraregional trade. In times of global war, the Middle East would be in less danger of starvation, and the pressure on the shipping facilities of combatants responsible for feeding the area would be greatly reduced.

4. Although the economy will continue to be based on agriculture, Iraq will no longer be exclusively a producer of primary products. Limited industrialization has already set in and, for the immediate future, the development program contemplates the creation of a light industry which uses mostly local raw materials and produces principally for the domestic market.

The authorities in Iraq have been wise in not launching grandiose but uneconomic industrial schemes. The lure of industrialization is almost irresistible in underdeveloped countries, for historically this economic process has been associated with political prestige and dominance, military might, a high standard of living, and a high order of technology, civilized existence, and cultural achievement. Later Iraq will no doubt follow the same path of industrialization that the Western world has taken, but, in the meantime, it would seem that she would be well advised, since land and water are her most valuable assets, to concentrate her efforts mainly on developing and utilizing her agricultural resources.

The creation of light industry should result in many benefits. It will supply the country with many of its basic needs of manufactured goods at low prices, thus giving Iraq a measure of independence from outside sources—a fact especially important in times of war. It will provide a secure market for some agricultural products, and employment for a large number of workers. It will assist in the expansion of the domestic market and pave the way for new industries. Finally, it will provide technical training facilities for Iraqi workers. In addition, the contemplated petrochemical industry, which is designed to produce for both the domestic and export markets, will utilize some of the natural gas now going to waste and gain for Iraq not insignificant sums of money in foreign exchange.

5. One of Iraq's perennial problems is its unfavorable balance of trade. At no time in its modern history has the value of its exports equalled that of its imports and, in some years, the value of the imports rose to more than twice that

of exports (excluding oil). Since 1950 the foreign exchange requirements to meet the deficit have been covered from oil royalties, mostly in sterling. The expected increase in agricultural and industrial production and in services should close this wide gap. This, in effect, means substantial "savings" for the country.

6. The program should result in increasing substantially the social capital reserves of the country. The curative and preventive health measures being taken should accelerate the rate of net natural increase. This should be regarded as an economic asset, since Iraq at present is underpopulated and requires a much larger labor force adequately to utilize its resources. These measures, along with the substantial increase in educational institutions and training centers, should gradually create a healthier and more vigorous population, produce a more intelligent labor force, increase the number of skilled workers, and raise the level of technical knowledge, resulting in a corresponding rise in the productive capacity of the individual.

*Social Impact*

Although the development program accelerates social change, most of the changes mentioned below would probably take place in one form or another even if there were no program. The difference is mainly one of pace.

1. Perhaps one of the most direct results of the program is the creation of a new class—hitherto virtually absent in Iraq—the independent small-farm owner-operator. Aside from its other ramifications, the emergence of such an economically independent class should give rise to a new set of social relationships in rural areas to supplant the traditional structure upon which the existing system of land tenure is based. It should also bring in its wake a re-evaluation of the *fallah's* place in society, and raise the horizon of his aspirations for the good life, thus releasing energies and potentialities which have hitherto been bottled up because the existing rigidly stratified social structure allowed them little room for creative expression.

2. As in most Arab countries, the urban middle class

in Iraq is numerically small. The program, through industrialization, new economic opportunities, increased population mobility and education, should cause a considerable increase in its ranks. This means a greater rate of social urbanization, the spread of middle class attitudes and way of life, a geographical redistribution of the population, the growth of urban areas, and an occupational redistribution of the labor force resulting in a relative decline of the number of those engaged in agriculture and a corresponding increase of those in industry, trade and services.

3. As mentioned previously, many aspects of society in Iraq, as in other Middle Eastern countries, have been undergoing change for many years. The program should soon become the main force speeding up this process. Secularization should reduce the differences among the various linguistic, ethnic, and religious segments of the population, and weld these blocs into a more cohesive unit with common beliefs, aspirations, and loyalties.

The above changes should also bring about a much greater degree of social mobility, both horizontal and vertical. For instance, to take an extreme case, a short time ago the chances of the son of a *fallah* receiving a university education and moving out of his class and up the social ladder were rather remote. Although still limited, such cases are now not infrequent. On the horizontal plane, social intercourse and intermixture between the various population groups is becoming more prevalent and should increase.

Iraqi society is also undergoing a cultural reorientation. Until recent years the aspirations of Iraqis, as well as those of most Arabs, were anchored in the past. Today, preoccupation with the glories of the past among the vocal public is restricted mainly to religious divines, historians, and antiquarians. Most educated young Iraqis are concerned with the future and are groping for solutions to immediate problems. Generally, they are interested in establishing a new kind of society that will equip them to live the good life in a twentieth century world.

*Political Impact*

The political effects of development in Iraq are of a two-fold nature: internal and external.

Internally, the short-term result of the program has been the maintenance of a measure of public peace. Many competent observers a few years ago believed that Iraq was on the eve of a revolutionary upheaval.

This is a very real possibility. In almost all countries of the Arab world, including Iraq, internal political issues have been reduced to one of two alternatives: immediate reform or revolution. In Iraq, in addition, there is considerable discontent in relation to foreign policy. Barring outside intervention or a revolution, the development program may give Iraq a "breathing spell" during which reform may be effected in an orderly manner.

The long-term results of the program are also obvious. It should bring about a redistribution of political power in favor of the masses and particularly the middle class, which includes the intelligentsia. This class today has considerable influence over the masses and is far more powerful than its representation in Parliament would indicate. The program will increase its membership and strengthen its economic position. As to the *fallaheen*, the landlords and the shaikhs will no longer be able to exert over them the same degree of political control which they do at present. It is, therefore, hard to escape the conclusion that the traditional ruling class will no longer have a monopoly on political power.

Finally, the social, economic, and cultural changes taking place should effectuate the transference of loyalties from the tribe, the religious group, etc., to the ideal of a nation.

Externally, the program requires that Iraq (at least for the time being) dedicate itself to the cause of peace and stability in the Middle East. An extended armed conflict in the region would result in the suspension of the flow of oil and oil revenue. The suspension of the program would cause chaos in the governmental machinery and bring in its wake hunger and poverty and severe public unrest.

On the other hand, Iraq, on the basis of its economic potential and barring international disturbances, should soon emerge as one of the major powers in the region.

*Significance for the Middle East*

Middle Eastern countries which may later initiate similar programs can benefit from Iraq's experience with intensive development. Successful experiments can be imitated, and mistakes avoided.

The development of Iraq, assuming political considerations permit, can provide a partial solution—through emigration—to the population problem of some Middle Eastern countries.

Finally, if at a later date a development plan for the Middle East is formulated and agreed upon, the program in Iraq will have laid some of the groundwork for the execution of the regional scheme.

**Appendix I**

## GENERAL POPULATION CENSUS: 1957*

The Preliminary Results for Enumeration of Population in Urban and Rural Areas
Classified According to Liwas

| Liwa | Urban | | | Rural | | | Grand Total |
|---|---|---|---|---|---|---|---|
| | Male | Female | Total | Male | Female | Total | |
| Mosul | 139,356 | 133,261 | 272,617 | 223,975 | 220,908 | 444,883 | 717,500 |
| Sulaimaniya | 41,299 | 37,969 | 79,268 | 114,866 | 105,844 | 220,710 | 299,978 |
| Arbil | 39,084 | 33,746 | 72,830 | 98,518 | 101,178 | 199,696 | 272,526 |
| Kirkuk | 78,648 | 74,524 | 153,172 | 117,900 | 117,840 | 235,740 | 388,912 |
| Diyala | 39,246 | 37,025 | 76,271 | 127,260 | 126,282 | 253,542 | 329,813 |
| Dulaim | 31,951 | 30,861 | 62,812 | 87,355 | 84,095 | 171,450 | 234,262 |
| Baghdad | 441,777 | 405,285 | 847,062 | 228,384 | 231,158 | 459,542 | 1,306,604 |
| Kut | 34,648 | 35,216 | 69,864 | 102,784 | 117,422 | 220,206 | 290,070 |
| Hilla | 52,987 | 51,258 | 104,245 | 124,556 | 124,813 | 249,369 | 353,614 |
| Karbala | 83,779 | 89,794 | 173,573 | 21,568 | 21,874 | 43,442 | 217,015 |
| Diwaniya | 60,088 | 62,386 | 122,474 | 186,379 | 198,695 | 385,074 | 507,548 |
| Amara | 42,027 | 41,291 | 83,318 | 120,161 | 126,168 | 246,329 | 329,647 |
| Muntafiq | 41,406 | 43,517 | 84,923 | 169,248 | 201,473 | 370,721 | 455,644 |
| Basrah | 119,764 | 115,445 | 235,209 | 132,618 | 135,057 | 267,675 | 502,884 |
| Deserts | — | — | — | 37,059 | 31,503 | 68,562 | 68,562 |
| Iraqi Communities Abroad | — | — | — | 30,750 | 11,714 | 42,464 | 42,464 |
| Delayed Registration | — | — | — | 124,632 | 96,434 | 221,066 | 221,066 |
| Grand Total | 1,246,060 | 1,191,578 | 2,437,638 | 2,048,013 | 2,052,458 | 4,100,471 | 6,538,109 |

*Source: Iraqi Government, Ministry of Social Affairs, Directorate General of Census.

# POPULATION OF CHIEF CITIES: 1957 *

| | |
|---|---|
| Greater Baghdad | 1,085,232 |
| Greater Mosul | 444,883 |
| Greater Basrah | 164,623 |
| Kirkuk | 120,593 |
| Karbala | 60,804 |
| Amara | 53,311 |
| Sulaimaniya | 48,450 |
| Nasiriyah | 39,060 |
| Arbil | 34,751 |

* Source: Embassy of Iraq, Press Attaché, Washington, D. C.

# INDEX

Abadan, 169
Abbassid Caliphate, 2, 30, 82
Abu Dibbis depression, 59, 64, 65, 68
Abu Ghraib canal, 77, 78, 228
Adams, Doris, 10, 16
afforestation, 55, 115
Afghans, 6
*aghas*, 80, 83
agriculture:
  Agricultural Machinery Administration (Directorate), 11, 106, 108, 115
  Agricultural Services, 105, 119
  capital invested in, 14, 89, 126, 140-141
  credit, 108-111
  development program, 78, 117, 120, 165-167, 173-175, 192, 203, 258-259
  experimental stations, 113-114
  extension service, 99, 102, 113, 114, 115, 122
  facilities for, 105-106, 114
  farm management, 63
  farming, dairy, 115
  farms, demonstration, 99, 102
  grain stores and silos, 20
  large-scale, 89, 121
  machinery, use and maintenance of, 106, 115, 183
  mechanization of, 11, 47, 60, 90, 106-110, 121-122, 166, 216, 222, 242
  percentage of population in, 12, 13, 18
  percentage of land cultivated, 18
  production, 18, 27, 78, 91, 177, 197, 251, 257-258
  reporting service, 114
  research and training, 113-114
  revenue from taxes on, 25-26
  Soils Laboratory, 115
  technical studies on, 117
  techniques of, 105, 106, 122
  *see also:* crops
Agriculture, Ministry of, 53, 95, 105, 110, 112, 114, 219, 250, 251
Ain Zala, 131, 133, 135, 137, 150, 152, 154

air transport, 44, 192, 200-201, 203-204
Alawand, 130, 169, 170
Alexandretta, 136
al-Mamun Town, 246
Alwan, Abdul Sahib, 53
Amara, 7, 8, 86, 88, 90, 197, 228, 237, 239
Ana, 55
Anglo-Iranian Oil Co.; *see* British Petroleum Co.
Ankara, 56
ankylostomiasis; *see* hookworm
Aramco, 132
Arbil, 3, 7, 74
Arizona, University of, 114
army personnel, 93, 96
Asia, 139
Asia, Southeast, 200
asphalt, 170
Assyrians, 5, 6, 7, 22
atomic energy development, 176
Australia, 79, 89, 120, 257
Awqaf Administration, 81

Baba Gurgur, 133
Babil canal and outfall, 71, 77
Babylonians, 70
Bad'a canal, 73
Baghdad, 4, 5, 6, 7, 8, 11, 12, 19, 54, 57, 58, 67, 86, 88, 104, 131, 136, 143, 146, 147, 150, 152, 161, 164, 165, 169, 170, 178, 181, 183, 189, 190, 191, 192, 193, 194, 195, 196, 197, 200, 201, 203, 204, 214, 217, 218, 219, 220, 224, 228, 230, 234, 236, 237, 238, 240, 241, 245, 246, 247, 248, 252
Baghdad Pact, 56
Bahrain, 137, 142, 200
Baiji, 135, 136, 170
Bani Hasan, 78
banking, 108, 110-111
banks:
  Agricultural, 53, 94, 107, 108, 110, 111, 247
  Agricultural-Industrial, 20, 184-185
  banking institutions, 168
  foreign, 108

endemic, 10, 124-125, 158, 231-239
epidemic, 12, 231, 242
infectious, 231-239
socio-economic origin of, 11, 232
*see also: bejel*; bilharzia; cholera;
diseases, venereal; d y s e n t e r y;
hookworm; malaria; plague;
smallpox; tuberculosis; typhus
diseases, venereal, 233
Diwaniya, 7, 86, 88, 104, 197
Diyala, 3, 7, 188, 237
Land Project, 77, 104
Diyala river, 54, 58, 69, 74, 78
Basin Project, 74, 75, 77
Barrage, 74
Dokan, 197
dam, 68, 69
gorge, 68, 73, 74
drainage, 44, 45, 50, 59, 61, 62, 63, 71,
72, 74, 75, 76, 77, 78, 89, 91, 95,
101, 103, 116, 117, 118, 123, 126,
227, 228, 231, 232, 234, 237
drought, 18, 54
Dujailah Settlement, 75, 77, 91, 96,
98, 99, 100, 101, 102, 122, 197, 235
outfall, 73, 77, 79, 99
*see also:* laws
Dulaim, 7, 104, 239
Dutch; *see* Royal Dutch Shell Group
dysentery, 233

Economics, Ministry of, 16, 95, 161,
177, 186, 250
economy:
agricultural domination of, 50
change from subsistence to money,
9, 115, 256, 257
development of, 140, 160
education, 1, 4, 5, 9, 17, 123, 126
adult, 156
bursary students, 32, 155, 221, 222,
224
centralization in, 212-213
efforts to improve, 206-210, 255,
259, 260
elementary, 213-214, 220
expenditures on, 46, 48, 53, 206-209
for boys, 210-212, 215, 219
for girls, 210-212, 215, 219
foreign study, 32, 155, 221-222, 224
fundamental (UNESCO), 100, 209
higher, 219-221, 260

inadequate facilities, 206, 208-210
intermediate, 213-214
non-bursary students abroad, 32,
221
preparatory, 213-214
progressive, 223
Provincial Administrative Councils, 206, 224
school construction, 206-209, 214
secondary, 213-214, 221
secular, 223
special problems; *see* Bedouins and
Yezidi
system of, 1, 25, 223-224
technical, 25
Education, Ministry of, 124, 155, 206-
208, 211-213, 215, 217, 218, 219,
221, 224, 240, 251
Egypt, 221, 236
Erbil, 88, 193, 194
erosion, 55, 57, 72
terracing, 89
Eski Mosul dam, 70
Euphrates river, 54, 55, 56, 77, 58, 59,
60, 61, 62, 63, 64, 65, 71, 76, 77, 78
tail regulators, 72, 77, 78
Europe, 5, 111, 112, 139, 159, 194, 214
exchange, foreign, 141, 203, 258, 259
experts and technicians, 25, 32, 42, 95,
118, 143, 196, 200, 202, 216, 222,
234, 248, 251, 255
exports, 26, 115, 116, 141, 162, 166,
167, 168, 177, 179, 184, 192, 203,
257, 258, 259
diversification of, 166
extension service; *see* agriculture

factories; *see* industry
Faisal I, King, 24
Faisal II, King, 23, 67
Faisal City, 246
*fallah, fallaheen*, 12, 14, 25, 75, 87, 88,
89, 90, 91, 92, 96, 103, 256, 257, 259,
261
fallow system, 59, 60, 61, 99, 102, 116
Falluja, 58
Fao, 135, 197, 199
Far East, 178, 200
farm owners:
small independent, 80, 86, 92
farms and farming; *see* agriculture
fats, 16, 26

Suq al-Shuyukh, 4
surveys:
    cadastral, 84, 85, 86, 92, 123
    of expenditures by economic groups,
        14-15, 182
    of road location, 198
    technical, 42, 44, 47, 48, 123, 168
syphilis; *see bejel*
Syria, 54, 55, 56, 58, 135, 136, 159, 194
Syrians, 6

Tanjero Valley, 234
*tapu* land, 81-82, 83, 85, 86, 93, 94
tariffs, 166, 167, 168, 178, 181, 187,
    188, 202
taxes:
    collectors of, 113, 256
    consumption, 26, 52
    exemption from, 30, 168, 187
    export, 52
    import, 52
    income, 25-26
    indirect, 25
    Land Tax, 25, 27
    on agriculture, 25, 26
technical assistance:
    from United Nations; *see* United
        Nations
    from United States; *see* United
        States
    from Western business firms, 32, 43,
        118-119
Teheran, 56, 200
telegraph system, 18, 20, 47
telephone system, 20, 47
tension, international, 139, 261
Tigris, 20, 54, 55, 56, 57, 58, 59, 60,
    61, 65, 67, 68, 69, 70, 73, 74, 76, 78,
    99, 131, 193
textile mills:
    cotton, 171
    rayon, 175, 176, 179
tobacco, 15, 16, 20, 116, 174
Topchi township, 245
trachoma, 231, 235-236
trade, 18, 27, 50, 79, 141, 151, 167,
    168, 260
    proportion of population engaged
        in, 12, 13
    unfavorable balance of, 258-259
traditions, 7, 11, 12, 25, 27, 28, 82, 108,
    112, 214, 222, 256

Treaty of Friendship and Neighborly
    Relations (Turkey and Iraq), 56
Tripoli (Lebanon), 135, 136, 138, 159
tuberculosis, 229, 233, 239
Turkey, 3, 5, 54, 55, 56, 57, 58, 136,
    159, 183, 186, 194, 257
    *see also:* Industrial Bank of Turkey;
        Treaty of Friendship and Neigh-
        borly Relations
Turkomans, 3
Turks, 4, 6, 23, 84
Tuwairij drain, 77
typhus, 231

Udhaim Basin, 73
Udhaim dam, 69, 73
Udhaim river, 58, 69
Umm Qasr, 199, 200
underdeveloped countries, 9, 22, 23,
    25, 42, 108, 168, 254, 256, 258
unemployment, 101, 108, 251, 255
unions, labor, 151-152, 160
United Nations, 48, 53, 95, 118, 234
    Department of Economic and Social
        Affairs, 16, 22, 161
    International Bank for Reconstruc-
        tion and Development (IBRD),
        Mission of, 13, 16, 32, 41-42, 50,
        53, 65, 87, 103, 105, 106, 166, 167,
        173, 174, 194, 199, 200, 204, 241,
        244, 253
    International Labor Organization,
        148
    Statistical Office, 13, 16
    UNESCO, 32, 100, 227, 235, 250
    UNICEF, 32, 209-210, 227, 234,
        235, 238
    WHO, 32, 227, 234, 238, 239
United States, 5, 32, 48, 79, 89, 105,
    112, 113, 114, 118, 120, 152, 181,
    221, 224, 234
    Lend-Lease Program, 106
    Point Four Program, 32, 35, 53, 95,
        110, 113, 114, 115, 159, 161, 227
unity, national, 1, 22
unrest, social, 30-31, 91
    " political, 17, 31
urban areas, 10, 11, 12, 27, 124, 189,
    242, 247, 252, 260
urbanization, 1, 11, 90, 107, 260
*ushr* (tithe-land), 82